MAHAGATHA

Celebrating
30 Years of Publishing
in India

Praise for *Mahagatha: 100 Tales from the Puranas*

'He [Satyarth] is truly a phenomenal storyteller.'

—Ashwin Sanghi, author

'An extremely readable book with beautiful illustrations.'

—Namita Gokhale, author

'The stories within this book ... and the way Satyarth has arranged all the tales from our Puranas in this very interesting chronological order, almost like you are going through the history of early Hinduism, is absolutely wonderful. I recommend it to everybody.'

—Ayan Mukerji, filmmaker

'*Mahagatha* is an excellent read.'

—*The Times of India*

'*Mahagatha* is a treasure trove for mytho-heads.'

—*The New Indian Express*

'*Mahagatha* has 100 mythological gems, handpicked through meticulous scholarly research.'

—*The Asian Age*

'Reading these curated stories can be an enriching experience that provides insight into Hindu culture, religion and philosophy. Also, some of these stories can provide individuals with a deeper connection to the divine, resulting in spiritual enrichment. This book provides an insightful journey into a magical world with mysticism, spirituality and divinity.'

—*Storizen*

MAHAGATHA

100 TALES
— FROM THE —
PURANAS

SATYARTH NAYAK

HarperCollins *Publishers* India

This edition first published in India by HarperCollins *Publishers* 2022
4th Floor, Tower A, Building No 10, DLF Cyber City,
DLF Phase II Gurugram – 122002
www.harpercollins.co.in

4 6 8 10 9 7 5 3

PISBN: 978-93-5629-449-3
EISBN: 978-93-5629-450-9

Typeset in ArnhemFine Normal by SÜRYA, New Delhi

Illustrations: Onkar Fondekar

Printed and bound at
Replika Press Pvt. Ltd.

MIX
Paper from
responsible sources
FSC® C016779

This book is produced from independently certified FSC® paper
to ensure responsible forest management.

For Bapa ...
For those hundreds of tales ...

CONTENTS

AUTHOR'S NOTE

The Puranas or 'ancient lore' of Hindu mythology are an encyclopaedic body of sacred literature that chronicles traditional legends of gods, demons, sages and kings and dwells upon subjects like cosmology, theology, genealogy and philosophy. Ascribed to varied sources and handed down orally for generations, they were recorded in writing roughly between 250 CE and 1500 CE, by numerous scholars who scripted and re-scripted these texts across centuries. Categorised into Mahapuranas and Upapuranas, they not only remain vital to Hindu culture but also bear testimony to the very evolution of Hindu thought.

Given that each Purana provides a different account of legends with varying details, the 100 tales presented here are simply one version of events out of multiple ones. Also, the structuring of this book, as can be seen, for example, in the way the Vishnu avatar stories have been sequenced, does not follow simplistic popular notions but adheres to the more complex and multi-dimensional narrative of the Puranas. As for the selection of these tales, a threefold criterion was employed to compile the final list. How fascinating was the story. Who were the entities involved. And, if the story was lesser-known and deserved a wider audience.

An attempt has also been made, for the first time, to create a semblance of chronology while narrating these tales. Although extremely difficult, given the cyclical nature of time in the Puranas, a timeline has been arrived at for many of these stories using prominent Puranic markers like the four yugas, the seven manvantaras, Vishnu's avatars, the generations of gods and demons and the family tree of kings. This is because I did not wish these tales to exist in isolation in the book but within a context of their past and future. Within a cycle of their cause and effect. Of karma and karma-phal which is how our universe functions. Hence, the book I present to you is not a random collection of stories but an epic narrative of continuous and connected action.

As is customary with recounting material like this, certain portions have been dramatised for effect. Creative liberties have been taken to enhance the bodies of some of these tales, but their souls remain untouched. Untainted. Unvarnished.

One of the biggest takeaways from these stories is the epiphany that the Puranas inhabit a gloriously grey zone. That there is no simplified dichotomy of good and evil but a highly complex cosmos where even devas can act vile and even asuras can act virtuous. Where the demonic can spawn the divine and the divine can bring forth the demonic. Where boons can often create chaos and curses can often lead to good. Where the Ocean of Milk that bestows amrita, also spews halahal. Where Sita curses a cow while Krishna blesses a snake. Where Vishnu, who debases the chaste Vrinda, also embraces the concubines of Naraka. Where Rama upholds but Krishna uproots. Where along with dharma, also exists Apad Dharma. This inexactitude allows for a million interpretations of these tales. Even raises queries that does our Brahmanda operate without rules. And yet, within this bewildering maze of dialectics, often glimmers a truth that is absolute. A moral that is supreme. An answer that is universal. A particle of the Parabrahman so enlightening that it takes us a little closer to him.

For me, the cardinal message of the Puranas has always been that nothing is haphazard about our universe. That everything occurs for a reason. For greater good. That we are all part of a monumental design, our fates entwined with each other, our lives impacting each other, our actions either ending a cycle or beginning a new one for each other.

I hope that you, my reader, shall go on to discover your own seminal truths in these pages.

1

BRAHMA BEGINS CREATION

In the beginning, there was nothing. Only the Parabrahman.

It was the supreme principle that had no beginning and no end. The absolute reality that was utterly indescribable. The divine essence with infinite potential. The cause and the effect blended into one. Timeless. Boundless. Self-created and self-contained. It had no form, nor was it formless. It had no traits, nor was it without any. Pure consciousness beyond the reach of thoughts and senses. A catalyst that was unchanging, yet it would bring forth every change.

It was only when the Parabrahman willed it, that creation of the material universe began.

A universe that would now be manifest. Observable. Discoverable. Distinguishable. This will of the Parabrahman produced a vibration which birthed the first sound, and it was Om. The sound that contained all the sounds. And the first to form was the Maha Tattva, or the primordial element from which originated the three gunas or the three attributes. Sattva Guna denoting preservation, Rajas Guna denoting action and Tamas Guna denoting destruction. The interplay of these three gunas brought forth the Pancha Tattva, or the five physical elements. Air. Water. Earth. Fire. Ether.

Together, they made Prakriti, or nature, manifest.

The gunas also gave rise to the five senses. Sight. Hearing. Touch. Smell. Taste. These would be determined by five sense organs which would be governed by the mind. With matter had come forth perception. Water now flowed and covered everything. Water, water everywhere, but nothing that would sink. The Parabrahman manifested itself as a divine entity who lay on these waters like a lily pad over a pond. Since water is 'nara' and abode is 'ayana', this entity acquired his name.

Narayana.

The Parabrahman now implanted its own seed in the water. Thus fertilised, the water nurtured the seed and, in due course, generated an egg. A golden egg that shone like an orb of light. Since this egg, or anda, had been spawned by the Parabrahman, it came to be known as Brahmanda. The cosmos. Narayana now entered the egg as Vishnu. The All-Pervading One. The Preserver, presiding over Sattva Guna. As this golden egg, or hiranya, enveloped him like a womb, or garbha, it acquired the name Hiranyagarbha.

A lotus with fourteen petals sprouted through Vishnu's navel, and out of this flower emerged Brahma. Another divine manifestation of the Parabrahman. The Creator, presiding over Rajas Guna. The progenitor bore a kamandala, or water bowl, and a mala, or rosary. Born thus of a lotus from the navel, he got other names, like Padmayoni and Nabhija.

After spending a year inside the Hiranyagarbha, like a pearl gestating in an oyster, Brahma split the egg into two. The upper half became heaven and the lower half, earth. Between the two stretched the sky. Brahma had begun the cycle and he knew how it would eventually end. Creation, or sarga, would lead to preservation, or sthiti and finally give way to dissolution, or pralay. But as soon as one cycle would die, a new one would be born. At the end of every cycle, when all would be reduced to the primeval ocean of chaos, he would initiate this process all over again.

An eternal sequence of cycles. A universe of interlocked circles.

Like a firework exploding in a dark sky, Brahmanda had come into being. Brahma sat gazing at what he had just created. Then he entered a state of meditation and from his depths originated the four Vedas. Rig Veda, Yajur Veda, Sama Veda and Atharva Veda. Little did the Creator know that four troubles were also about to rear their heads. Four troubles that would now endanger this very course of creation.

Would well-begun be half-done?

2

VISHNU KILLS MADHU AND KAITABHA

No sooner had Brahma brought forth the Vedas than two creatures crawled out from the earwax of Vishnu.

One of them began craving for honey to satiate his hunger and so got the name Madhu. The other brother resembled an insect, or kita, and came to be known as Kaitabha. Unaware of where they were, they glanced around in utter confusion. Feeling famished too, they searched for means of sustenance, but all they could see was infinite water surrounding them. Madhu and Kaitabha began feeding on this nourishing fluid and grew immensely mighty. As their bodies grew large, so did their heads, for they were now filled with arrogance. Supremely confident that they were the masters of this realm, the creatures began exploring the cosmos. As they wandered, they came upon Brahma sitting atop his lotus. The brothers instantly confronted the Creator.

'Who are you? How dare you occupy that floral seat meant only for the exalted?' they growled in fury.

Brahma kept quiet, which further inflamed them.

'Either come down and accept us as your sovereign or prove your worth by defeating us in combat.'

When the Creator did not comply, Madhu and Kaitabha began shaking the lotus stem to topple him. Poor Brahma clung to the flower, but the Vedas slipped from his hands. Gliding down, they fell one after the other through the cracks between the petals. The brothers hid them under water and began threatening to decimate everything that Brahma had brought into existence so far. Panicking, the Creator now turned to Vishnu.

'O Protector of the Universe. I beseech you to come to my aid. Are you not aware that I am no match for creatures born even from your dirt? How can I carry out my appointed task of creation if you do not ensure my safety? Why must we draw a circle if the ends cannot meet? Do you hear me, lord? Do you hear me?'

Alas, the Preserver had already entered Yoga Nidra, that dreamless state between being awake and asleep that made him oblivious to everything. Brahma kept shrieking, but Vishnu barely stirred. Madhu and Kaitabha began cackling, but Vishnu remained impervious. Finding no other recourse, the Creator now invoked Nidra, or sleep, to awaken the god.

'O Nidra! It's by your power that Narayana has fallen asleep. Pray, liberate him from your embrace. Let him rid us of these two brothers, whose senses have overpowered them. Who are so smitten with what they are seeing that they are wrongfully coveting it. Release him, Nidra. Release him.'

Nidra responded to the plea and the Preserver opened his lotus eyes. Seeing Brahma's predicament, he realised at once that all of creation was in peril. Vishnu immediately began assuming a new form to combat Madhu and Kaitabha. Brahma gazed at that lustrous mane. That equine avatar. The god had become Hayagriva.

The Horse-Headed One.

As the battle raged, Vishnu found himself unable to slay the pair. When one brother would tire out, the other would engage. Five thousand years elapsed and the Preserver became completely exhausted. He fathomed now that physical strength would no longer work. These two creatures would have to be foiled using games of the mind. Laying down his mace, Vishnu folded his hands and addressed them in a tone most honeyed.

'Bravo! I bow before your skill. You both are truly incomparable.

Unconquerable. Paying homage to your power, I would like to grant you both a boon. Name anything and it shall be yours.'

'A boon from you?' Madhu and Kaitabha sneered. 'From a weakling who stands petrified before us? Whose blue skin has turned even bluer out of fright? We are victors, and victors do not beg for boons. They hand them out in charity. Ask *us* for a boon. Ask and you shall have it.'

'Anything?'

'Anything.'

This was the exact turn of events Vishnu was awaiting. The cue had arrived. His face creased into a disarming smile.

'Grant me then that I may kill you both.'

Silence.

As his words sunk in, the brothers realised that they had walked into a trap with eyes wide open. But word had been given and there was no going back. With death looming large, their instinct for survival kicked in. Looking down, Madhu and Kaitabha saw how the waters were stretching around them endlessly in every direction. Making one last bid to save themselves, they chorused, 'You may take our lives but on one condition. Slay us in a place where there is no water.'

The Hayagriva smiled again. Spreading his arms, he began growing in size. Larger and larger. Larger and larger. Larger and larger until they could no longer see his face. Only his form, towering above the water like a blue mountain. Blending with the blue sky. Placing Madhu and Kaitabha on each thigh, he beheaded them. Born from his ears, they perished on his thighs.

Since Vishnu thus killed Madhu, he acquired the name Madhusudan.

'Looks like the more I create, the more forces shall arise to annihilate,' Brahma said. 'Keep saving us, Narayana, like you just did.'

'Perhaps I did nothing,' the Preserver replied. 'Perhaps Brahmanda saved itself through me.'

Retrieving the Vedas, Vishnu now removed meda, or fat, from the corpses of both the brothers and instructed Brahma to use it to create land on Earth. Hence, Earth would be called Medini and its soil would be considered unfit for consumption. The remaining portions of the two bodies disintegrated into six pieces each, forming the twelve seismic plates of the Earth. Perched atop his lotus, Brahma resumed creation, hoping that his path ahead would be tranquil from hereon.

But his troubles had only just begun.

3

SHIVA EMERGES

Earth had been moulded with the body fat of Madhu and Kaitabha, and it was now time to garnish it. Brahma created eight primary mountains, including Sumeru, Kailash, Himalaya and Malay, and seven island continents, including Jambudwipa, Kusadwipa and Pushkaradwipa. Rivers and oceans began flowing to suckle this newborn world. Everything had been embryonic inside the golden egg and the Creator was making them manifest now. Trees and plants and fruits and flowers. The Earth was taking shape, sprouting limbs and organs. It came to be known as Bhuloka, while the heavens above became Swargaloka. The netherworld below was split into seven regions, including Atala, Vitala, Sutala and Patala. And above these three realms lay Vaikuntha, Vishnu's abode. Time began ticking and Brahma divided it into four yugas, or eras. The white Satya Yuga, the red Treta Yuga, the yellow Dwapar Yuga and the black Kali Yuga. Together, they would constitute a mahayuga. The eyes of the Parabrahman were unblinking now, keeping an eternal watch over Brahmanda.

The moment had arrived for Brahma to plant the highest form of life in Bhuloka. To create man in his own image. And that's where the next trouble confronted him.

He closed his eyes and from his mind issued forth Kumaras, or four child sages. Named Sanaka, Sanatana, Sanandana and Sanatkumara, they were the first sons of the Creator. The first beings born out of his divine aura. Projecting from his manas, or mind, they came to be known as his Manasputras. And since they were four in number, they were also called Chatursana. As Brahma experienced the first pangs of paternal love, he informed the brothers that he had produced them for a purpose. They were to aid him in his task of creation. Populate Brahmanda through the act of procreation.

The Kumaras folded their hands and said, 'No!'

'No?' The Creator frowned.

'No.'

'Do you dare refuse to do your father's bidding? Disobey the one who gave you life?'

'Pardon us, Param Pita,' they answered. 'We are grateful that you created us, but we do not wish to remain confined within the circle of life and death. Why be dedicated to something so finite when the universe around us is infinite? We would rather meditate upon it. Upon the alluring nature of the Parabrahman. We are expressions of truth and purity, and those alone can fulfil us. Not this mortal world but the worlds beyond. Don't you hear the four directions calling out to the four of us?'

An alarmed Brahma began pleading with them for the sake of creation. Reminding them that their refusal would render everything useless, but the Chatursana did not budge. More than propagating, they were interested in interrogating. They begged the Creator to bestow a boon upon them.

'Bless us, Param Pita, that we may never age. That we may forever remain Kumaras. Child saints receiving and transferring knowledge for all eternity.'

Brahma argued some more, but finally yielded. Watching his Manasputras leave, he felt an intense rage surging inside him. In that violent emotion lurked the third trouble.

As his anger mounted, it sparked from his forehead in the form of a fiery beam and from that inferno emerged a being. A celestial being with eyes blazing red. Roaring ferociously, he demanded, 'What is my name?'

Brahma sat in awe, wondering what to reply. The being's eyes turned sulphuric now as he roared louder.

'Tell me my name.'

Recalling that the root word for both red and roaring is 'Rud', the Creator replied, 'Rudra. I name you Rudra.'

Rudra was Shiva. Mahadeva. Another divine manifestation of the Parabrahman. Presiding over Tamas Guna, he now completed the cosmic trinity.

Brahma, the Creator.

Vishnu, the Preserver.

Shiva, the Destroyer.

Energies dark and turbulent were arising in his terrifying form. Brahma calmed the god down with folded hands and requested him to aid in the process of creation. Shiva agreed and instantly started generating one being after another. Brahma's joy knew no bounds. He had found a companion. One who was readily sharing his burden. A radiant smile creased the Creator's face, only to freeze the next moment.

What is Maharudra doing?

The god was multiplying his own self. Like a cell undergoing mitosis, he was spawning his own replicas. All Rudras, one by one. An assembly line of mirror images. And as if that was not confounding enough, they were all immortal like him! Each one of them. Eleven Rudras were standing before Brahma now as he raised his arms in horror.

'Stop! Stop! You cannot do that, Mahadeva.'

'Do what?'

'Bring forth immortals.'

'Why not?'

'The whole cosmic balance will tilt. Creation must give rise to mortals. They must die to be born again like this very universe they inhabit. That alone shall sustain the cycle of creation, preservation and destruction. We cannot have immortals living on Earth. Can you not produce mortal beings?'

Shiva shook his head. 'I can only generate immortals. If that nullifies your process, then I cannot be a part of it. I would rather meditate.'

As the god departed, leaving the eleven Rudras behind, Brahma gazed at them. On the one hand, his Manasputras had refused to spawn a single being, and on the other, Shiva had brought forth multiple beings. Neither paucity nor plenty had helped his Brahmanda. The Rudras were now clamouring for a place to live and the Creator designated eleven sites for them. One was allotted the heart. Five were given the sense organs and the remaining five got the elements. The Rudras left and Brahma was all by himself again. Chiding himself for not knowing better. For not comprehending that Mahadeva, whose hallowed task was to destroy, cannot create. That the triple division of labour between Brahma, Vishnu and Shiva was sacrosanct and the cosmos would never blur those lines. Creation was his karma alone and he would have to own it.

He picked up the reins again, making way for the final trouble.

4

BRAHMA AND NARADA FIGHT

Brahma began meditating once more and seven celestial sages now emanated from him. They were Vashishtha, Marichi, Atri, Angira, Pulastya, Pulaha and Kratu. Collectively, they became the Saptarishi.

Following this, Dharma was born from the heart of the Creator in the form of a bull. And Brahma made a prophecy, foretelling its fate as time would pass.

'You, Dharma, are standing on four feet, which symbolise four virtues. Satya or truth, Tapas or austerity, Swachha or purity and Karuna or compassion. In Satya Yuga now, you shall remain four-footed as all of these virtues will be readily practised. But as each yuga progresses, you shall keep losing a foot. You will have three feet in Treta Yuga.'

'Three, father?'

'Yes, since many will stop practising austerities. Two in Dwapar Yuga.'

'Two, father?'

'Yes, since many shall forego purity. And only one in Kali Yuga.'

'One, father?'

'Yes, since many will no longer be compassionate. I have created you from my heart, Dharma, but you won't last long in the hearts of others.'

Soon, more beings came into existence. Agni sprang from the Creator's eyebrow and Kamadeva emerged from his bosom. Daksha from his right thumb, Vishwakarma from his navel and Narada from his neck. Brahma was feeling sapped again. He turned and gazed at Narada with fatherly affection and made that same request that he had to the Kumaras.

'Go, my son. Continue the process of creation.'

Alas, like the Kumaras, Narada, too, shook his head.

'I must decline. This temporal world caught in an endless vortex of living and dying means nothing to me. I prefer the realm of Narayana where time and space do not exist. You are offering me the joys of flesh, but I seek the bliss of consciousness.'

The Creator had had it now!

First, Madhu and Kaitabha had put him in great danger. Then his own Chatursana had bluntly refused to shoulder responsibility. Shiva had added to his troubles eleven-fold and now Narada, too, was abandoning him. Brahma felt that flare of anger swelling inside him again. Overpowering his mind and heart again. Blinding him to everything else. His lips parted and out fell a curse.

'You, Narada, shall become a gandharva. A minstrel. If everyone shuns the physical world, how will Brahmanda function? How will creation attain its purpose?'

Narada stood stunned. Refusing to take it lying down, he did the unimaginable. The son cursed his father back!

'Just as you have failed to curb your fury, you shall fail to curb your lust. You shall desire that which must not be desired and pay the price for it.'

The cosmos shrank. The three realms trembled. Never had a father cursed his son and never had a son cursed his father. As his words reverberated throughout Brahmanda, Narada stormed off, leaving the future of creation in peril once again.

Tears rolled down from Brahma's eyes now. Such was his anguish that even the petals of his lotus began to wilt. He was almost convinced that this was a doomed enterprise, when help arrived. Arrived from a quarter most unexpected.

5

MAN IS CREATED

Having been born from the Creator's right thumb, Daksha now organised a ceremony. The seven sages participated and were assigned specific duties. Vishnu came out of hibernation to attend and so did Brahma. The rituals commenced as the Saptarishi began to chant. Their words were winging through the cosmos. Permeating its veins. Smearing it with a layer of piety. Brahmanda was swaying now, drunk with devotion. The mantras were sanctifying everything they were touching when suddenly a furore broke out at the entrance of the yagna hall.

Shiva!

After bidding Brahma farewell, Shiva had found a beautiful spot and begun meditating. But the resounding mantras of the sages today had shattered his peace. Jolted out of his contemplation, the infuriated god had arrived at the gates of the ceremony. Storming the site, Shiva now began turning it upside down. Daksha and the Saptarishi fled in terror, but Vishnu stood up against this divine vandal. Seeing the Preserver protesting, Shiva's rage spiralled and a battle erupted between the two. Galaxies shuddered. Time froze. The elements covered their eyes as the two devas clashed, threatening to rip apart the universe. Fearing an irreversible catastrophe, Brahma folded his hands.

'I beseech you both. End this combat or it will never end. You are both equal to each other. Opposite of each other. This will be an infinite war. Everything around you shall perish but you will go on fighting. Either resolve your anger or dissolve my cosmos. What will you choose?'

The gods halted as better sense prevailed. The Creator smiled.

'You both have removed fear from my heart. Removed the threat upon Brahmanda. Hereafter, Vishnu will also be called Hari, and Shiva will also be called Hara. Both names mean the same. One who removes. They shall always remind you that you both are each other's synonyms. Hari and Hara shall together be Harihara.'

Shiva departed and Daksha's ceremony was completed. As everyone began to leave, Vishnu called Brahma aside.

'I have been noticing, lord. Your face appears troubled and you have hardly enjoyed the rituals. Speak to me. What causes you such grief?'

Finding a sympathetic ear, Brahma unspooled his woes. His words came gushing forth like a stream, recounting every frustration. How the process of creation was destroying him. How his own sons had rejected him. How he was in perpetual agony while Vishnu was slumbering in peace.

'Perhaps I should be discarded for I have failed to deliver,' he lamented.

The Preserver stood gazing at a pillar. A pillar of white gold. An alloy of gold and silver. Then he spoke.

'Mahadeva.'

'Mahadeva?'

'Go to him. He alone can solve this.'

'I tried but he kept breeding immortals. He's the Destroyer. How can he create?'

'He may not create but he shall surely counsel. Go to Mahadeva.'

The Creator did as instructed only to find that Shiva had resumed meditation. Having witnessed the havoc that he had wreaked at Daksha's ceremony, Brahma was too fearful of interrupting him again. But he knew that he could not leave without an answer. Sitting down, he began praying to the god. Praying from the very pith of his soul. Time passed but the Creator did not stir. So earnest was his plea that Shiva now opened his eyes.

'I know why you are here.'

'Guide me, lord.' Brahma's eyes welled up. 'Creation is at stake and I am lost. Show me the way. Tell me where I have gone wrong.'

'Reproduction cannot happen the way you generated your sons. What you need is Shakti.'

'Shakti?'

'Power of the feminine.'

Shiva stood up and the Creator watched mesmerised. Watched as the god's body acquired a new form. A magnificent composite form that was half-male and half-female. The right side was masculine, while the left was feminine. Split evenly down the middle upon a central axis. A union in division. A perfect symbiosis of opposing energies. A divine duality that he had never seen before. A fusion that was whispering the secret of creation to him. So powerful was this sight that the Creator sat both petrified and euphoric. Since ardha or half of this form of Shiva was nari, or female, it became known as the Ardhanarishwara. The Androgynous One.

The avatar addressed Brahma. 'This is what creation needs. A synthesis of Shiva and Shakti. Dev and Devi. Static and dynamic. Being and becoming. Masculine and feminine are the two halves of your Brahmanda and one cannot function without the other. Only when these binaries integrate can there be propagation. This union will not only initiate creation but also ensure that the process sustains itself until the end of time. Hail Adishakti. Divine Mother. The Sacred Feminine.'

Brahma bowed. 'I worship you, Devi, for you have opened my eyes. Bless me that I may be able to create the female agency. Bring forth the human pair who shall procreate on Earth.'

Adishakti smiled, bestowing the generative force upon him. Thus empowered, Brahma now created a man and a woman from his own body. The first pair on Earth. The man was named Manu and the woman, Brahmi. Since maithuna, or copulation, became the source of sustaining srishti, or procreation, this process came to be known as Maithuna Srishti. The human race would now descend from Manu and hence man would be called manushya or manava.

Brahma was elated. Creation would take care of itself now. He had created man. The highest form. God's own image. The intent of the universe.

So rapturous was the deva that he forgot every trouble he had encountered thus far. Every hurdle that had seemed insurmountable. Even the terrible curse that Narada had laid upon him.

You shall desire that which must not be desired ...

Words that were about to come true.

6

SHIVA BEHEADS BRAHMA

Emerging from Brahma's body, Manu was his son and Brahmi his daughter. But a curse is a curse and it knows no ties. Once uttered, it becomes a part of natural law and must come to pass. Inexorable as an arrow inching closer and closer. Narada had spoken and his words, like unripe fruit, had been waiting for the right season.

You shall desire that which must not be desired ...

The curse came into effect now as Brahma began desiring his own daughter. Brahmi was a woman of exceeding beauty and the Creator became besotted with his own creation. His flesh was now craving his own flesh. As soon as Brahmi stood before him to pay her respects, she realised his intentions. His eyes were not exuding love but lust. Insatiable lust.

The daughter immediately moved to Brahma's right to avoid his gaze. Lo and behold, a second head sprouted on that side of the god, so that he could continue looking at her. She shifted to his left and a third head sprung forth. She moved again to stand behind him and a fourth head emerged there. Thoroughly exasperated now, Brahmi rose high up in the air, but the Creator's passion knew no bounds. A fifth head bloomed right atop his other four heads, yearning for her. Finding their sister in distress and their father shaming himself, Marichi and Atri hastened to warn him.

'Do not succumb to the words of Narada. You are the Creator supreme.

How can you harbour impious feelings towards your own daughter? How can you impose your will upon Prakriti herself? You have produced Brahmi for a divine purpose. Do not give in to actions that may render your entire creation inauspicious.'

Alas, Narada's curse was way more potent. Its claws so fastened over Brahma that he began to chase Brahmi. She kept running hither and tither but there seemed to be no escape from her father. In a desperate bid to foil him, the woman began transforming herself into animal forms. She turned into a cow, but Brahma turned himself into a bull. She became a mare and he became a stallion. She became a duck and he became a drake. She turned into a doe and he turned into a buck. This went on and on as she morphed into one hundred creatures. Reptiles, insects, birds and mammals. Animals of air, land, river and sea. And every time, the bewitched Creator kept turning into her male counterpart, tarnishing that hallowed binary of Nara and Nari that had been revealed to him.

Since Brahmi thus took hundred forms, she acquired the name Shatarupa. And this is how all the animals now came into existence on Earth.

A furious Shiva materialised and began to condemn Brahma. The Creator came to his senses now. He begged forgiveness, but the Destroyer's rage boiled over and he severed Brahma's fifth head on top, leaving him with only four.

'Such vile thoughts are unworthy of pardon,' Shiva hissed. 'From now on, your four mouths shall forever keep reciting the Vedas to repent for today.'

Suddenly, the Destroyer paused. Something was clinging to his left hand. He glanced down to find the Creator's severed head stuck to him. Shiva frowned, but the next moment he realised that decapitating Brahma had amounted to Brahmahatya. Killing of a Brahmin. Hence the head had attached itself to him as a penalty for his sin.

'But what Mahadeva did was justified,' Shatarupa argued. 'Why must he be punished?'

'An action will always give birth to a reaction independent of its context,'

Atri explained. 'Our father lusted because he was under the influence of a curse and yet he paid the price. Similarly, Mahadeva, too, faces the consequence of his deed, no matter how valid. The rules of Brahmanda apply equally to all.'

The Destroyer began roaming throughout the universe now but found no remedy. The head remained stuck. Soon its flesh began to rot and fall, leaving only bones. As Shiva wandered thus with a skull clinging to his hand, he earned the name Kapali. Time passed and he set foot on Earth. Suddenly, a miracle came to pass. At one place, the skull detached from his hand and fell on the ground. The god had been purged. He realised that this land here offered salvation. That anyone who came here would be absolved of every sin. The site became Kashi or Varanasi.

Not long after, Manu found Shatarupa in a pensive mood. Clasping her gently, he lay her head on his heart.

'What ails you, beloved?'

'I fear,' replied the mother of mankind. 'I fear now to beget the female race. If a father can endanger his own daughter, who shall keep them safe? Who shall heal them if everyone wounds them?'

He remained silent but she trembled.

'I fear now. I fear now to give them beauty for men might disrobe them. I fear now to give them wisdom for men might degrade them. I fear now to give them choices for men might disown them. I fear now to give them power for men might destroy them.'

She moved away from him.

'I fear, Manu. I fear.'

7

NARADA AND MAYA

'Four heads! My father has four heads now.'

Hearing how monumentally his curse had fructified, Narada had made his way to Vaikuntha to recount the events to Vishnu. The Preserver smiled.

'It's all maya.'

'Maya? What is maya?'

'I feel thirsty. Get me some water and I shall tell you,' Vishnu answered.

The Devarshi made his way to the river outside and suddenly froze. He had spied a maiden by the banks and his eyes were refusing to look away. So ethereal was the woman that Narada forgot Vishnu and his thirst. Forgot everything else. He married her then and there and made a house on those sands by the river. Years came and years went, and the Devarshi became a father and a grandfather. As his tribe increased so did his love for each one of them. For this household that had now become his universe. Everything seemed forever blissful when one day, without warning, the sky turned grey. Thunder roared and rain poured, flooding the river. Its waters came crashing and swept Narada's family away. As he swirled helplessly in that current, he suddenly found himself back in Vaikuntha, standing before Vishnu.

'Where's the water, Narada? I told you I am thirsty.'

The young sage stood confounded.

My wife? My children? My home?

It pierced him like an arrow now.

Maya ...

It had all been one giant illusion.

Maya ...

'Do you see?' The Preserver smiled. 'This suffering comes from maya. From attachment to a material world that is transient. Attachment to the physical, just as Brahmadeva experienced with Shatarupa. Maya deludes us. Makes us forget the infinite and pursue the finite. Makes us forget that the Parabrahman is the only reality. The singular truth. All else is sand that slips through the fingers. Only when one loses maya will one find moksha.'

Vishnu looked at Brahmanda getting populated now. He smiled again.

'Prepare yourself, Narada. There's going to be much maya.'

8

JAYA AND VIJAYA

The four Kumaras of Brahma had been exploring the universe, admiring their father's handiwork. Bowing before Shiva. Conversing with the Saptarishi. Absorbing knowledge that every realm had to offer. Roaming through all the lokas, they had now reached the gates of Vaikuntha, the abode of Vishnu. Land of the liberated. The truly enlightened. Passing through six portals, they were about to cross the seventh one when two voices rumbled.

'Halt!'

Two pairs of arms were barring their way. Two beings were glaring at them.

'Who are you to stop us from entering?' the sons of Brahma asked.

'We are the gatekeepers of Vaikuntha.'

The Chatursana tried to walk past them but in vain. The two guards continued to deny them passage, unaware that they were wise souls blessed by the Creator to remain forever child-like.

'You cannot come wandering into Vaikuntha. Entry here is for a privileged few.'

'What are your names?' the Kumaras asked them.

'Jaya and Vijaya.'

'What's the difference?'

'Vijaya is victory over others. Jaya is victory over one's own self. One's own mind and heart, thoughts and actions. Vijaya is external but Jaya is internal and that's always the hardest. Only those who have conquered themselves can achieve Vaikuntha. You four are too young and have hardly engaged with the world. You cannot be here.'

'Our bodies appear infantile but we are the Manasputras of Brahma. Chatursana, in quest of perpetual knowledge. Kindly inform Sri Hari that we would like to pay our respects to him.'

But Jaya and Vijaya refused to believe them and insisted that Vishnu was resting.

'Kindly leave. He cannot see you.'

'He sees everything. Don't you know that?'

'You boys are not even suitably attired. He will not receive you. Leave.'

The Kumaras frowned in anger now. 'How can you both be so ignorant despite being so close to divinity? A god never denies audience to his devotees. He is forever available. It's you both who are keeping us away from him. Your impudence springs from your exalted position. Vaikuntha is all about harmony, but you two are notes of discord. Unworthy to stand here. You have sinned by coming in the way of our pilgrimage and you shall suffer for it.'

Four tiny palms sprinkled water on them.

'We curse you both that you shall lose your celestial form and be born as mortals on Earth. You prevented us from standing in the presence of Sri Hari. Now you, too, shall undergo separation from him.'

As soon as the Kumaras left, Jaya and Vijaya fell at the feet of the Preserver. He was aware of what they had done and shook his head in pain.

'Brahma's Manasputras are pure souls. You should not have offended them.'

'Save us, lord.'

'I cannot reverse their curse but I can assign it a period of time,' Vishnu consoled them. 'You can either take seven births as my devotees or three births as my enemies. Once you have served those lifetimes on Earth, you shall be free to return to Vaikuntha.'

The brothers stood up.

'Seven births to love me or three births to loathe me. What will you choose?' asked Vishnu.

Jaya folded his hands. 'Seven lifetimes on Earth is too long a duration, lord. We cannot bear to be away from you for so many years. We would rather be reborn only three times even if it means that we shall be your foes.'

'But the world will revile you. Forever mock you and burn you.'

Vijaya smiled. 'Let them all hate us if it means that we can return sooner to your love.'

'But grant us a favour,' Jaya begged. 'Destroy us yourself when we stand before you as your enemies. End each of our three mortal lives with your own hands so that we may once again enter Vaikuntha.'

Vishnu nodded. 'So it shall be.'

As the pair departed, the Preserver gazed into their future. Their three lifetimes on Earth as his foes. In this Satya Yuga, they would be reincarnated as brothers Hiranyaksha and Hiranyakashipu. In Treta Yuga, they would be brothers Ravana and Kumbhakarna. And in Dwapar Yuga, they would be cousins Shishupala and Dantavakra.

Reborn every time to be killed by him.

Vishnu closed his eyes. Three lives for them to lose their bodies but gain their souls. Three lives to learn that Jaya and Vijaya were not mere words to be explained. Not titles to be defined. Not names to be paraded.

They were ends to be achieved.

9

DAKSHA CURSES NARADA

Manu and Shatarupa now begot sons, Priyavrata and Uttanapada, and daughters, Akuti, Devahuti and Prasuti. Prasuti's hand was given in marriage to Brahma's son, Daksha.

The Capable One.

Daksha took another wife called Asikli, who gave birth to five thousand sons. They were collectively named the Haryashvas. Daksha instructed all of them to become rulers of the Earth and continue procreating. The princes were a dutiful lot and readily agreed. Before carrying out their father's command, they congregated at a point where River Sindhu met the sea to offer oblations. But neither they nor Daksha knew that someone was headed their way. Someone with mischief in his heart and the drug of persuasion in his voice.

The troublemaker, Narada!

He approached the Haryashvas and began dissuading them from doing their father's bidding.

'Kings? How can you become kings of Bhuloka when you have no knowledge about her history or geography? Are you familiar with her circumference? How will you know if you are under-populating her or overpopulating?'

The brothers had no answer. The Devarshi smirked.

'First, seek out every detail about Earth and then stake your right to rule. You may even come across knowledge so transcendental that you might wish to pursue a different path. A higher path.'

Narada's words seemed to exert mass hypnosis over the Haryashvas. All five thousand faces were now creasing with doubt. All five thousand heads were soon nodding in agreement. They dispersed to explore Bhuloka and no one saw them again. Like the River Sindhu losing herself in the sea, they never came back. Failing to trace them, Daksha and Asikli gave birth to another thousand sons and named them Shavalashvas. But Narada was not done yet. He discouraged these princes, too, in exactly the same manner, and this batch also vanished, never to return.

'How could you do this?' their hapless father roared. 'Who will build homes, Narada, if everyone becomes a hermit?'

'I only showed them a path to supreme truth,' the Devarshi defended himself. 'It was their choice to walk upon it.'

Unable to control his pain and fury, Daksha now uttered words most terrible.

'Our father, Brahma, was right to curse you and I shall do the same. You, Narada, have scattered my sons throughout Earth and instigated them to become wanderers. From now on, your life shall be the same. You, too, shall forever wander through these three realms and never find an abode. Never find sanctuary. You shall keep drifting through Brahmanda for all eternity so that everyone realises the value of civilisation.'

Having lost all their sons, Daksha and Asikli now produced sixty daughters. Twenty-seven of them were the nakshatras, or stars, who married Chandra, the moon god. Ten married Dharma and thirteen married Marichi's son, Kashyapa. These thirteen unions went on to become the primary source of the rest of creation.

Out of the thirteen sisters, Aditi's children were called adityas. One of them was Surya, who became the source of heat and light in Brahmanda, while another was Indra, who became Devaraja, the ruler of the gods. Diti's children were called daityas. The eldest two were Hiranyaksha and

Hiranyakashipu. Danu brought forth danavas, and Arishta brought forth gandharvas. Muni gave birth to apsaras, while Khasa gave birth to yakshas and Kadru gave birth to nagas. Since Daksha was the father of these thirteen women, he was hailed as the pati, or lord of all the praja, or living beings, that his daughters had begotten.

He was henceforth addressed as Prajapati.

Daksha's other wife, Prasuti, was an ardent devotee of Adishakti, the mother deity of the universe. The feminine half of Ardhanarishwara who had enlightened Brahma about procreation. Prasuti persuaded her husband to pray to the goddess to be born as their daughter. They performed austerities for years and finally Adishakti agreed.

'However, I must warn you,' the goddess said. 'If you ever affront me, I will leave you and you shall face dire consequences.'

In time, Prasuti gave birth to twenty-four daughters and the most radiant of them all was the youngest one. The incarnation of Adishakti.

Daksha named her Sati.

And the first word she uttered was Shiva.

10

THE GODS GO HUNGRY

A new dawn had just broken when the Creator saw all the gods marching towards Brahmaloka. He smiled as they entered, but the next moment he turned tense. Everyone appeared frail and famished. Their faces were hardly luminous and their bodies were more bone than flesh. On enquiring, the devas informed Brahma that they had nothing to eat.

'I don't understand. Nothing to eat?'

'Down below on Bhuloka, the good earth is providing food for humans. They don't have to toil in any way as she keeps bearing roots and fruits. But up here in heaven, there's nothing to feed us. How do we sustain ourselves?'

'Through yagnas,' Brahma answered. 'The Vedas decree that when men perform yagnas on Earth, they make offerings through Agni, the mouth of the gods. Those oblations poured into the fire are carried directly to you and, in return, you grant them boons and blessings. A yagna is but a barter of energies that benefits everyone. A symbiosis that nurtures both gods and humans.'

'We know that,' Indra said. 'Humans are regularly conducting yagnas on Earth but none of their offerings are reaching us here.'

'Why not?'

'It's the fire god. He's failing us,' Kamadeva protested.

Agni came forward and folded his hands. 'I am truly to blame, Param Pita. I can burn the offerings made by men but I am unable to transport them to the devas. I do not possess that skill. Everyone here is starving because of me. What should I do?'

Brahma was puzzled now. He scratched his four heads but they yielded no solution. He then consulted Vishnu, who advised him, 'Pray to Prakriti. Mother Nature. She will come to our aid.'

The Creator invoked Prakriti, who immediately spawned a young goddess to preside over the ritual offerings. She would become the cosmic conduit to transmute oblations and make this vital exchange possible between Earth and heaven.

'You are our lifeline now,' Brahma blessed her. 'What has Prakriti named you?'

'Swaha.'

The Creator announced, 'Henceforth, every offering made to Agni in a yagna must end with the word "Swaha". If her name is not chanted, the libation poured into the fire will not reach the gods. Any incantation without "Swaha" shall be like a tree without fruit, a snake without venom and a man without knowledge. The yagna shall remain incomplete and prove inauspicious.'

The devi had saved the devas. Brahma gave Swaha in marriage to Agni and the two remained forever united.

11

BRAHMA AND VISHNU RACE

The devas woke up one day to hear that a quarrel had erupted between Brahma and Vishnu. They rushed to the spot to find both of them baring their teeth at each other. Tempers were rising and so were the decibels. Seeing the gods assembled around them, Brahma griped, 'I came this way and he wouldn't even greet me. I am the Creator. The first of the triumvirate. Am I not worthy of a modicum of respect?'

'You may be the Creator but I am the Preserver,' Vishnu shot back.

'You preserve only because I make it possible. Without me, you would have nothing to do. No role in the scheme of things, if I did not initiate creation.'

'Creation so fragile that it needs me to sustain it. Recall how I slew Madhu and Kaitabha. The one who protects is always greater. What power do you have if you cannot safeguard what you create?'

'Power?' Brahma inched forward. 'You wish to see the extent of my power? Enter my body and see what I encompass.'

'Your body?'

'Enter it.'

Vishnu permeated inside him to discover a million worlds throbbing. There were oceans raging and mountains soaring. Life forms of every kind were inhabiting that space. Ecosystems of overwhelming magnificence were breathing all around. Embryos were gestating and multiplying while elements were nourishing and nurturing. Every dimension was soaked with wondrous sights and sounds that he had never seen before. Every vista was proclaiming that a vacuum was a lie, for even the voids were hiding secrets in their wombs. Walking out of the Creator's body, he addressed him. 'You are indeed the lord of everything. But why don't you take a look at what my body envelops?'

Brahma stepped inside him and stood dazed. He was standing before the truly infinite. The boundless and the limitless. An interstellar space cradling a million galaxies. Giant planets, and shimmering constellations. Times past, present and future. Dimensions manifest and unmanifest. His multiple eyes were failing to contain what they were seeing. His multiple heads were failing to process what they were absorbing. Not one universe but manifold. Multiverses like a cosmic kaleidoscope, changing and yet unchanging. Asking him to lose himself to find himself. To locate the absolute truth. Traversing through every plane of existence, the Creator now wanted to come out but failed to find an exit. Searching high and low, he finally made his way through the lotus stalk and once again emerged from Vishnu's navel.

With both of them proving how divine they were, the argument picked up again. Running out of abuses now, they began brandishing weapons at each other. As the assembly quaked, suddenly a towering column of fire manifested before them. Blazing like a pillar of gold, that inferno reached far up and far down as if it neither began nor ended. So hypnotic was this vision that the Creator and the Preserver paused to gape at it. Finding an opportunity now, the gathering made a proposal. They asked Vishnu to find the base of this column and Brahma to locate its top. Whoever succeeded first would be hailed as the greater one.

The two gods agreed.

Vishnu turned himself into a boar and sprinted down to dig into the earth, while Brahma became a swan and soared up high. They searched and searched but neither could come even remotely close to either end. The pillar appeared to stretch ceaselessly on both sides, spanning through earth and sky like the very spine of the cosmos. Feeling thoroughly exhausted now, Brahma was about to turn back when his eyes fell on something floating down. A ketaki flower.

'Where are you coming from?' the Creator asked, catching it in his beak.

'I was on the upper reaches of this column but I slipped.'

Brahma barely caught the whole sentence. Only a phrase.

... upper reaches of this column ...

The words were jangling inside him. He was no longer holding a flower but the key to his victory. A piece of evidence that no one could possibly deny. Overpowered by his desire to trounce Vishnu, the Creator did the unthinkable. He asked the ketaki to bear false testimony before everyone that he had reached the top of the pillar and picked it up from there.

'You want me to lie?'

'I created you,' Brahma argued. 'I am only asking you to return the favour.'

'But a lie?'

'If you do so, I can assert my worth.'

The ketaki agreed. Coming down, they saw Vishnu returning as well. The Preserver hung his head and confessed that he had failed to locate the base. Brahma smiled. His four mouths began narrating how he had scaled the summit of the pillar, pecked at its peak and returned triumphant with proof. He presented the flower and it endorsed his story word for word.

'Brahmadeva is indeed the greatest,' the ketaki affirmed.

Vishnu admitted defeat. He had barely folded his hands when that column of fire cracked. It was splitting right through the middle. The sound of Om was reverberating aloud. The flames were turning a deeper and deeper red. In that burning haze stood Shiva. A furious Shiva. Pointing at Brahma, he thundered, 'Liar!'

Everyone froze. Shiva hissed, 'You say that you found the top of this pillar? This Sadashiva? This endless Parashiva? Do you know what it is that you both were trying to explore? Shivalinga. A Jyotirlinga.'

Brahma tuned pale.

'A Jyotirlinga is everlasting. Immeasurable like the Parabrahman it symbolises. Beyond every sensual perception. It only manifested here to tell you both how trivial your argument was. Remind you both that nothing is higher than the Parabrahman and we are but equal components of that cosmic principle. Sri Hari embraced his failure but you, Brahmadeva, were so afraid of losing that you tried to deceive. How can you remove fear from the hearts of others when you yourself are filled with fear?'

Shiva struck his trident.

'This is not a curse, Brahmadeva. This is natural law. You denied the truth and now everyone shall deny you. Henceforth, no one shall worship you.'

Turning to the ketaki flower, he roared, 'You were dear to me but you bore false witness. I pronounce now that no one shall offer you to worship me anymore.'

As the Destroyer walked away, Daksha stood glaring at him. His eyes were flooding. His soul was flaming.

First you behead my father ...

Now you deny him worship ...

A wave of hatred for Shiva was swallowing him from tip to toe.

12

BALA CREATES NINE WONDERS

Daksha's daughters, Diti and Danu, had married Kashyapa to give birth to daityas and danavas respectively. Both were demonic races who were constantly battling the devas. Constantly trying to capture Swargaloka or Bhuloka. Although fruits of the same family tree, the gods and demons were forever baying for each other's blood.

Once, heaven witnessed all the devas fleeing for their lives. An invincible asura called Bala had routed Indra and taken over. Driven out of their abode, the gods were standing helplessly by the gates. No longer masters of their realm. Simmering with shame. As they began to depart, they saw the demon approach. Although possessing a vicious mind, Bala had a virtuous heart. A generous spirit that never refused a request. Standing amidst the devas, he made an announcement.

'You may have lost all authority but not my helping hand. In the past I have donated freely and will continue to do so. You can always count on my cooperation whenever you perform a yagna.'

As he left, Indra glanced at everyone and smirked. The gods were wondering what had given their banished Devaraja such joy when it dawned upon them. Bala had made an innocent error. He had handed them the key to his defeat.

A yagna ...

Preparations began immediately and soon the day of the yagna arrived. The sacrificial fire was soaring high. Mantras were resounding. The hour had come to execute their plan. Indra and the gods trooped back to the palace and greeted the demon humbly.

'We have organised a yagna, sire. We need a being who can be sacrificed to complete the ritual.'

'Absolutely.'

'We request you to kindly offer yourself so that the yagna may be accomplished and ...'

The assembly paused. Bala had stood up. His face was striking terror. His shadow was devouring them. Had they just uttered the last words of their lives? Was the asura advancing to butcher them one by one? Were his gleaming eyes the last thing that they would see? They knew how benevolent he was, but could someone be generous enough to offer himself for others? They shrank as he came closer. Closer. Closer. What was going on in that demonic mind?

Bala folded his hands. 'I am willing.'

Soon, ritual flames were feeding upon his body. Burning his bones. Melting his flesh. Their ruse had worked. Bala was dead. Swargaloka belonged to them once more. The gods were revelling. Dancing around his corpse, when someone screamed.

'Look!'

What miracle was this? The asura's charred body was transforming. Every portion was solidifying. Turning into objects so magnificent that they could barely tear their faces away.

What are these things?

They inched nearer to gaze at them. To touch the colours taking birth in that corpse. Red and green and blue and yellow. Unseen shades that were dazzling their eyes. Seizing their hearts. The demon's remains appeared to have become a rainbow that was glistening with the glow of a million stars.

A heavenly voice now proclaimed, 'Bala's final selfless act has sanctified his flesh. Turned it into a repository of the most precious substances that can occur in Brahmanda.'

The devas gawked as if unable to believe that an asura's body could be so wondrous. They instantly tried carting it back but, despite every effort, it slipped and fell towards Bhuloka. As the corpse plunged, it began to split. The fragments scattered all over Earth and formed deposits. A total of eighty-four body parts had landed across mountains, forests, rivers and oceans. Of these, twenty-one emerged as the most brilliant objects that could be found in nature. They became known as jewels. Of these, nine came to be regarded as the most precious. Diamonds that had formed from his bones and emeralds from his bile. Rubies from his blood and sapphires from his eyes. Pearls from his teeth and topaz from his skin. Garnets from his nails, corals from his guts and cat's eye from his voice.

These became the Navaratnas.

13

VISHNU GETS THE SUDARSHANA CHAKRA

Alas, not every demon was as benevolent as Bala. Most were afflicting gods and slaying humans. Disrupting yagnas and defiling women. As their darkness began blinding the realms, the devas pleaded with Vishnu to deliver them. But the god himself had turned weary with these constant onslaughts. Preservation appeared to have become a tad heavy now for those blue shoulders. As havoc mounted, Vishnu realised that he needed to take extreme measures.

'I must invoke Mahadeva. Invoke him like no one has ever done before.'

Journeying into the wilderness, Vishnu began worshipping Shiva. Years came and years went but the Destroyer did not materialise. Mantras flowed endlessly from Vishnu's mouth. Odes that would please any god in Brahmanda, and yet they did not conjure the vision that he was seeking. The voice that held the answers. Vishnu paused. Sifting through the earth now, he sculpted a lingam. Seated before it, he began chanting the thousand names of Shiva.

Ashutosh ... Bhairava ... Mahakaal ... Rudradeva ...

For each name that he uttered, he placed a lotus flower on the lingam. Thus, when the chants ended, the lingam had been adorned with a thousand blooms. An enchanting spectacle. This became the god's daily ritual.

Every day, Vishnu would recite the thousand names and offer a thousand lotuses.

Shiva was touched.

He was about to manifest himself when he decided to test the Preserver one last time. Watching him anointing the lingam, Shiva stole a single lotus. As a result, when Vishnu finished arranging the flowers, he counted only nine hundred and ninety-nine. The god was thoroughly perplexed. He looked here and there, but the lotus was nowhere to be found. Missing even a single flower meant that the ritual would remain incomplete. Years of austerities would amount to nothing.

Was Hari going to fail before Hara?

As Vishnu pondered, his face lit up with a thought. While chanting the names of Shiva, he had forgotten that he, too, had multiple names. Beautiful ones given by his devotees that celebrated his own splendour. One of them was Kamalanayana.

The Lotus-Eyed One.

'If my eyes resemble the lotus flower, surely one of them can be offered to the lingam,' he said joyously.

Shiva watched. The gods watched. The whole of creation watched as Vishnu plucked out his eye and placed it on the lingam. The thousandth lotus. Glinting now on top of all the flowers. Far more resplendent than any jewel generated by Bala. Prettier than every lotus in Brahmanda. Flushed with the dew of devotion. Shiva instantly appeared and healed the god. He knew what Vishnu desired and presented him with a golden disc. It had two concentric circles spinning in opposite directions and carrying one hundred and eight serrated edges.

'It's the only mobile weapon in the universe,' he said. 'Bound to your will, it shall fly out and come flying back after destroying its target. You can combat every chaos in Brahmanda with this.'

'What do we call the chakra?' Vishnu asked.

'Sudarshana.' Shiva touched his eyes. 'Virtuous vision.'

14

SANGYA CREATES HER TWIN

Surya, the sun god, had married Sangya, the daughter of Vishwakarma, the divine craftsman of Brahmanda. She had given birth to Vaivasvata, Yamuna and Yama, the future deity of death.

Life appeared beautiful, but Sangya was hiding a secret.

No matter how much she adored Surya, she found his heat and light too harsh to bear. What nurtured life during the day became the death of her every night. The good wife endured meekly for years, but one day she decided not to be good anymore. The burns on her flesh had far outweighed the affection in her heart. She toyed with the thought of leaving Surya, but she knew he would be devastated. He loved her too much. Standing before her mirror, Sangya came up with a ruse. A charade so sly that it would not only provide her escape but also take care of her husband. She spawned a woman who was her exact replica. Since she looked like her own reflection, she named her Chhaya.

'I can no longer withstand Surya's radiance,' Sangya confided in her. 'I love him with all my soul but my body shuns him now. I am leaving for my father's house.'

'What about your duty to look after your family?' Chhaya asked.

'Right now, it's about looking after myself. I no longer relish my husband but he relishes me and so I have created you. Take my place. Look after him and my children and never reveal your identity to anyone.'

'I will not,' Chhaya assured her. 'But the moment someone tugs at my hair, I shall speak the truth.'

Sangya reached Vishwakarma's house and recounted everything. Her father tried persuading her to return but to no avail. Since she had arrived without informing her husband, Vishwakarma refused to shelter her. Sangya journeyed to a nearby kingdom called Uttarakuru and began living there in the form of a mare. Back home, unaware of this duplication, Surya begot three more children with Chhaya. A daughter, Tapti, and sons, Savarni and Shani. Alas, blood soon proved thicker as Chhaya's love for Sangya's children dried up. She began neglecting them to dote only on her own. While Vaivasvata was too upright to protest, the other two siblings did not take this well. Yamuna began a terrible fight with Tapti and cursed her right away.

'May you turn into a river on Earth.'

'And may the same happen to you.'

No sooner had they spoken than both maidens dissolved into streams of water. Yamuna flowed through the north, while Tapti coursed along the west. Seeing this, Chhaya began venting her rage on Yama. But Yama had long been suspecting her. A voice inside him had been growing louder every day that this woman was not their mother but a mirage. Outraged with her behaviour now, Yama threatened to kick Chhaya. Her lips shivered with fury and she, too, pronounced a curse.

'You dare to kick me? May your legs wither and fall off!'

Yama was convinced now that she was not the real Sangya. He immediately shared his doubts with his father.

'I had only raised my leg and she cursed me. What mother blights the body of her own son?'

The question baffled Surya. Later that night, he confronted Chhaya, but she had her defence ready.

'I feel terrible that my temper overpowered me and I cursed Yama. I cannot retract it, but I shall reduce its impact. His legs will remain unharmed but bits of their flesh will fall on Earth and be consumed by worms. I shall leash my tongue hereafter.'

She kept speaking, forgetting that she was standing before Surya. Forgetting that no one could keep the sun in the dark. He began questioning her now and Chhaya began to fumble. Concoct more lies. Contradict her own words. Surya was soon burning holes in her story. Melting her entire narrative even as she clung on to it. But when he grasped her by the hair, she crumbled.

'Not Sangya ... Chhaya ....'

'How could you be so cold towards my children?' the god asked.

'I was afraid for my own. Afraid that they might end up as mere shadows like me.'

Seething with rage at being deceived by both women, the sun sped towards Vishwakarma's house. His father-in-law apologised and tried reasoning with him.

'I am not saying Sangya acted wisely, but you are also to blame. Your heat was too much to bear. Did you ever consider how your touch was terrorising her?'

Surya gazed at himself in a vessel of water. It dawned on him now that, all these years, he had not been pleasuring Sangya but only himself. Blinding her and blistering her and never once noticing. His face darkened as if a cloud had covered it.

'I must bring her back. What do I do?'

'We can try something. The culprit here is the excessive energy you radiate. I can chip away much of that with my tools. Then she shall be able to look at you and hold you in her arms.'

The solution worked. Surya was now left with only one-sixteenth of his original brilliance. He reached Uttarakuru and, seeing through Sangya's illusion as a mare, he changed into a stallion. As soon as Sangya recognised her husband, she began to flee in horror. Then she paused.

Something had changed.

His fire was not searing her anymore. It was a tender lustre now, fondling her face. Kissing her eyes. A gentle glow that was warming her loins. The flares were still magnificent but so mellow now. So inviting. So pleasing.

She clasped him and knew that she would never part with him again.

Savouring each other in that animal form, they produced a pair of twins. Since the couple was in the form of ashwa or horses when they gave birth, the twins came to be known as Ashwini Kumaras. Physicians to the gods. Soon after, the pair converted to their original form and returned home. And Sangya never needed another Chhaya.

15

DHRUVA BECOMES A STAR

Manu and Shatarupa's eldest son, Priyavrata, was more inclined towards piety than politics. As a result, their younger son, Uttanapada, was crowned king of the Earth. He had two wives, Suruchi and Suniti. The former was the more beautiful of the two, and Uttanapada adored her excessively. Knowing she had the upper hand, Suruchi soon relegated Suniti to a life outside the palace. The king, although aware, remained too enchanted by Suruchi to oppose her. Before long, both queens bore a son each. Suruchi's son was called Uttama, while Suniti's son was called Dhruva.

The Immovable One.

Uttanapada's unequal affection for his wives began colouring his relationship with his sons. He cared more for Uttama than Dhruva and, in time, declared him Yuvaraja, the crown prince. Dhruva had just turned five when, one day, he entered the court to find the king on his throne and Uttama on his lap. It had been a while since he had felt his father's love. Longing to experience it again, Dhruva began climbing those gilded steps when Suruchi's voice arrested him.

'Where do you think you are going, boy?'

'To sit on father's lap.'

'On his lap or on his throne?'

The queen lowered her face close to the child and hissed, 'You have your eyes on the throne. You wish to be king. Monarch of Bhuloka. Forget it, boy. The highest seat is not for everyone. You have to be worthy enough. Do not aspire for what you cannot acquire.'

Dhruva glanced at Uttanapada, but his father remained silent. Boiling with pain and humiliation, Dhruva fled and buried his face in his mother's lap. Between sobs, he narrated the entire incident. A solitary tear oozed from the corner of Suniti's eye, but she had learnt long ago that those amounted to nothing. Time had come to teach the same to her little one. Wiping the tear away, she kissed Dhruva.

'Grieve not, my son. One can only accept one's fate. You came from my womb and so you are tied to my misery.'

'But why are we miserable, mother?'

'I cannot answer that. Everything is willed by Lord Vishnu. Maybe he is pleased with Suruchi and Uttama and hence they have been rewarded with a better life.'

Dhruva stopped crying. His eyes lit up as he looked at the queen. 'Lord Vishnu blesses those who please him?'

'Indeed. Do not grudge your brother anything. Try to please the almighty and he may bless you with his grace in your next life.'

The fire in the child's eyes flared brighter. His mother's words seemed to be clutching at his hand and pulling him hard. Asking him to walk a beautiful path that had opened up. Dhruva nodded.

'Not the next life. I shall please Lord Vishnu in this life so that he fulfils my desire.'

Suniti gasped. Her five-year-old was prattling about making god happy. What did he have in mind?

'Your desire? What are you seeking? Your father's throne? That Suruchi be punished?'

'No, mother,' Dhruva assured her. 'Uttama can have the throne. If I can please Lord Vishnu, why would I ask for something so measly? So momentary? I shall ask for something more lasting. A boon like no other. A boon inaccessible to everyone else. You have always found your life empty. I shall strive for an honour that will fill you with pride.'

The queen could hardly believe the words coming from her cherub. Her confusion gave way to terror now. Terror of losing her child. Terror of where this zeal might lead him. She tried hard to dissuade him but to no avail. Dhruva was unbending. He began questioning her about ways to please the Preserver. When Suniti could provide no answer, he took her blessings and left. Reaching the forest, Dhruva came across seven sages and asked them the same question. Like his mother, the sages, too, tried to deter him and failed. This degree of resolve in someone so young was astounding them. Their chorus of voices finally revealed that the best way to please Vishnu was to perform austerities. Rigorous austerities.

'Only when you stop seeing everything else can you see him. Can you do that, child?'

Dhruva smiled. Choosing a spot, he began meditating. Meditating long and hard. Days passed but nothing happened. His body was turning weary. His morale was starting to dip. Suniti's face was looming large before his eyes. But the elements had recognised how noble his quest was. How incandescent his soul was. The child heard footsteps. Turning around, he saw a sage draped in saffron and carrying a veena and khartal. As Dhruva got up to pay his respects, the man touched his forehead.

'I know all about you, son. You want to please him whose very presence pleases the universe. But the summer has turned hot and the winter shall be cold. How will you cope with the seasons here?'

'I can, for I have my mother's blessings.'

'But this forest is filled with beasts and you are a tender morsel. How will you secure yourself?'

'I can if I have your blessings.'

The sage laughed. 'I see that you are unshakeable like your name. You have my blessings, but you shall please Narayana faster if you chant the right mantra.'

'Right mantra?'

'The one with twelve syllables.'

Closing his eyes, the sage asked Dhruva to repeat after him. The air swayed as his melodious voice swirled through it.

Om Namo Bhagwate Vasudevaya
Om Namo Bhagwate Vasudevaya
Om Namo Bhagwate Vasudevaya

As he was leaving, the child asked him his name. He smiled. 'I am he who wanders around singing praises of the lord. They call me Narada.'

Imbued with the mantra, Dhruva was feeling strangely renewed. A nameless energy was spreading through his cells, igniting his blood. Walking ahead, he arrived at Madhuvana, by the banks of the Yamuna. Standing on one foot under a kadamba tree, he began invoking Vishnu with the mantra. His fervour was now springing from the core of his being. Vibrating through the very matrix of his self. His mind and heart were joining hands as every ounce of Dhruva serenaded the Preserver. Time passed and he stopped having food. More time passed and he gave up water. So intense was this adulation that it soon began sending tremors across Brahmanda. Across every realm. As the cosmic spine shivered, the devas hastened to convene. They had never seen such devotion and feared that the child was pursuing a devious goal. His success could make him master of the universe. Topple Devaraja Indra. Their decision was unanimous.

Dhruva had to be stopped!

Every possible hurdle was sent his way now. They dispatched demons with terrifying faces. Tigers roared during the day and jackals howled through the night. The sun scorched his body and rain lashed his skin. Indra even descended in the form of Suniti to jolt him awake. But Dhruva did not budge. He had become that rock against which waves crashed only to shatter. His equilibrium was foiling every foe. His inner vision was merging with the divine. Thwarted by the child, the gods turned to Vishnu, who gently dispelled their fears.

'He does not crave material things. There are higher rewards that can be acquired if one makes the effort. It's time I grant him what he deserves.'

Silence fell around the meditating figure. No more animals or demons or wind or rain. Not even the song of Yamuna rippling by. Just a cosmic voice calling out his name.

'Dhruva.'

The boy opened his eyes to see what they were showing him. Blue skin. Yellow robes. White conch. Pink lotus. Tears were blurring Dhruva's vision and yet he kept gazing. The sight was saturating him and yet making him crave for more. Inducing an exhilaration that he had never known before. And just like that, a delightful verse of twelve stanzas poured from his mouth. Words that the world would call Dhruva Stuti. Finishing it, he asked, 'Have I pleased you, lord?'

'You have.'

'Can I touch your feet?'

'You have touched my heart. What do you wish for?'

But Dhruva could no longer speak. That image of Vishnu had gratified every desire. Validated all of his life. He could think of nothing else. He shook his head, but the god touched him with his conch shell.

'Ask, O Grandson of Manu.'

Dhruva was about to refuse again when he recalled the words Suruchi had flung at his face.

The highest seat is not for everyone ...

Vishnu smiled.

'Go back to your kingdom. When the times comes for you to leave your mortal body, I shall place you there.'

The god pointed above.

'The highest place in the whole of Brahmanda. Exalted above all creation. There you shall twinkle as a star. The brightest star. Firm in its place just as you have remained throughout this ordeal. Men will look at you with faith in their eyes, for you shall guide them in the dark. They shall bless you and call you Dhruva Tara.'

16

BHARAT ADOPTS A DEER

One of the descendants of Manu's elder son, Priyavrata, was King Bharat. He was an exemplary ruler. The welfare of people was his primary karma, and devotion to Vishnu his only dharma. So virtuous were his actions that he soon cleansed his soul of every fault. Every bond. When old age finally beckoned, he transferred his kingdom to his sons, removed every piece of regalia from his body and left for Pulahshrama along River Gandaki. The place offered a solitude that would steer him closer to god and Bharat was looking for nothing more. His mantras soon began dousing the hermitage with reverence.

Om Namo Narayanaya ...

Om Namo Narayanaya ...

One morning, he was offering water to Surya when a pregnant doe approached Gandaki on the opposite bank. As she drank, they heard a lion roar. Terrified, the doe bounded across the river to save her life. Alas, both her fear and exertion proved fatal and she collapsed dead in the middle of the stream. As her body slumped, the fawn fell out of her womb. Bharat's heart melted at the sight of that infant animal thrashing about in the current. Its eyes terrorised by sunlight as it groped for that tender darkness encasing it a moment ago. Bharat carried the deer into the ashram. Laying it down, he hacked the umbilical cord, unaware that an invisible one had begun sprouting between him and the animal. As days passed, he became exceedingly fond of the deer. He would bathe it and feed it with his own hands. Narrate stories and sing songs. Cradle it by the Gandaki as if reminiscing about the day when it had entered his life. As if wondering where this tributary of love had been hiding inside him that the deer had dug out.

'Helping the helpless is a virtue. This poor creature has no one but me and I shall foster it,' he would keep telling himself.

But with time, Bharat's affection swelled into obsession. It reached a point where it occupied him so entirely that he turned oblivious to everything else. Even Vishnu. The man who had come unfettered to Pulahshrama had now yoked himself to another. Tending to the deer's needs had become the sole purpose of his existence. He loved how the creature would often poke him with its horns or frolic with his objects of worship. The deer had begun roaming outside and Bharat would remain restless until it returned. Dreading that it might fall prey to a beast, he would open his eyes in the middle of meditation to look for it. Gazing at similar spots on the moon, he would wonder if Chandra might have abducted it. Leaping at every sound, he would pine to hear its footsteps returning home. Everything appeared futile to him until the deer was back in his arms.

'Why must you go wandering around?' He would fondle it. 'I miss you as I miss my own sons now.'

Bharat's last days arrived to find him still unwilling to part with the animal. Wondering who would care for it once he was gone, he remained clinging to its body until the very end. So profound was his sorrow that in his next life, he went on to take birth as a deer.

A Jatismara. Beings who remembered everything about their past lives.

Bharat realised now that he had failed to differentiate between affection and attachment. Strayed at the last moment by weighing down his soul with maya. Regretting his actions, he abandoned his herd and reached Pulahshrama again. There, he spent the rest of his days yearning to be born as a human once more. His prayers were answered and he reincarnated as a Brahmin. A Jatismara again.

His new life was dedicated now to the quest of supreme knowledge. Communion with the Parabrahman. So absorbed was he in his own world that he again became detached from everyone. He would hardly speak, hardly move, and preferred to remain stationary with just his thoughts. This inertia earned him a peculiar name.

Jadabharata, the Immobile One.

Finally unburdened, his soul floated free.

17

BHRIGU CURSES VISHNU

The gods and demons continued to fight incessantly. At times, the cause of the devas was justified, and at times that of the asuras. Sometimes the former would gain an upper hand, and sometimes the latter. And yet, those battlefields had begun reeking more of demonic blood than divine. Alarmed at their dwindling numbers, the tribe approached their guru, Shukracharya, also known as Asuracharya.

The guru agreed that there was indeed cause for concern. He had been hearing the daityas and danavas mourning a lot more than the devas. He outlined a plan.

'I shall pray to Mahadeva. Perform austerities to gain secrets that shall make you all deathless. Armed with that knowledge, we shall foil the gods like never before.'

'But what shall we do while you are gone?' the demons asked.

'Nothing.'

'Nothing?'

'Yes. Do not engage in any combat until I return. Give up your arms and coexist peacefully with the gods.'

'They will never respect such a truce. The moment we disarm ourselves, they will come charging at us. Who will safeguard our lives?'

'My father,' Shukracharya replied. 'Sage Bhrigu. Go and seek shelter from my parents. They will provide you sanctuary.'

As the demons travelled towards Bhrigu's hermitage, their guru began invoking Shiva. When the Destroyer appeared, Shukracharya asked for a boon.

'A mantra, lord. Teach me a mantra that can revive the dead. The asuras shall have no fear of dying then, and the devas will be unable to wipe out their race.'

'An antidote for death is not easy to acquire,' Shiva told him. 'You will need to observe austerities for a thousand years. And during that time, you must live solely on smoke. Only if you succeed can I grant you that elixir.'

Shukracharya began meditating right away while the demons arrived at Bhrigu's abode. The sage and his wife, Kavyamata, opened their doors and hearts to them. They knew why their son had sent the asuras and assured them complete security. As news began to circulate that Shukracharya was performing austerities for the next thousand years, the gods instantly spied an opportunity. The guru was away and the demons had disarmed. Once Shukracharya returned, the asuras would turn deathless.

The time to act was now.

Led by Vishnu and Indra, the devas stormed the hermitage. Blood began to spill. Bodies began to pile. Such was the carnage by the gods that it seemed as if the demonic clan would turn extinct today. With Bhrigu away from the ashram, the remaining asuras rushed to Kavyamata in panic.

'Do not stand in our way,' Indra threatened the sage's wife. 'We mean you no harm. We are here only for these demons.'

'They are disciples of my son and have sought refuge under my roof,' she asserted. 'My husband and I have vowed to keep them safe until Shukra returns. I cannot sin by betraying their faith.'

Vishnu folded his hands. 'I respect your words, mother. But daityas and danavas are a threat to the cosmic order and Shukracharya is attempting to make them invincible. If that happens, chaos will run amok. Vice shall infect Brahmanda and all that's good will be doomed. Just as your son has an obligation as a guru, so have I as Narayana. His dharma is towards the demons, but mine is towards the entire cosmos. Towards greater good, which always demands a price.'

'What price? When Mahadeva himself is prepared to fulfil Shukra's request, how can you object?'

'Mahadeva is a yogi. A neutral soul who does not engage with Brahmanda. Gods and demons are alike for him, but I cannot remain indifferent. I must act, and so should you.'

But Kavyamata refused to budge. She even turned hostile as the gods inched closer. Using her mystic powers, she froze Indra's limbs. Seeing their king paralysed, fear filled the devas and many began to flee. Vishnu asked the Devaraja to enter his body but Kavyamata hissed like a female python.

'Beware! I shall reduce you both to ashes.'

'Kill her,' Indra shrieked. 'She's preventing the cosmos from purging itself. We cannot achieve our goal as long as she stands in our way.'

Vishnu closed his eyes. He lifted his hand and the Sudarshana materialised. The disc, light as a feather for him, weighed on his finger today. His final hope was that the sight of the chakra might terrorise the woman, but she continued to hold her ground. Her head erect. Gaze unflinching. Prepared to be a martyr. The disc sprang and the demons watched as the god beheaded a woman. Her blood was staining his hand. Her torso kept standing awhile as if still defying the Preserver, and then collapsed.

An eerie silence fell, only to be ruptured by Bhrigu's scream.

'Kavya!'

Staggering towards her body, the sage realised what had occurred. Corpses of asuras littered his ground. The chakra reeked of his wife's blood. Bhrigu spun towards Vishnu.

'What have you done?'

'What had to be done for the sake of dharma. Just as Mahadeva had to behead Brahmadeva, I had to behead her. Often gods must also kill so that Brahmanda can live.'

'But those who kill must also atone, Narayana. Mahadeva had to wander with a skull stuck to his hand, and now you, too, shall pay. You have filled me with pain and I curse you that you will undergo the same. You shall take birth on Earth. Take birth as human avatars on Bhuloka. You shall go through life and death and suffer the very pain that you inflict on mortals.'

The Preserver folded his hands again. 'I accept.'

Far away from the hermitage, Shukracharya sat lost in meditation. Oblivious to everything. Counting the years. One thousand years. Waiting for the mantra that Shiva had promised him. It had such a lyrical name.

Mritasanjivani.

18

SHIVA KILLS YAMA

One of the many ways gods toyed with men was to bring someone to a point where two roads diverged and make him choose. Rarely would both roads be equally divine. More often, they would be equally diabolical. But most of the time, they would be paved with equal amounts of heaven and hell. Sage Mrikandu and his wife, Marudvati, were in the throes of a similar dilemma right now. He was another son of Bhrigu and the couple had been performing a severe penance to gratify Shiva and obtain a child. The Destroyer was standing before them to grant the boon. But he was asking them to make a choice.

'Listen carefully, for I am repeating my words. You can either have a son who shall be unwise but will live for many years or a son who shall be wise but will live for sixteen years. What do you choose?'

Marikandu and Marudvati peered into each other's eyes. Shiva asked again.

'Age or acclaim? What will it be?'

The sage turned and folded his hands.

'We both wish for the same, Mahadeva. The prospect of a son who shall live long is enticing. His presence will surely comfort us in our ripe years, but his own life shall be hell if he's unwise. It would be a selfish choice to make. We would rather have a son who is wise for his mind shall outlive his body.'

In due course, Marudvati gave birth to a boy and they named him Markandeya. So fertile was his mind that even as a child he began sowing it with words from the scriptures. Sages from far away would arrive to debate with him and leave enlightened. By the time he entered adolescence, he had mastered the Vedas and the Shastras. The whole land was hailing him now but time was ticking on indifferently, and it soon arrived at Markandeya's sixteenth birthday. Marikandu had been celebrating it every year with a yagna, but today the boy woke up to a strange gloom. He could neither hear the sound of mantras nor smell the scent of offerings. Instead, his father was building a funeral pyre.

'Who's dead?' he enquired.

'No one yet,' Marikandu smiled. 'It's for you.'

'For me?'

'Yes. Mahadeva created our bond only for sixteen years. Today, that comes to an end.'

'And none of you are mourning?' he exclaimed as his mother walked out of the hut holding an urn.

'We made our choice,' Marudvati clasped him lovingly. 'And we would choose the same again and again if Mahadeva asked us. You may perish today but your fame shall live on. And so will our names, forever linked with yours. You are mortal but you have made us immortal.'

Markandeya stood staring at his pyre. Then he sat down and began to sculpt a lingam out of soil.

'I shall pray to Mahadeva as I have been praying all these years. He's the most benevolent of gods and will surely spare my life.'

'But he has ordained your death,' said Mrikandu. 'Why will he alter that?'

'He might, for he knows that I still have so much to learn. So much to love.'

Closing his eyes, the boy began to chant a mantra. Meditate upon Shiva. The deeper he was descending into that name, the higher he was ascending towards bliss. It was flooding his every cell. Transcending his five senses. Conjoining his seven chakras. Igniting a fervour so intense that he was dissolving into the Destroyer now. Becoming one with the One. For Markandeya, the three realms of Brahmanda had condensed into three words.

Om Namah Shivay
Om Namah Shivay
Om Namah Shivay

Shadows were encircling him now. The minions of Yama were manifesting like vultures eying a chunk of meat. As one of them pounced upon Markandeya, he instantly fell back as if repelled by an invisible force. He tried again, only to crash harder. They all tried now but were foiled one by one. Markandeya's communion with Shiva had encased him like an armour. Given rise to a barrier so ferocious that even the aides of death were failing to breach it. They hastened to inform Yama.

'Looks like I will have to collect this one myself,' he muttered.

Markandeya choked at once. He could feel a rope clenching his throat. Binding his breath. He opened his eyes to see Death incarnate standing before him. Yama had flung a lasso around his neck and was dragging him along with the lingam. The boy tried to chant again but the rope constricted him like a python. It was knotting tighter and tighter. His soul was loosening faster and faster. As his body began to give up, Markandeya embraced the lingam with a final plea.

I surrender before your will, Mahadeva ...

Yama halted. The sound of a thousand damrus was surrounding him. Rattling before him. Rattling behind him. Rattling above him. Rattling below him. Shiva was standing in his way.

'Let go of the boy,' he commanded.

The god of death bowed. 'Markandeya's time on Earth has come to an end. You had granted him sixteen years and he has lived them all.'

'I am here to grant him many more years. To make him immortal.'

Yama trembled. 'Immortal?'

'Indeed.'

'But you had destined his death. How can you grant him life?'

Shiva stepped closer.

'Look at me. I smear myself with ash but I also wear the rudraksha. I am decked with both the seed of life and the dust of death. In this paradox lies your answer. Just as my body harmonises both, I, who had given him death, am now granting him life. Destroying every rule for his sake. Few on Earth are luminous like Markandeya, and his everlasting presence will do everyone good.'

'Granting immortality flouts the very cardinal of cosmic laws.' Yama shook his head. 'You have already promised Bhrigu's other son, Shukracharya, the Mritasanjivani, and now you are granting Bhrigu's grandson eternal life? As the deity of death, I cannot allow someone to be made deathless. I have a prescribed role in Brahmanda, which I must fulfil, or I shall no longer be Dharmaraja. My father, Surya, remains unshakeable on his path and so must I. Pray, allow me my dharma. Allow me to claim what's mine.'

As he took another step, the damrus began rattling louder. Their echoes were turning fiercer. They were closing in on Yama now. Strangulating him with invisible hands. He was twisting. He was clawing. Screaming for a gulp of air. The echoes were digging. Their nails were piercing. Gouging his throat. Perforating his windpipe. His eyes were bulging. The damrus were blaring. As he arched violently, they snapped his neck. The universe gasped.

Death himself has died!

Catastrophe! Gods began to descend. They were pacifying Shiva. Imploring him to bring back Yama. Reminding him of how vital he was to Brahmanda. To the rhythm of rebirth. How he alone could mete out justice based on karma. The Destroyer offered them a simple barter.

'Yama comes back to life only if Markandeya gets eternal life.'

The gods gave in. As Yama opened his eyes, they all bowed before Shiva.

'You have done what no god has ever done before, Mahadeva. You not only killed Death himself but have also made your devotee deathless. We mark this event by bestowing upon you the name Kalantaka. He who triumphed over death. He who showed the universe what true devotion can attain. The words chanted by Markandeya to invoke you will now be called the Mahamrityunjaya mantra, and anyone who recites it will have no fear of Yama.'

The Destroyer fondled the boy's face. 'Your parents chose wisely.'

'Do we humans really choose anything, lord?' he asked. 'Was it my parents who chose? Was it not you who had already made that choice for them?'

The damrus were laughing. Shiva smiled.

19

CHANDRA LOSES HIS LIGHT

Born of brilliant fluid oozing from the eyes of Sage Atri, Chandra had become the cosmic night lamp. Married to twenty-seven daughters of Daksha, those nakshatras, or stars, twinkled lustrously around him to make the night sky prettier. But the moon had eyes for only one of them.

Rohini. The Red One.

Chandra's passion for her soon soared to a point where he began neglecting his other wives. As his love for them began dimming, so did their radiance. Their light no longer illuminated the dark, no longer adorned Brahmanda. Those nakshatras now began making every possible attempt to rekindle their husband's love. They sang the sweetest verses and made him the choicest food. Dressed in exquisite robes and invited him to undress them. Clustered into incredible constellations to delight his heart. Employed every other ruse but nothing worked. The moon was no longer dividing his love into twenty-seven parts. It was all for Rohini. Unable to bear his continuing disregard, the wives complained to their father. Daksha reasoned with his son-in-law, but Chandra was too bewitched by the Red One.

'I give my light to all, but I can surely choose whom to give my love.'

Outraged, the Prajapati pronounced a curse.

'Your indifference has robbed my daughters of their sparkle. Why should you continue to shine? I curse you that you shall lose all your light and all your beauty that fills you with pride. Like blindness spreading through the eyes, your radiance shall decline. You have darkened their lives and now a darkness, twenty-six times greater, will blot you out of the sky.'

The moon god laughed. He was confident that nothing could obscure him. But the next moment, he saw Rohini staring at him with dread.

'Your glow. It's fading.'

It had only just begun. That majestic sheen began to dwindle every day. More and more. Faster and faster. The moonbeams were vanishing as if someone was sucking them out of him. Ripping chunks of incandescence to leave him cold and pale. The nakshatras were terrified now to see their lord wasting away. Chandra was the presiding deity of plant life on Earth and, if he withered, all vegetation would die. Nights would turn dark and humans would lose their way. They advised him to speak to Brahma. When the moon sought his counsel, the Creator could only think of one name.

'Mahadeva. Pray to him and he shall revitalise you.'

Chandra journeyed towards the western coast. There, he built a lingam by the sea and began chanting the Mahamrityunjaya mantra. Sitting motionless as if he, too, had been sculpted by someone. Waves would come and crash against his body. Salt water would sting his skin. The sea would try to pull him away, but he held on. His flesh was decomposing but not his soul. Then, one day, he opened his eyes to see footprints on the sand. Shiva was standing before him.

'What do you seek?'

'Myself, lord. My true self. Daksha's curse is killing my splendour. Pray, restore me to my glory.'

'A curse cannot be revoked.' Shiva shook his head. 'And a curse from the Prajapati is quite potent. Like an object flung into this sea, it will keep returning. I cannot undo it but will modify it. You shall keep losing more and more of yourself and eventually fade out as Daksha had pronounced. But that will not be permanent. You shall regain your light the very next day. You will gradually become resplendent again only to start dwindling once more. Thus, you shall keep waxing and waning till the end of time. Bright and dark. Full and half. You shall now be a continuous process.'

'Like birth and death. Creation and destruction.'

'Yes. When you are wholly dark, it shall be Amavasya, and when you are full of light again, it will be Poornima. Thus, you shall be in a state of eternal flux, which will influence Bhuloka, for as you wax and wane, these sea tides everywhere will crest and ebb with you. You shall also bedeck my forehead now and I shall be called Chandrashekhar.'

The moon bowed before the god and so did that coast. It had become a revered place that could grant a new lease of life. Since Chandra was also called Soma, both Shiva and that seaside pilgrimage acquired a hallowed name.

Somnath.

Chandra opened his heart to all his wives now and even vowed to remain forever faithful. Alas, that was not to be.

20

DADHICHI BATTLES THE GODS

Sage Dadhichi and King Kshuva shared a tender friendship. Although the unlikeliest of bonds, it had remained steadfast for years until one day the two began debating over whose varna was superior. While Dadhichi argued in favour of Brahmins, Kshuva exalted the Kshatriyas. So enamoured were they of their own varna that the banter soon turned into battle. Competition displaced all affection and Kshuva now borrowed Indra's deadliest weapon.

The Vajra.

Crafted by Vishwakarma out of the excess energy that he had chipped from Surya, the Vajra could annihilate anything in the cosmos. Kshuva hurled the weapon at Dadhichi, and it instantly ripped the sage's body apart. Dadhichi was dead. The king walked away feeling jubilant that he had been validated. That a Kshatriya had trounced a Brahmin. Unaware that another Brahmin was about to foil everything. A Brahmin who had been meditating for the past thousand years. A Brahmin who had now acquired a mantra more lethal than a hundred Vajras.

Shukracharya.

The guru of the demons had succeeded in appeasing Shiva and returned with Mritasanjivani, the mantra that could reanimate the dead. As soon as Shukracharya heard about Dadhichi, he reached the spot where his corpse lay. Mritasanjivani blew life into the sage and Dadhichi at once questioned Shukracharya about this miracle he had performed.

'Mahadeva,' he replied. 'Nothing is impossible if your devotion can touch him. Just as he blessed Markandeya with eternal life, he has blessed me that I can bring the dead back to life.'

Dadhichi was still bristling with humiliation. Mritasanjivani had healed his body but not his soul. He was not only determined to crush Kshuva but to also restore the pride of his varna. Instructed by Shukracharya, the sage now began terrible austerities to gratify Shiva. When the god manifested, Dadhichi asked for three boons.

'Make my bones mightier than the Vajra.'

'So be it.'

'Grant me that no one can ever kill me again.'

'So be it.'

'And grant me that no one can ever dishonour me again.'

'So be it.'

Thus fortified, the sage stormed into Kshuva's palace and kicked him brutally. Stunned to see Dadhichi alive, the king flung the Vajra at him again. The weapon struck him, only to be repelled right away. Kshuva kept launching the weapon again and again but in vain. The sage stood unscathed, as if the Vajra was terrified to touch him now.

'Witness the power of a Brahmin.' Dadhichi laughed. 'Mahadeva himself has made me invincible.'

Hearing this, the king instantly began invoking Vishnu. He was an ardent devotee and realised that the Preserver alone could counter the sage. But when Vishnu found out that Shiva had blessed Dadhichi, he advised Kshuva to be tactful.

'You can no longer defeat him. The only way to save yourself is to call for a truce.'

Vishnu turned towards the sage.

'It's time to end this conflict. Both Brahmins and Kshatriyas are equally relevant to the scheme of things. No one is lesser or greater than the other. No one needs to be afraid of the other.'

'Afraid?' Dadhichi sneered. 'Mahadeva has made me unconquerable. I am afraid of no one anymore. Not even you.'

'Not even me?'

'Not even you.'

The Preserver glowered. He realised that Shiva's boons had filled the sage with arrogance. That the need to establish his supremacy had so blinded Dadhichi that he was challenging even the gods. If not subdued, he could breed chaos. Vishnu had arrived to broker peace, but he knew that war was inevitable now. He summoned the Sudarshana and hurled it at the sage. The blades made resounding contact with Dadhichi's throat but failed to even nick his skin. Its edges buckled and it came crashing to the ground.

'Is this the chakra you are so proud of?' the sage taunted. 'Perhaps it's only good enough to behead women.'

A livid Vishnu now flung his mace at Dadhichi, but that, too, proved impotent. The god kept using one divine weapon after another: not one of them could override Shiva's boons. Several devas had begun materialising around Vishnu to aid him. They launched their own artillery at the sage but to no avail. It was as if every weapon was mortally afraid of making contact with Dadhichi. He smiled.

It was his turn now.

Picking a handful of Kusha grass, he tossed them at the devas. Lo and behold, each blade of grass transformed into a fiery trident threatening to vaporise the gods. They began to flee in terror but not Vishnu. He conjured multiple replicas of himself, all of whom Dadhichi dissolved. With nothing else left to attempt, the god now assumed Vishwaroop, his cosmic form supreme. The whole of Brahmanda was breathing inside him. Innumerable forms. Matter animate and inanimate. The living and the dying. Endless possibilities across endless dimensions. Gazing in wonder, the universe bowed. But not the sage.

'Illusion. Mere illusion. Your spectacle will not overpower me, Narayana. Nothing you do can overpower me now.'

Finally, Brahma appeared and advised Kshuva to seek Dadhichi's forgiveness. The sage relented but not before uttering a curse.

'All you gods shall soon face the wrath of Mahadeva. Each one of you.'

The words were haunting them as they watched him leave.

Each one of you ...

21

SATI KILLS HERSELF

Daksha's youngest daughter, Sati, had grown into an alluring woman. An incarnation of Adishakti, she refused every suitor that her parents approved for her. With the Prajapati attempting esteemed alliances, her continuous refusal had begun to peeve him. When he finally asked her whom she wished to marry, Sati uttered the name she had been chanting since childhood.

'Mahadeva.'

Daksha erupted. He had not forgotten how Shiva had decapitated his father, Brahma. How he had pronounced him unworthy of worship. How he had alleviated his curse on Chandra. Recently, the Destroyer had again incensed the Prajapati. Daksha had entered Brahma's assembly and everyone had stood up out of respect. Everyone but Shiva. A furious Daksha had laid down a cardinal rule.

'Shiva is not civilised enough to mingle with gods. Henceforth, no one shall invite that uncouth to any gathering.'

The Destroyer's mount, Nandi, had instantly retorted, 'Mahadeva is not concerned with worldly rituals. Anyone abusing him can only be an animal. Check your words, Prajapati, or you may soon end up looking like one.'

But Sati had no inkling of these events. All she knew was that she was existing only partially and Shiva alone could complete her. Retiring to the forest, she started severe austerities to win over the god. So fiercely did her soul burn for Mahadeva that the ice on Kailash began to melt. Overwhelmed by her love, Shiva consented to make her his bride. Daksha fumed but Brahma intervened.

'Sati was born for Shiva.'

'He roams around in animal hide. Smokes hemp and smears ash. Rides a bull and wears a snake. How can a princess live with a hermit?'

'He's a free spirit. Their union is natural law. You cannot keep them apart.'

'Don't you remember how Shiva shamed you? Shamed you not once but twice?'

He argued more and more but Brahma declared that the marriage was inevitable. The Prajapati knuckled under his father's will. And it came to pass that as the couple circled the holy fire, something burned and died inside Daksha.

I shall show them their place ...

No sooner had Sati and Shiva settled into conjugal bliss than news arrived that the Prajapati was organising a grand yagna at Kankhala. All the gods would be invited and all the sages would be honoured. The choicest oblations would be offered and enormous merit would be earned. Sati was rapturous. The prospect of seeing her parents and sisters filled her with joy and she began to make preparations. Days passed but no invitation landed at her door. Neither did Daksha arrive nor her mother. Not even a priest or a messenger. Gradually her delight gave way to dread. She no longer ventured out in the morning or fell asleep at night lest she missed her summons. Her eyes were afloat with hope but her heart had begun to sink with every passing hour.

Shiva barely uttered a word.

The day of the yagna arrived and Sati watched the gods leaving for Kankhala. Were they taunting her as they passed? Or were they pitying her that she had become an outcaste for Daksha?

'Why is father doing this?' She broke down before her husband. 'How can he not invite his own daughter? Invite every deva and not you who are Mahadeva?'

'Prajapati's hatred for me has singed his love for you. For him, you are no longer his daughter. Only my wife.'

'A father can never hate his own child. I must go and speak to him.'

'We are not welcome there, Sati. An unwanted person is always disgraced in such assemblies. Besides, your presence will stir negative emotions in the Prajapati, which will contaminate his yagna. Render the whole ceremony futile. Harm may even befall you and there won't be anyone to protect you.'

'Harm?' Her eyes widened. 'What harm can come to me in my own house? In the presence of my own family? I cannot let this injustice pass. You say my father hates me, but he will love me again when I stand before him.'

Shiva tried to deter her again, but Sati was adamant. Finally, the god instructed Nandi to carry her to Kankhala. Sati arrived at the yagna and stood aghast. While her mother, Prasuti, embraced her, Daksha was displaying nothing but contempt. Even her sisters were scorning her for showing up uninvited. Mocking her for the wild flowers she had bedecked herself with. The ceremony site further heightened Sati's pain. All the gods were present but no seat had been assigned for Shiva. No share of the oblations had been reserved for him. No mantras featuring his name were being chanted. The yagna had boycotted the Destroyer and no one was protesting, not even Brahma or Vishnu. As Nandi shed silent tears, Sati confronted her father.

'How can you conduct this yagna without the presence of Mahadeva? I see gods and demons here. Yakshas and gandharvas. Even souls and spirits. Why have you barred your own son-in-law?'

'Because he belongs to none of these categories,' the Prajapati cackled. 'He's neither divine nor demonic. Neither a human nor an animal. Inferior to every creature. The lowest form of life. Has he sent you here to beg for an invitation?'

'You are insulting my husband, father.'

'Yes. The husband you took against my wish. Look around. My civilisation celebrates culture. Rites and customs. It has no place for that anarchist. That half-naked addict who remains indifferent to what we have so painstakingly created. You died the day you married him and the dead are no longer invited.'

Disbelief seared Sati's face. Her tone was wounded as she spoke. 'You, who condemned Chandra for what he did to your daughters, are condemning your own daughter today? My own are shunning me today? Mahadeva was right. I should not have come to this place. This yagna where Brahma and Vishnu sit silently while Shiva is being reviled. Have both of you forgotten that you are the triumvirate? Agents of the same supreme will? Isn't the Prajapati abusing you by abusing my lord? Or has your hunger for these oblations gagged you both?'

'How dare you?' Daksha raised his hand as if to strike her. 'They are worthy, unlike your Shiva. They both engage. One creates and the other preserves, but your husband rejects. He blights Param Pita Brahma but blesses the demons with Mritasanjivani. Why should I include him when he has excluded himself from us? I have nothing but hatred for him.'

'You do not hate him,' Sati snarled. 'You fear him. You fear that you cannot tame him. That he does not conform to anything you have designed.'

'Hence a pariah who does not deserve my ceremony. Not even the leftovers of my ceremony.'

'Enough!'

The assembly froze. It was Dadhichi. He got up from his seat.

'Any yagna that maligns Mahadeva is a blot on the face of Brahmanda. Sitting here will be a sin now and I shall not be a sinner.'

As he left, Prasuti screamed. All eyes had been on Dadhichi, and no one had noticed that Sati was standing now by the edge of the sacrificial fire.

'I cannot leave like the sage,' she said as tears flooded her face. 'I can no longer go back to Mahadeva as Sati. This body is a curse. Being the Prajapati's daughter is a curse. My lord has been shamed today because of me. Because I am Daksha's seed. I must destroy this identity, this body of mine. Only then can I truly reunite with him. Only then will you comprehend the true meaning of Shiva. Your yagna has no offerings for my lord so I offer myself. Forgive me, Mahadeva. Forgive me.'

Her father gnashed his teeth. 'Stop chanting his name. You are polluting my altar.'

'Vile Daksha,' Sati roared. Her eyes inflamed now. Her voice scalding.

'You forget that I am Adishakti. Born to you and Prasuti because you both had invoked me. I had warned you that the day you dishonour me, I shall disown you.'

The gathering recoiled as Sati leapt into the fire. As her flesh burnt, terrible omens began to manifest. The skies turned dark. Vultures swooped and jackals howled. The wind screeched like an angry spirit blowing out every flame. As Sati took her last breath, Shiva's eyes sprung open. Quaking with pain and fury, he wrenched a strand of hair off his head and hurled it. Hitting the ground, it sparked a horrific being with three eyes and a thousand arms named Veerbhadra. He bowed as Shiva commanded him.

'Tear Daksha's yagna to pieces!'

Moments later, everyone at the ceremony was fleeing in horror. Veerbhadra had spawned more terrifying entities from the pores of his skin and they were wreaking havoc. Maiming gods and killing humans. Urinating on oblations and spilling blood. Torching the place and frolicking with the ashes. All that was feral in Brahmanda seemed to have pounced upon the yagna. Bhrigu brought forth warriors called Ribhus to counter them but in vain. Veerbhadra's army was relentless, like a boulder in motion, grinding the ceremony to dust. The ice of Kailash was choking the flames of Kankhala. Daksha pleaded with Vishnu now to use his Sudarshana, but the god refused.

'Veerbhadra is the energy of Shiva himself. As potent as my chakra. If they both collide, the universe will explode.'

Before the Prajapati could utter another word, Veerbhadra charged. Seizing Daksha by the hair, he hacked his head and tossed it into the fire. The gods realised that Dadhichi's curse had come true.

You shall face the wrath of Mahadeva ... each one of you ...

The yagna had been defiled and this was highly inauspicious. Consequences for the three realms would be devastating now. Brahma and Vishnu were consulted and their verdict was unanimous.

'Mahadeva must be pacified. Only he can revive Daksha to complete the ceremony.'

The gods rushed to Shiva and prostrated themselves. Sought his

forgiveness and brought him to Kankhala. Since Veerbhadra had burnt Daksha's head, the Destroyer asked them to find a substitute. Finally, a ram's head was implanted on the Prajapati's body, proving Nandi's words true as well. He who had called Shiva beastly had been reanimated using a beast. The Destroyer now foretold that Daksha would soon be reborn on Earth in his true form. The yagna was accomplished and merit ensured.

Suddenly, tremors began passing through Brahmanda.

The universe was shuddering as if someone was pounding it without mercy. The two halves of the cosmic egg appeared on the verge of cracking. The assembly rushed out to see and stood catatonic. Shiva was dancing with Sati's charred corpse slung over his shoulder. His eyes bloodshot. His face livid. His limbs writhing. His body flailing. Pulsating with that savage choreography that wanted to crush everything to death.

The Rudra Tandava ...

Mahadeva was wailing. Mourning the death of his love.

All eyes turned towards Vishnu to save the cosmos. The Preserver realised that Sati's remains were torturing Shiva. Scorching the yogi with flames of maya. Weighing upon the Kapali like a thousand skulls. Vishnu hurled the Sudarshana. As the Destroyer gyrated, the chakra dismembered Sati's corpse into fifty-one pieces. One by one, they fell at various locations across Earth, giving rise to Shakti Peeths. Shiva halted. The weight was off his body but his heart was still heavy.

He walked away. He was alone again.

22

VISHNU SAVES THE ELEPHANT

Ksheersagar, or the Ocean of Milk, cradled a towering mountain known as Trikuta. Waves would lap at its feet and secretly aspire to rise as high. Its peaks, capped with gold, silver and iron, would turn so luminous under the sun and the moon that the valley was perpetually filled with light. Adjoining it was a forest named Ritumata, which contained a beautiful pond. Lotuses covered its surface and the water was pure ambrosia. It was the haunt of the elephants of Ritumata and they would visit every day to drink and bathe. The herd was headed by an elephant that was devoted to Vishnu.

Gajendra, the king tusker.

One day, as the elephants were frolicking in the water, they heard their king trumpet in terror. Mortal terror. They shrank as they realised what had happened.

A graha, or crocodile, had seized one of his legs.

The reptile's teeth were digging deep as Gajendra writhed in agony. He kept straining to pull his leg away but it only ripped his skin. Tore his flesh. The crocodile's jaws were clamping tighter. Blood was gushing and sullying the pond. The herd stared helplessly, for they knew that the reptile was far mightier in water. Its teeth were piercing the tusker's tendons now. Inching dangerously close to the bone. As the noose of death tightened around Gajendra, he saw the elephants departing. Leaving him to his fate. All alone now, his tears cleared his vision. Told him that his end had perhaps arrived. He stopped thrashing about. There was only one thing to be done. Lifting his eyes up, he sent a prayer to Vishnu.

'I surrender to you, Sri Hari. There's nothing more I can do to save myself. Protect me if you wish that I should remain alive. Or liberate me if my hour of death is here. I bow before your will.'

Holding aloft a white lotus in his trunk, Gajendra spoke again. 'I seek shelter in you who permeates Brahmanda. Omnipotent and omnipresent. The end and the very beginning. I take refuge in you.'

The morning turned dark. Trikuta was no longer radiant. The sun was no longer visible. Only a celestial form was spreading across the horizon. Blue face. Blue body. A blue finger holding the Sudarshana. As the tusker watched in awe, the chakra came swooping and sliced the crocodile's head. Vishnu was smiling.

'Have you learnt your lesson, Indradyumna?'

Gajendra froze.

Indradyumna ...

Like a stone in a pond, that name was creating ripples in his mind. Like an echo far away, it was awakening sights and sounds of his past. His previous birth. The elephant recalled now that he had been born as a human back then.

Born as King Indradyumna.

Recalled now that he had not greeted Sage Agastya when he had visited his court. Lost in his own thoughts, he had not even deigned to open his eyes. And so, the sage had cursed him to be born as an elephant. To learn how to renounce the Self. To surrender to a higher power as he had done today.

'Are you wiser now, Indradyumna?' the Preserver was asking again. 'That crocodile was a gandharva named Huhu in its past life. Huhu had insulted Sage Deval and has paid the price for it. What about you?'

The peaks of Trikuta watched as Gajendra prostrated himself before Vishnu.

23

PRITHU FEEDS MANKIND

One of the great emperors in the lineage of Dhruva was Anga. He was a pious man who followed every tenet of the Vedas. The gods were pleased and the Earth was flourishing. His wife, Suneeta, was the daughter of Mrityu, or death, whose soul was dark and twisted. Unfortunately, Anga's son was born with less of his father's virtues and more of Mrityu's vices. The lad also spent much time with Mrityu, which further corrupted him.

His name was Vena.

When Vena turned sovereign, the law of the land turned wicked. He abolished Vedic rites and thoughts. Banned yagnas and penalised anyone found conducting them. Declaring himself as the only god, he began forcing Bhuloka to venerate him. As his atrocities mounted, the Saptarishi advised him to mend his ways. Reinstate the scriptures and accept the supremacy of Brahma, Vishnu and Shiva. Allow rituals since they benefited both the ruler and the ruled. But Vena had fallen hopelessly in love with himself.

'I am Brahmanda,' he declared. 'The Yagna Purusha. Greater than the greatest. My body houses all your gods. Why must I bow to anyone?'

The sages realised that the man's own darkness had devoured him. If he lived on, he would seriously threaten order. Picking up a straw, they charged it with mantras and flung it at him. Vena died instantly. The Saptarishi had untangled one knot but tangled another. While they had rid Earth of a tyrant, they had also deprived her of a king. Vena had no son and the Vedas stipulated that a land without a monarch would never thrive. With no other solution in sight, Marichi advised the sages to carry out the only measure possible now.

They would have to harvest a ruler from Vena's corpse.

The sages began to knead his right thigh and out came a being with an appearance most foul. A dwarf with skin like a moonless night. Atri identified that all that was vile inside Vena had surfaced from his body in this terrible form. The sage screamed 'Nishada', which meant 'sit', but the dwarf stormed out. That became his name, and eventually a race of hunters descending from him would be known as the Nishadas. With evil thus leaving Vena's flesh, his corpse had turned pure. The sages kneaded his right arm now and it yielded a young man. Clad in resplendent armour, he emitted an aura so luminous that it dazzled the seven of them. Marichi gave this new king of Bhuloka his name.

Prithu. The Great One.

Earth rejoiced. Oceans and rivers anointed him and brought exquisite corals and jewels. Brahma himself arrived to crown him and discovered that he had a birthmark resembling the Sudarshana chakra.

'Your monarch has been blessed by Vishnu,' he proclaimed. 'He shall be the first Chakravarti Samrat. Ruler of the four directions.'

To prove his point, the Creator now commanded Prithu to conduct an Ashwamedha Yagna. A royal horse would be let loose to roam Bhuloka freely, proclaiming the king's dominance everywhere. Anyone challenging the animal would have to declare war. Prithu agreed and the horse set out.

Alas, these celebrations were filling another being with envy. Indra had never seen Earth embracing a human like this. Never seen Brahma adoring a mortal like this. He began dreading now that this new ruler may not remain content with his own loka. That thus exalted by everyone, he may try to seize Indraloka. Consumed with panic, he did the unimaginable.

Indra stole the Ashwamedha horse.

As soon as Prithu was informed, he commanded his forces to kill the Devaraja. His might was being questioned and he was not pleased. The army charged but Indra had already prepared his defence. Smearing his body with ash, he stood before them in the garb of a hermit. The soldiers turned fearful now of attacking a saintly being and retreated right away.

Learning about the Devaraja's trickery, Prithu's anger exploded. He began baying for his blood, but the sages stopped him. 'You need not battle. We shall chant mantras here that will pull Indra to this yagna altar. Drawn to our sacrificial fire, he shall burn to death.'

The chanting began and as they were about to make the final offering, Brahma appeared again. Indra was his great-grandson and he requested Prithu to forgive him. The four Kumaras also walked in and cautioned him against starting his reign with such a violent deed. The horse was duly recovered and the Ashwamedha Yagna was completed.

But before Prithu could revel, a larger crisis now reared its head.

His subjects rushed in to inform him that the Earth had stopped producing food. Roots were withering and trees were no longer bearing fruit. Animals were dying and humans were nearing starvation. The ruler gaped at the Saptarishi, who explained in solemn tones. 'This was bound to happen. There has been a considerable time gap between Vena's death and your coronation. Natural law dictates that a land without a king shall not yield anything. Since Bhuloka was devoid of a ruler for a while, all her vegetation has dried up. She has entered a state of limbo and nothing is germinating. Everything is concealed inside her now.'

'Concealed?'

'Yes. All the food is lying dormant in her womb.'

Prithu leapt to his feet. 'I shall kill Bhuloka then and retrieve it.'

The assembly gazed with horror as he loaded his bow.

'What good is her life if she can no longer keep us alive?'

Bhuloka was listening to every word. Seeing the king approach, she took the form of a cow and began to flee. But no matter where she ran, Prithu was right behind, his arrow threatening to tear into her. Exhausted at last, the Earth pleaded with him.

'How can you consider killing me? I am like your mother and you shall be sinning. And where will mankind reside if you destroy me? You have been blessed by Sri Hari and your duty should be to preserve.'

'And your duty should be to nourish, but you are concealing food. What if Surya and Chandra follow your example and hide their light? What if every element renounces its duty because you did the same? How will Brahmanda function? If you can forsake your dharma, so can I. You are killing my people and now I must kill you. Pierce your belly and release every resource.'

'I have never refused to share my bounty. Even when the gods were starving in Swargaloka, I was filling everyone here with what I could produce. But I can only generate food when there's a ruler. The presence of divine kingship. Vena's death created a vacuum and I could no longer yield anything. But you are my master now and I shall provide again.'

Prithu's face turned thoughtful. Looking at Bhuloka, he nodded.

'You shall not only provide. We shall also extract now.'

'Extract?'

'Yes. We shall also derive from you now just as I was derived from my father's body.'

'I don't understand.'

The king had been pondering over the law that the Earth could only produce food in the shadow of a ruler. He realised now that the only way to counter this was to make humans self-reliant. Free them from this dependency on a monarch to fill their bellies. It was time to teach men to grow food. To not only eat what Bhuloka was bearing but to also draw from the depths of her womb. And draw constantly so that this cycle would never end. Prithu beamed.

'You are right. Blessed by Lord Vishnu, I must preserve.'

He pulled his bowstring and released the arrow. Travelling throughout Earth, it levelled mountains and created plains. Prithu milked Bhuloka and received seeds. He instructed his people and soon they were turning those patches into farmlands. Creating settlements and domesticating animals. The human race was cultivating now. Growing grains and cereals. Harvesting crops. Earth was still bountiful, but man was no longer passive.

Prithu had changed Bhuloka. He had introduced agriculture. She borrowed a new name from this Chakravati monarch.

Earth would now also be called Prithvi.

24

MARISHA TAKES TEN HUSBANDS

Prithu's great-grandson, Prachinvarhi, went on to marry the daughter of the ocean and produce ten sons. Collectively, they were called the Prachetas, and they grew up to become fervent devotees of Vishnu. Soon, the day dawned for Prachinvarhi to pass on his throne. He sent the ten brothers an uprooted plant, symbolising the need for a new ruler, but they sent it back.

'How can we rule when we are ourselves ruled by Narayana?' they chorused. 'Our adoration for him permeates us and there's no place for anything else. Contemplating upon him is our only purpose. The highest purpose. We are content and need nothing more.'

But the old king was not one to give up easily. He reminded them of the duties of a monarch. Stressed upon their obligation towards the people and this Earth. The debate went on and the Prachetas now offered a proposal.

'We shall meditate upon Narayana. Invoke him to guide us. If he commands us to rule, we shall obey. But if he wishes us to continue on our spiritual quest, you will not object.'

Prachinvarhi agreed and the brothers left for the coast. Diving down into the waters, they sat on the ocean floor in deep meditation. Years passed and the king grew weary. He would walk towards the shore every day and return with nothing more than sand on his feet. He would plead with the ocean every night and hear nothing but the waves laughing at him. He kept waiting for them and they kept waiting for Him.

Thus elapsed ten thousand years.

Touched by the affection of the Prachetas, Vishnu finally appeared in a haze of blue. While he blessed them for their undying devotion, he endorsed what Prachinvarhi had said.

'Your great forefather, Prithu, gave Bhuloka a new identity. Descending from his bloodline, you are bound to your throne. Dharma and karma are forever inseparable. How can you attain one without the other? Make me your source of strength, not your means to escape.'

'You have shown us the way, lord. We shall strive for the good of our Earth.'

'You must. Bhuloka needs you more than ever now.' The Preserver's words struck a chill into their hearts. 'More than ever now? Why do you say that, lord?'

But Vishnu was no longer there. As the brothers rose from the ocean floor, his words kept floating around them.

Needs you more than ever now ...

Surfacing from the water, they stared in disbelief. Was this true or were the elements conjuring a mirage? The shore and sand had vanished. Their city and fortress were gone. In their place now stretched an infinite wilderness. Giant trees covered the land as far as they could see. Piercing the ocean below and the sky above. Spreading everywhere with not a clearing in sight. Entering this jungle, the Prachetas kept walking for days but did not come across a single man or woman. Only endless foliage that was sprouting around them like green fungi. Choking everything but itself. Seeing the plight of the brothers, Surya now recounted what had happened in their absence.

'You were underwater for ten thousand years. You father died and the Earth had no ruler. Anarchy erupted. Civilisation collapsed. I saw how that chaos killed all the humans. Only plants and trees survived. They have sprung everywhere, shrouding Bhuloka in dense overgrowth. Prithu had cleared the Earth but she is infested again.'

The Prachetas shuddered with rage and remorse. This forest now seemed to them like a daitya that had spread its leafy tentacles everywhere. The brothers joined hands. Stood in a circle and opened their mouths. They were breathing fire. Scorching the trees. Blowing wind. Scattering them away. A savage force was sweeping through Bhuloka, stripping her bare. Turning that green cover into billowing smoke. As they kept demolishing, a voice shrieked from above.

'Stop!'

They looked up to see Chandra pleading.

'I nurture vegetation on Earth and you are killing it all. Pray, end this horror. How can you punish the forest when it was your absence that caused it to breed? Trees and plants are your subjects, too, and you must protect them.'

But the Prachetas refused. They pointed out that with mankind extinct now, it was no longer possible for them to procreate. Once they were dead, the human race would come to an end. Hence, they were ravaging everything.

'What if I tell you that your lineage will continue?' Chandra asked.

'What do you mean?'

'It's true that all humans have perished, but there's someone still alive. Someone who shall carry your race forward.'

The brothers heard footsteps. The sound of anklets. They turned to see a woman.

'Who is she?' they asked.

'Marisha. Daughter of Sage Kandu. The sage had cohabited with an apsara who gave birth to her. Being half-divine, she survived and has been nourished by these trees. I see now that Earth was ensuring the survival of your ilk through her. This vegetation you are destroying has been cradling the womb that shall bring forth humans again. Bhuloka has played her part and now you must, too. Mankind has perished because of you and now you must right that wrong. The ten of you must marry her and repopulate Earth.'

'All ten of us?'

'All of you,' Marisha affirmed. 'In my former life, I was married to a king who fell ill and died young. I had prayed to Lord Vishnu and asked for two boons. First, that my son would be like Brahmadeva, and second, that I would have ten healthy husbands in my next ten lives. The lord granted the first one but altered the second. He blessed me that I would have ten husbands in a single life.'

She smiled. 'His second blessing has come true.'

'And so will his first,' Chandra assured her. 'Your son will indeed be like Param Pita Brahma, for he shall be the Creator's own son. The mighty Daksha.'

'Daksha? Sati's father?'

'Yes. Mahadeva had given him his word that he would be reborn. That time is near. Your union with the Prachetas shall beget the Prajapati again.'

The fires died. The winds ceased. The ten brothers held out their hands towards Marisha.

25

THE MATSYA AVATAR

Vaivasvata, the eldest son of Surya and Sangya, had now become one of the rulers of Earth. One day, he was standing in the middle of River Kritamala, making offerings to Vishnu. As he lifted his hands filled with water, a glint of silver stung his eye. A tiny minnow was shimmering in his palms. Bending down to put it back in the stream, Vaivasvata heard the fish plead.

'Take me with you, Benevolent Soul. I am small and the river frightens me.'

'But isn't this your habitat?'

'Any large fish can prey upon me. You are the sovereign of this land. Will you not protect your subject?'

Feeling drawn towards it now, he nodded. 'I shall take you to my palace.'

'Is it big enough for me?'

Vaivasvata smiled and put the minnow in his copper pot. But the fish began to grow and, by sunset, it was sixteen fingers long.

'Save me, Noble Soul. Your vessel is woefully small.'

The king put it in a pitcher, but the minnow was soon too large for that as well. He dropped it in a well and the same thing happened again. He placed it inside a pond next, but it outgrew that too. The fish was tossed back into Kritamala, but even the river failed to contain its growth now.

In the end, it was transferred to the ocean. As it touched the waves, the minnow kept expanding and covered the entire ocean. Vaivasvata fell on his knees.

'You are no fish.'

'I am not.'

'What supernatural being are you? No place on Bhuloka is able to encompass your stature. Are you Lord Vishnu? You can only be Vishnu. Have I unwittingly been trying to protect him who protects us all?'

'I am Vishnu. And you shall be the new Manu.'

Vaivasvata stood up in awe. There had been six Manus so far, beginning with the very first one created by Brahma. Husband of Shatarupa. Progenitor of mankind. The time period of every Manu's lifespan was called a manvantara. Six manvantaras had come one after the other, presided by six Manus. And now Vishnu was declaring him the seventh Manu. Vaivasvata Manu.

'In seven days, Earth will be flooded and all her life forms shall perish,' the god revealed. 'It will be time for a new cycle to begin. As the Manu of the next manvantara, it's your task to see it through.'

'Guide me, O Saviour.'

'Construct a large floating vessel and take on board all the seeds of life. Plants and grains. Herbs and medicines. Fruits and flowers. Animal pairs. Take the Saptarishi, your wife and all the wisdom written down by men. When the deluge comes, I will arrive again in this avatar. Then you shall tether the vessel to me and I will tow you to safety.'

The fish vanished and a terrible drought descended upon Bhuloka. Everything dried up as if water had never existed. Someone seemed to be sucking the very marrow out of Earth. Every drop of her nectar, leaving her veins dry. Land cracked. Men died. The world became a mass graveyard where nothing was green. Nothing was breathing. The only signs of life were inside Vaivasvata's vessel. For six days, he sat still. On the seventh day, his skin throbbed. Something had landed on it. Something was making love to it.

A drop of water.

He glanced at the sky to see dark clouds rallying. Nimbus ones, licking up the sun. Smudging the horizon. Lightning lashed. Thunder wailed. Wailed louder and louder and then began to shed tears. More tears. Bigger tears. Faster tears. Streams and rivers and oceans of rain were pouring down now. It was as if all the water that had been snatched from Earth had found its way home. Rushing back wildly, it embraced Bhuloka until not a speck of land was visible. Only water here and water there. Water and water everywhere. As the world sank, Vaivasvata's vessel rose. It was all that was left of Bhuloka now. Bits and pieces of everything that man had attained.

Culture. Knowledge. Nutrition. Conception.

Floating now on that endless expanse as designed by Manu. Charting a strange course as devised by Vishnu. Cradling life like the cosmic egg had once done over primordial waters. Was the ocean glaring at the vessel? Salivating to gulp it like it had gulped everything else? Vaivasvata looked around in fear. Looked for the avatar who had given him its word. He saw the seven sages pointing. A horn was emerging from under the sea.

The Matsya.

Slicing the waves, it was soaring higher and higher. The head of the golden fish, surfacing like an aquatic deity. Vaivasvata tied the vessel to its horn and it began steering them towards the north. The ocean was bowing before this leviathan as it tore right through its heart. Navigating them across a divine path. Manu had saved the fish and now the fish was saving Manu. Gods appeared in the sky to marvel at this vision. At how Vishnu was preserving the relics of Earth, revealing his profound love for man. How he was riding those waters majestically but cautiously for he knew how precious his burden was. As the Saptarishi chanted praises of his glory, night turned into dawn. Vaivasvata saw a mountain jutting out of the ocean. Its snow-laden peak was proclaiming that the avatar was anchoring them to the Himalayas.

As they stepped on land, Vishnu addressed the new Manu again.

'O Son of Surya! From you shall eventually spring the illustrious

Suryavanshi clan. Bring forth your descendants and populate Bhuloka once more. Just as you had safeguarded me as a fish, create a society that will safeguard all.'

The Matsya was blessing him. The seven sages were standing against the horizon. And birds were singing songs about building new nests.

26

THE VARAHA AVATAR

The eldest two of the daityas that Diti had birthed were Hiranyaksha and Hiranyakashipu. The Golden-Eyed One and the Golden-Clothed One. Hiranyaksha soon submerged himself in austerities to gain a boon from Brahma. When the Creator was pleased, he demanded immortality.

'Not possible.' Brahma shook his four heads. 'Unlike Mahadeva, I cannot make anyone deathless. Ask for something else.'

'Make me the ruler of Bhuloka then. Her sovereign absolute. Unconquerable by every form of life. Bless me that neither humans nor animals can kill me.'

'Which animals? You will need to identify the species.'

The demon began rattling off names. Creatures of every possible habitat. Subterranean. Terrestrial. Aquatic. Aerial.

The Creator nodded. 'So be it.'

As soon as the devas heard what Brahma had done, they hastened towards him in rage. A daitya being granted authority over Earth was unheard of. And a reckless demon like Hiranyaksha was bound to abuse that power. Wreck the very soul of Bhuloka.

'I see your point but you don't see mine,' the Creator told them. 'Unwavering effort cannot go unrewarded. It's natural law. Hiranyaksha's devotion was fierce and I had to bless him accordingly, just as Mahadeva had to reveal the Mritasanjivani to Shukracharya. It has happened in the past and will keep happening in the future. Rigorous quest for a boon will always be fulfilled whether it's a deva or a daitya.'

'Even if the boon itself is evil?' the gods questioned.

'A boon is never evil or good. It's simply an opportunity that empowers. How the seeker chooses to use it makes the difference. As the master of Earth now, Hiranyaksha can either cherish her or cripple her. If he walks the latter path, he shall be destroyed.'

'But no creature can harm him. You have yourself guaranteed that.'

'Not quite,' Brahma's tone was enigmatic. 'You shall know when the time comes. Let's see what the demon does with my boon.'

The fear of the devas soon came true. Hiranyaksha let loose fumes of tyranny and Bhuloka began to choke. Cries of every living being began to resound through the skies. The daitya not only remained unmoved but went further to do the unthinkable. He wrenched the Earth from her axis and dragged her to the bottom of the primordial Garbhodaka Ocean.

'Catastrophe! Catastrophe!' the gods screamed as the Creator watched. 'Power granted to the unworthy never inspires. Only intoxicates. How do we retrieve Bhuloka from these depths?'

They saw the spirit of Earth approaching them as a cow. Her eyes were burning with sea water. Her face was beseeching them to liberate her. The devas turned towards Brahma again.

'You had assured us that Hiranyaksha was not invincible. Tell us how? Did he not safeguard himself against every creature?'

'Not all of them,' the Creator said and smiled. 'That's why I had asked him to specify the species. So prolific is my creation that no one can catalogue every animal form. The demon failed as well. He named every creature on Earth except one.'

'Which one?'

'Varaha. The boar. That shall be his nemesis.' Brahma stood up with folded hands. 'Watch! Watch how Sri Hari takes avatar again. How he, who renewed as Matsya, now restores as Varaha.'

The cow looked as the Preserver entered the ocean in that magnificent form. A boar, lofty as a cosmic column. Its tusks, massive as twin hills. It challenged the daitya and battle erupted. The waters began to froth and foam. Boil and freeze. Spin in a gigantic vortex of fury as Vishnu and Hiranyaksha clashed for a thousand years. In the end, Varaha gored the demon to death. The ocean was choking with blood and yet rejoicing. Cheering at that wondrous sight as the boar lifted Bhuloka. Cradled her on its tusks like palms holding a flower and reinstalled her on the axis. Brahma was exulting. The gods were celebrating.

Vishnu did not join them. Hiranyaksha was dead but Hiranyakashipu was alive.

27

THE NARASIMHA AVATAR

A fiendish fanfare was soon rocking every tier of Brahmanda. The asuras had coronated the elder son of Diti. Shukracharya himself had placed the crown on his head. As the new demon king, Hiranyakashipu's foremost thought now was to safeguard his own life. Treading Hiranyaksha's path, he, too, began to propitiate Brahma on Mount Mandara. Eleven thousand years later, the Creator materialised.

'What boon do you seek?'

Hiranyakashipu paused. The fate of his brother was flashing before his eyes. Hiranyaksha had been confident that he had insulated himself against every danger. Blissfully unaware that he had left a loophole through which his death had sneaked in and consumed him. Hiranyakashipu was not going to make that error. He began composing the boon in his mind with caution. He was sifting words. Adding clauses. Modifying details. Making sure that every possibility had been accounted for. Every peril taken care of. The boon had to be an impregnable fort and he was not going to leave any door open.

'Bless me, O Creator, that I cannot be killed by gods or demons. Humans or animals. Neither during the day nor at night. Neither indoor nor outdoor. Neither in the sky nor on earth. Neither in water nor on land.

Bless me that no weapon made of metal, stone or wood can do me any harm. Bless me, O Creator.'

Brahma granted him his wish and the daitya emerged twice as malevolent as his brother. He not only tormented earthlings but also drove Indra out of heaven. Conquered the three realms. Sole master of the universe now, his chaos began to paralyse Brahmanda. But in this very cesspool had bloomed a lotus. Hiranyakashipu's youngest son, whose name denoted excessive joy.

Prahlad.

Although springing from demonic seed, the boy's mind and heart belonged to Vishnu. While Hiranyakashipu had been away invoking Brahma, Indra had abducted his pregnant wife, Kayadu. Narada had intervened and saved the queen and her newborn son. The child had grown up hearing the glories of Narayana from Narada and had embraced him as his only reality. On coming back, Hiranyakashipu had sent Prahlad to Shukracharya to learn about the daitya race. But the boy had returned, still chanting that one name.

'Vishnu?' Hiranyakashipu growled. 'Don't you know how insignificant he is? A self-proclaimed god who needed the form of a lowly animal to kill my brother.'

'A compassionate god in whose eyes all life forms are equal.'

'You are disgracing your clan. Who taught you the name of our foe?'

'Lord Vishnu himself, for he's the teacher of all teachers. Ruler of all rulers. Sole guide to attaining dharma, artha, kama and moksha.'

The demon was livid. The universe cowered before him, but his own son was rejecting his might. He tried every trick to stamp out his devotion but failed. The name of the Preserver had become embedded in the very pith of Prahlad's being. Days later, when Hiranyakashipu asked him the purpose of his life again, his answer had not changed.

'To worship Lord Vishnu.'

'What breed are you? You are certainly no deva but also not a daitya if you worship him. How can you extol that wretched thing when I stand here before you?'

'He's the singular truth. Above everyone. Even you.'

'You are disowning your father?'

'I am revering the one who has fathered us all.'

Gnashing his teeth, the demon now ordered Prahlad to be put to death. But this turned out to be a divine impossibility. They got him trampled by elephants and bitten by snakes but to no avail. They pushed him down a cliff, but he remained unhurt, as if he had landed on the invisible palms of Vishnu. They flung him into the sea, but the waves brought him back. Venom added to his food turned into ambrosia. Weapons feared to strike him and assassins refused to slay him. The ogress, Kritya, was summoned to take his life, but her trident shattered as it touched his body. Like Shiva shielding Markandeya, Vishnu was shielding Prahlad. With Hiranyakashipu's patience wearing thin, his sister, Holika, now proposed a diabolical scheme.

'You forget that I, too, have been blessed with a boon,' she reminded him. 'My body is immune to fire. Prepare a pyre and I shall sit on it with Prahlad on my lap. When you ignite it, he shall burn to death while I will remain unscathed.'

Her instructions were carried out at once. Prahlad realised what was happening but did not utter a word of protest. He was only chanting the lord's name. Chanting louder and louder as the flames crept higher and higher.

Vande Vishnu ... Vande Vishnu ... Vande Vishnu ...

Surrendering himself to Him.

Vande Vishnu ... Vande Vishnu ... Vande Vishnu ...

Screams were erupting now from the pyre but it was not Prahlad. It was Holika. The fire was devouring her skin. Dissolving her flesh. But not harming a hair on Prahlad's head, as if something beatific was encasing him again. The woman was turning into ash. Succumbing to the horror that the powers above had revoked her boon for trying to misuse it. As the flames faded, Hiranyakashipu froze. The boy was sitting alive while Holika had been charred to death. Trembling with rage, he dragged Prahlad and hurled him before a moonstone pillar.

'Enough. Looks like I will have to end your miserable life with my own hands.'

'You can do so only if my lord wills. If he does not, you can do nothing.'

'I shall bind you to this pillar and disembowel you. Will your Vishnu arrive in time to stop me?'

'He need not arrive anywhere.' The boy smiled. 'He permeates everything. He is everywhere. In every element. In every cell. In you. In me. In this very pillar.'

'In this pillar?' Hiranyakashipu snickered.

'Yes, father. He was. He is. He will be.'

'Show me.'

Prahlad closed his eyes as the daitya struck the pillar with his mace.

'Invoke your god. Show me his presence. His ver—'

Words died inside his throat. The pillar was splitting right through the middle. The two halves were tumbling down, releasing a wave of light. Revealing a creature that they had perhaps been incubating. A towering chimera that defied every description. Every anatomy. It was neither human nor animal. Neither a deva nor a danava. It was none of them and yet all of them. An amalgamation of all forms possible. A transcendental hybrid, horrific yet hypnotic.

Narasimha. Vishnu as the humanoid lion. Fulfilling every condition of the demon's death.

Gathering Hiranyakashipu in its arms, the avatar now carried him to the threshold of the palace entrance. Thus, the daitya was neither indoor nor outdoor. Twilight had descended, making it neither day nor night. And Narasimha placed him on its lap, suspending him between earth and sky. Away from land and water.

'You have been blessed that you cannot be killed by metal, stone or wood,' the avatar roared. 'I shall use none of those. My claws will rip your flesh.'

The demon howled as Narasimha dug its nails into him. Tore his belly and pulled out his intestines. Hung them around its neck and licked his blood. Prahlad lay prostrate before the god. Vishnu was laughing because both the brothers were dead. Because he had saved Prahlad.

Because the first lifetime of Jaya and Vijaya on Earth was over.

28

NARASIMHA FACES SHIVA

Every realm was ecstatic at the fall of Hiranyakashipu. Gods were rejoicing. Men were revelling. Even the five elements were celebrating, when suddenly everyone froze. And then began huddling. Pointing. Listening. Listening to the roars that were rattling the very bones of Brahmanda.

Moments ago, that sound had filled them with joy. Now it was sending a chill down their core.

Vishnu had slain one crisis but spawned another. A far more menacing one. Instead of reverting to his original form, the god now seemed locked in his Narasimha state. Locked in that fury that had wrenched the demon's entrails out. That brutal killing appeared to have inflamed the lion avatar for it was pacing fiercely through Brahmanda. Threatening to rip everything apart. The cosmic spine was shivering. Wondering if those claws would tear it to shreds, too. Brahma immediately asked Prahlad to pray to Vishnu. The boy made every attempt but it was fruitless. The Creator turned to Shiva.

'Sri Hari calmed your Rudra Tandava. It's your turn now to restrain him.'

'The avatar is engorged with Rajas Guna since it has tasted Hiranyakashipu's blood,' Shiva explained. 'That is generating its rage. If we do not demolish this body, Sri Hari could remain forever trapped in this violent form.'

The Destroyer pulled out his hair and produced Veerbhadra.

'Narasimha is roaming wildly through the universe. Pacify it.'

Veerbhadra found the avatar snarling by the stars. Trying to pluck them out one by one. He folded his hands.

'Calm down, lord. You are the Preserver supreme who has been taking avatars for the sake of dharma. Your purpose as Narasimha has been accomplished. This avatar is just a mask. Do not allow it to melt into your face. Do not bury your soul beneath this savage body. Cast it off and return to your benevolent self.'

But Narasimha scratched the sky. It pounced at Veerbhadra, who instantly surrendered for he knew that he could not combat Vishnu. As he began to retreat, he paused. Something was happening. The sun was getting obscured. The moon was no longer visible. The stars were fading away. The galaxies were being eclipsed. Something was manifesting before him. Wings of enormous proportions were stretching across the firmament. Their plumes were rustling louder than the roars of Narasimha. Gleaming brighter than all the nakshatras. Veerbhadra fell to his knees. He was looking at Mahadeva.

But not as he had always seen him. Not as he had always known him.

The Destroyer, too, had assumed an avatar. A glorious hybrid form like Narasimha. One half was a lion with eight legs. The other half was a golden bird with a thousand arms. Its crest was flaring. Its eyes were glinting. Its claws were piercing.

Shiva had become Sharabh.

Finding a new being looming above it, Narasimha leapt to slash its feathers. To poke its eyes. To gash its beak. But the more the lion leapt, the more that bird rose. Hovering right above. Always out of reach.

Higher. Higher. Higher. Higher.

Then Sharabh swooped. Diving down, it grasped Narasimha in its talons and soared up again.

Higher. Higher. Higher. Higher.

Ascending every realm. Passing every dimension. Every sphere possible.

Higher. Higher. Higher. Higher.

Rising above everything in Brahmanda, Sharabh let go of Narasimha. The cosmos watched as it fell towards the Earth. Plunging faster and faster like a giant meteor. As it crashed, Narasimha snapped out of its rage. Sharabh proceeded to decapitate it. Then it skinned the lion's body and released everything that lay within.

Thus was Vishnu liberated from his own avatar.

29

INDRA ATTEMPTS FOETICIDE

Diti was standing by a river. Its waters were blue like the sky it mirrored, but her eyes could only see red. See the blood of her sons, Hiranyaksha and Hiranyakashipu, killed by Vishnu. Blood of her innumerable daityas, slain by devas. Telling her that they were not at peace. Asking her to avenge them all. She sat down and invoked Kashyapa.

'What do you want, Diti?' her husband asked.

'A son. Bless me with a son who shall kill Indra.'

'Why Indra?'

'Because Vishnu is deathless, but Indra is not. He's Devaraja. Ruler of the gods. It was under his command that so many of my sons were butchered. He must die now. Will you grant this to the mother of your children?'

Kashyapa sighed. Indra was also his son, born to him and Diti's sister, Aditi. But the sage was a fair soul and realised that Diti's pain needed to be soothed. He gave in to her demand but laid down the sternest conditions.

'The embryo shall gestate in your womb for a hundred years. And throughout that period, you must live as an ascetic. Practice non-violence in word and action. Observe every rite of cleanliness and stay away from impure objects. Never wear unclean clothes and never lay down without washing your feet. If you succeed, your son shall destroy Indra. But if you fail, he will befriend him instead.'

Diti laughed. She was not going to spawn a mate for the Devaraja but his murderer. She began following the rituals devoutly. Observing every rule. Every detail. Her adherence to her cause reached such intense levels that word began to spread. The gandharvas told the gods and the yakshas told the demons. It reached Aditi's ears and she instantly alerted Indra.

'The life growing inside Diti could be your death, my son. Act fast.'

The Devaraja realised how severe the threat was. Conquering the daityas had been easy, but Diti was a woman. Diti was a mother. Indra knew the power of a mother's resolve. Knew that a mother could hate just as ferociously as she loved. That she could seize from the gods what she craved and they would stand powerless before her. Indra's instincts kicked in. The only solution was to invade Diti's body and neutralise the peril, but it seemed like an impossible task. Her rigorous austerities had turned her womb impregnable.

Her austerities ...

The Devaraja sat up. A thought had crept into his mind. The success of Diti's quest hinged entirely on fulfilling Kashyapa's conditions. Her body had become a fortress only because she had been upholding every ritual so far.

But what if she erred in some way?

Indra descended. He began lurking around her hermitage. Observing in case she made even the slightest blunder. But Diti proved to be impeccable. Asceticism had become her way of life and she was following every rite flawlessly. The Devaraja's hopes were rising every day with the sun and sinking each night with the moon. He was watching Diti's belly growing bigger and bigger. Watching his end inching closer and closer. Thus passed all the years, and only three days now remained.

Three days ...

Indra surrendered. He had almost started composing his own elegy when suddenly the new day dawned in his favour. With Diti's pregnancy full-term now, she had become prone to fatigue, and austerities had begun to take a toll on her body. That evening, feeling more drained than ever, she fell asleep without having washed her feet. The Devaraja leapt! That one act of uncleanliness had done what he had been waiting for. Lowered Diti's defences, rendering her vulnerable.

The next moment he was inside her womb.

Summoning his Vajra, Indra sliced the foetus into seven pieces. He was panting. He was laughing. Suddenly, he choked. The foetus had not aborted. The seven chunks were still alive. They were wriggling. They were wailing. Gaping with rage and confusion, Indra screamed, 'Ma ruda', meaning 'Don't cry', but in vain. Their decibels were growing louder and louder. The Devaraja desperately mutilated each piece into seven more pieces, but they were still refusing to die. Their commotion now increasing sevenfold. As Diti woke up hearing all that racket inside her, Indra vanished. Clutching her belly, she knew.

She had lost.

A single moment had erased a hundred years.

With the foetus fragmented into forty-nine parts, she gave birth to forty-nine beings. No longer a threat to Indra but his companions now, as stipulated by Kashyapa. Since he had yelled, 'Ma ruda', they became collectively known as Marutas.

The storm deities.

Soon, they abandoned their mother to become demigods in heaven, but Diti was not alone. She still had her anger clinging to her breast. She begged Kashyapa again for another son to destroy Indra. A son who would be invincible to his Vajra. The sage yielded once more.

'You do realise what you are asking for? Withstanding the Vajra is almost impossible. You can get such a son only if you meditate for ten thousand years.

'I will.'

'Ten thousand years, Diti. Can you really do that?'

She spoke no more. Sitting down in padmasana, she lay a curse upon Aditi.

'You are no sister of mine for you sent your son to kill my unborn. You are unworthy of being a mother. Of being Devamata. May you watch your sons die before your eyes like I have.'

As soon as Aditi heard this, she broke down before Kashyapa.

'Grieve not,' he consoled her. 'Her curse will not come true in this yuga but in Dwapar Yuga. You shall be reborn as Devaki. Your brother, Kansa, will imprison you and kill your sons one by one. All but one, since your womb shall finally bear He who cannot be killed.'

'Who's he?'

'Mahavishnu. His Krishna Avatar.'

Far away from them, Diti was breathing deep. It was time to begin meditating for the next ten thousand years. Before closing her eyes, she looked up and hissed.

'It's not over, Indra. Not yet.'

30

PRAHLAD IS HUMBLED

Sage Chyavan was gazing at the prince curiously. That royal face seemed to be in search of something.

'You shall be king now, Prahlad. What are you looking for?'

'An answer.'

'That word misleads. An answer is nothing but another question. It struts around in disguise, but those with the truest eyes can see through it. I am keen to enlighten you. Ask.'

'Which is the greatest pilgrimage on Earth? The most blessed patch of land?'

'Naimisharanya,' the sage replied.

'Fascinating name. What does it mean?'

'It's derived from a miracle performed by Lord Vishnu. Long ago, the sages of Brahmanda implored him to locate a place where they could conduct yagnas unhindered. The Preserver let loose his Sudarshana and instructed them to walk behind it. He proclaimed that when they arrived at the right spot, one of the circles of the chakra would detach itself and fall.'

The prince watched as Chyavan drew a disc on the floor.

'Imagine, Prahlad! What an ethereal sight it must have been. A cluster of sages following the Sudarshana. Their hearts filled with nothing but faith.

That lethal weapon holding their hands and pulling them with invisible strings. Leading them to a pious land. As soon as they reached the right place, a circle came crashing down. The chakra had chosen.'

'Just as the skull fell from Mahadeva's hand at Kashi.'

'Indeed. Since the circumference of the concentric circles of the Sudarshana is called Naimi, the sages named that spot Naimisharanya.'

Overwhelmed by the story of that place, Prahlad left for it the very next day. He knew how formidable the chakra was. How terrifying a tool. A land that could make that disc disintegrate itself had to be beyond extraordinary. As he entered Naimisharanya, he got down from his horse, took off his sandals, and began walking barefoot. His toes were tingling. His breath was deepening. He was on hallowed ground. Were the footprints of those sages still around, he wondered. Was that broken circle of the chakra still buried here? Was it going to gash his feet as he moved? Or had its gold melted into this soil to forever anoint Naimisharanya?

He paused.

Two hermits were seated under a tree whose trunk had been stabbed with multiple arrows. Prahlad peered at the bows and quivers lying next to both of them.

'You look like saints but your actions are those of archers. What are you? Brahmins or Kshatriyas?'

'We are what we are.'

'What does that mean?' Prahlad frowned. 'If you are sages, why have you riddled this tree with shafts?'

'One must do what one is capable of. That alone earns respect.'

Their words were baffling him. Their indifference was angering him.

'You seem unaware of whom you are addressing. I am Prince Prahlad. I am the one for whom Lord Vishnu became Narasimha Avatar.'

'As he would do for anyone who desires refuge in him.'

He glared, pointing at their bows, 'Your rustic arms hardly measure up to your tone. If I challenge you both, your blood will stain this land.'

The hermits stood up. 'But we are indomitable.'

Prahlad's temper exploded. As he began battling them, he invoked one lethal weapon after another. Contemplated upon Vishnu to empower his arrows and rout them both. But exactly the reverse was happening. The hermits' meagre bows were repelling everything that he was launching at them. Counteracting every missile with an equally potent one. The prince's strength was depleting now like his ammunition, but the hermits seemed blessed with an infinite arsenal. Believing it to be the sorcery of Naimisharanya, Prahlad fled and sought refuge in Vaikuntha.

'Who are those men?' he yelped. 'Why can't I defeat them?'

'Can a devotee defeat the divine?' Vishnu asked.

'Divine? But only you are divine.'

The Preserver smiled. The prince cowered.

'You? Were they you, lord? Both of them?'

'Yes. Nara and Narayana. My twin avatars.'

Prahlad's eyes widened as he flung himself at the god's feet. 'How could I be so blind? How could I not see your face in their faces? How could I aspire to defeat you?'

'You cannot defeat me, Prahlad. You can only conquer me.'

'Not defeat but conquer?'

'Yes. Solve this riddle and you shall be dearer to me.'

Prahlad racked his brain but could find no answer. So, he asked another question.

'You say Nara and Narayana are your twin avatars. Will you be manifesting again on Earth in those forms? Again in another yuga?'

'I will. In Dwapar Yuga.'

'And who shall they be?'

'I shall be Narayana. And Nara shall be Arjuna. I shall sing a song for him in the middle of a war.'

31

TARAKA INVADES HEAVEN

Surya was hesitating to rise.

If he did, ten thousand years would finally come to an end. A mother's pursuit would come to an end. Waiting for this very hour, she would give birth to chaos. Suckle her seed with the milk of vengeance against his brother. But Surya knew that he was chained to natural law. To the wheels of his chariot that had begun to move. A red smear was spreading through the sky as if somewhere a wound was still bleeding. The day broke and glanced at her in terror.

Diti.

She was opening her eyes. Touching her womb. She knew Kashyapa's word had come true. She had asked for a son who would slay Indra. Stand invincible before his Vajra. She could feel him germinating inside her now. Warming himself with the fire that was still raging in her heart. Taking a pledge that he will not be vanquished like the other daityas or betray her like the Marutas. That he will drag the Devaraja by his hair and hurl him at her feet. She smiled as she named him.

Vajranga. He whose body was like the Vajra.

Not long after, it all came true when her son trounced Indra. The king of gods was kneeling before her. Quaking with fear as her eyes seemed to slowly dissect him. Then her lips moved.

'Chop his head off.'

Vajranga raised his sword but Brahma intervened.

'Halt! Don't do this, Diti. He's the Devaraja. Integral to the functioning of Brahmanda. His death may gratify you but it will create a terrible vacuum. Your son has already decimated his pride. If you spare his life, that shall further add to his shame. Disgrace him across every realm. Isn't that the foulest punishment possible?'

Diti was not swayed, but Vajranga liked what he was hearing.

'I agree. Why kill him when we can give him a life worse than death? I obey you, Param Pita.'

Pleased with Vajranga, Brahma created a beautiful woman for him called Vajrangi. The two got married and Vajranga retired to the forest to perform austerities. Seeing her husband's devotion, Vajrangi also decided to meditate until his return. Such was their piety that everyone soon began marvelling at the couple. Everyone but Indra. The Devaraja was still sore and, finding an opportunity for revenge, he targeted Vajrangi. Turning into a snake, he bit her again and again, but the grace of Brahma prevented her from dying. Unable to kill Vajrangi this way, Indra summoned clouds to rain relentlessly over her. The torrent began and, seated in meditation, the hapless woman endured the downpour. By the time Vajranga returned, his wife was soaking and his mother was simmering.

'You silenced the daitya inside you and tried to act benignly,' Diti shrieked. 'Vajrangi now pays the price.'

A furious Vajranga approached the Creator and threatened to decapitate Indra. Panicking once more, Brahma did the only thing that he could. He doled out another boon.

'I bless you with a son. Since your family has been tormented by a god, your son shall grow up to be the scourge of all gods. He shall be called Taraka.'

Years later, the demon took birth and came to know about this prophecy. Coming of age, Taraka journeyed to the Paripatra mountains to propitiate Brahma. Choosing a patch of ice where nothing grew, he began to observe the strictest penance. He stood on one leg for a hundred years, and then only on his toes. Sat under water for a hundred years, and then inside fire. Astounded by the depth of his resolve, the Creator materialised.

'You are beyond compare. But I have already blessed you that you shall loom as a terror that will be hard to defeat. What more do you want?'

'To defeat my death.'

'If you are seeking immortality, that's out of bounds.'

'Grant me something else then. Grant me that only a child will be able to kill me.'

'A child?'

'Yes. Only the son of Mahadeva.'

'Mahadeva? I don't und—'

Brahma paused.

Son of Mahadeva ...

It cleaved him like a sword. Taraka was casting a crafty dice. Like Hiranyaksha and Hiranyakashipu, this daitya too was attempting to come as close as possible to everlasting life. The Creator blessed him and Taraka stormed heaven. The gods battled along with Indra, but their combined resistance collapsed before Brahma's boon. The Devaraja was captured, his head was shaven and his body was marked with the feet of dogs. With even Vishnu failing to overpower Taraka, the devas now rushed to the Creator.

'The demon shall be destroyed,' he assured them all. 'But we need Mahadeva's son.'

'Mahadeva is still in mourning for Sati,' the gods chorused. 'He has withdrawn from all affairs of Brahmanda and locked himself in infinite meditation. He may never procreate.'

'That's exactly what Taraka is counting on. That's why he asked me for such a boon that renders him practically deathless. But we have to thwart him. Mahadeva can no longer remain indifferent. He must engage now. He must produce an offspring who shall be Taraka's nemesis.'

'But Adishakti ...'

'Adishakti has been reborn.'

'Reborn?'

'Yes. Sati has reincarnated and is again burning for Shiva. She alone can induce him to reproduce. The question is ...'

He fell silent. The same words were clanging inside all of them now.

Will that hermit father a son?

32

PARVATI WINS OVER SHIVA

Brahma was fondling the flowers that wreathed the arrows. Lotus, ashoka, mango and mallika. Fondling that bow made of sugarcane and its string of honeybees. He smiled.

'How do you keep these blossoms so radiant, Kamadeva?'

The god of love folded his hands. 'It's not me, Param Pita. It's you. Your vital energy which created me keeps my arrows alive.'

'Do you know from which part of my body you have sprung?'

'Your bosom.'

'Indeed. That's why your presiding emotion is love. You emerged from my heart, so that you can enter the hearts of others.'

'Nothing gives me greater joy. That twang of my bow. That first flush of love when my arrow strikes someone. That emotion unfolding in them like petals of a flower. Leading to a union that creates a new world. Whenever that happens, I become you, Param Pita. I become Brahma.'

'You need to do it again.'

'I shall be honoured. Who's my target? My arrows can pierce any heart in Brahmanda.'

'Can they touch the heart of Mahadeva?'

Kamadeva shrank. His face was wilting. His voice was drying. He was sputtering about Sati's death and Shiva's agony.

'Mahadeva had punished you for your carnality, Param Pita, and now you wish to induce the same in him?'

The Creator informed him about Taraka's boon and the rebirth of Adishakti.

'Adishakti has reincarnated?'

'Yes, Kama. They were three sisters. The first one, Kutila, was too arrogant and I cursed her to become a river. The second one, Ragini, was too weak, and I cursed her to become dusk. But the third one is Adishakti reborn.'

'What's her name?'

'Parvati.' Brahma pointed into the distance. 'There she sits, meditating for Mahadeva. And only you, Kama, can jolt him out of contemplation. Kindle in him the flames of desire. Make him fall in love once again.'

Not long ago, Parvati had begun invoking the Destroyer. Born to the Himalayan king, Himavanta, and his wife, Maina, the princess had left them behind. Her parents had been still grieving for her sisters, who had been cursed by the Creator. Maina had beseeched Parvati to stay back, but she had reminded her mother of the prophecy attached to her birth.

'Have you forgotten what the venerable Narada told you when he saw my astral chart? I am born to be fused with Shiva. To be his eternal consort. I have grown up dreaming about Kailash. Seeing visions of myself with Mahadeva. He is my destiny and I must put myself on that path now. Do not mourn, mother. Bless me that I may realise the meaning of my existence.'

Scaling the Himalayas, Parvati had begun to propitiate Shiva. Kamadeva was looking at her now. Then his gaze turned fearfully towards Mahadeva. That mahayogi, sitting still. His eyes closed. Arms taut. Body erect. Encased in his own sorrow as if a slab of stone was bleeding silently. Kamadeva trembled again. His fingers were refusing to pick up the arrow, but Brahma's words seemed to be holding his hand and loading his bow.

For Taraka ...

He aimed and released. As his shaft winged towards Shiva, bees hummed and birds cooed. A fragrant breeze began ruffling the Destroyer's hair. Diffusing through his nostrils. Saturating his senses. Kamadeva had conjured spring. The season of mating. Of nature copulating. The arrow was infiltrating the god's heart. The four flowers were trying to take root in that chunk of rock. Arouse his affection. Awaken emotion in that debris of pain. Shiva stirred. Opened both his eyes.

Then he opened his third eye.

An inferno leapt and swallowed Kamadeva. Charred the birds and all the flowers. The universe quailed. The arrow crumbled. It had not inflamed his passion but instead detonated an explosion. The god of Kailash was raging. Generating flames that were scorching the spring. Shiva's yoga had been intruded upon by that shaft of bhoga, and his blaze was licking every pore of Kamadeva now.

'What have you done?'

It was Brahma's cry. As he came rushing, other devas also materialised, lamenting Kamadeva's ghastly end. Informing Shiva about Taraka and his boon that was endangering the cosmos.

'You killed Yama, who presides over death,' the Creator said as he shuddered. 'And now you have killed Kama, whose love begets life.'

The Destroyer sat in silence. Then he got up and walked towards Rati. Wife of Kamadeva. She was crouching on the ground. Her fists full of ash.

'Sati and Rati.' Her eyes poured water. 'Looks like Agni craves us both. Sati burnt then. Rati burns now. But Sati burnt and died. Rati will burn forever.'

'No.' Shiva touched her head. 'Kamadeva shall take birth again in Dwapar Yuga, and you will be united with him once more.'

As Rati smeared herself with her husband's remains, Brahma handed the Destroyer his trishul.

'You must also reunite with Sati now. She has begun rigid austerities.'

'I cannot desire anyone again. I have seen the maya it leads to.'

'But she is your Sati. Your own. Reborn to never part with you. You had given me the mantra of creation and now your child alone can safeguard it. This union of Shiva and Shakti is everlasting. Let it come to pass. Not only to foil Taraka but also to foster Brahmanda.'

'Not yet. Not yet.'

Shiva began watching Parvati. Observing how she was meditating on that frigid peak. How she was turning into ice every night and thawing every morning. How she was cursing those whom he had deliberately sent to slur his name. How she was renouncing food and water to survive only on a single leaf a day. How she was gradually forsaking that too to subsist only on his name. How her body was begging to collapse but her zeal was propping it up.

'Aparna.'

Parvati did not move.

'Aparna.'

She looked. The word was echoing as if the snow was whispering it. Shiva was standing before her. He who had rejected Kama's lust had responded to her love. Her yoga had compelled him to accept bhoga again. He caressed her in such a way that she no longer felt starved.

'Aparna?' she asked.

'Yes. You are Aparna. The Leafless One.'

'But my parents named me Parvati, my lord.'

'Parvati. Sati. Aparna. Uma.' He embraced her. 'You are all of them. And they are all mine.'

33

MOTHERS OF KARTIKEYA

Parvati and Mahadeva had become one. Shiva and Shakti had reunited. Parvati's mother, Maina, had threatened to halt their wedding on seeing the groom enter. He had appeared with three eyes, five faces and countless arms. Mounted on a bull and decked with a snake. Matted hair like an ant-hill and tiger skin below. Coated with ash and high on hemp. But then Shiva had transformed and his aura had lit up Brahmanda. More effulgent now than the sun and the moon. More enchanting than every god, as if all that was sublime had become a part of him. Maina had wept tears of joy and sought forgiveness for her lack of vision. Shiva had become Shankar. The hermit had become a householder. The universe had celebrated a new beginning. It was now awaiting an end.

Taraka's end.

Days passed but no news came of Shiva's child. With the daitya's sins now becoming too immense for Brahmanda, the gods were losing patience. Turning desperate. Refusing to wait any longer, they dispatched Agni to Kailash. But an unexpected guest often walks right into an awkward situation. As the fire god arrived at the mountain, he stumbled upon the worst one possible. Shiva and Parvati in the middle of coitus! Agni hastened to retreat, but it was too late. Finding a sudden intruder there, the couple disengaged abruptly and Shiva's semen spilled on the ground.

Disaster!

With Mahadeva remaining celibate since Sati's death, his seminal fluid had accumulated inside him, becoming highly potent. It also contained the vital seed that would produce Taraka's adversary. Alas, all of it was lying spilt now. Realising what he had done, Agni immediately changed into a pigeon and consumed it. But the fluid generated such heat that it began to scorch even the fire god. Unable to fly with it any longer, Agni deposited the semen in River Kutila. But her waters began to boil, too, making the river sweat. Writhing in pain, Kutila hastily transported all of that essence to Sara Vana, a thicket of reeds by her bank.

Thus, that seed had been cradled first by fire, then by water and now by earth. And there, on the sixth day of the Margasheera month, a child manifested. A boy whose radiance dyed Sara Vana with a golden hue.

As he lay wailing among the reeds, six Krittikas, or stars, of the Pleiades constellation, chanced upon him. One look at the infant and they stood bewitched. They were soon rushing towards him. Fighting over him. Their breasts had begun oozing with milk and each one wanted to suckle him. As they clamoured, lo and behold, the child grew six heads. One for each of them to nurse, giving him the name Shadanana or Shanmukha. The Six-Faced One. Some called him Agneya, as fire had borne him, and others Saravana, as he had materialised in the reed forest. But since the six stars were the first to nourish him, he acquired his primary name from them.

Kartikeya. The one fostered by the Krittikas.

Several beings now began to claim parenthood. Agni, who had carried him from Kailash, and Kutila, who had held him in her waters. Sara Vana, who had nestled him, and the Krittikas, who had suckled him. News soon travelled to Shiva that his seed had flowered and Parvati reached Sara Vana to bring him back. No sooner did she hold the infant in her arms than his six heads fused into one. The heavens rejoiced. The devas cheered. Kartikeya was declared mahasena or commander of the gods. He chose the peacock as his mount and the rooster for his banner. Merely seven days after his birth, the young one thundered from the peaks of Kailash.

'Taraka! Here I come.'

34

KARTIKEYA BATTLES TARAKA

The scion of Shiva was on the warpath.

His peacock was screaming. Its plumes were flashing green and gold. The rooster banner was beckoning the foe. A battered Brahmanda watched in awe as the devas rallied behind the child. Indra, Agni, Yama and Varuna. Even Surya, Chandra and Veerbhadra. Following him where he was leading them. Or perhaps not him but that prophecy of Brahma. The promise that he would deliver them was making every god walk behind that seven-day-old.

Kartikeya struck his lance now and a spasm ran through the cosmos. His knuckles were roaring to seize what had been destined for him. Taraka's insides were quivering, but he laughed aloud.

'Are there no warriors left in Swargaloka? Have my demons wiped out all of them?'

'You had asked for Shiva's seed. Here I am.'

The armies charged. While the demons brandished terrible weapons, Taraka began to employ sorcery. Master of the dark arts, he conjured visions. Mirages of horrific monsters. Illusions of death and doom. A phantasmagoria so chilling that even the blood of the gods turned into ice. The daitya turned Indra unconscious and routed Yama. Veerbhadra engaged him for a while but ultimately collapsed. With even Agni and

Varuna bowing out, the devas began to retreat. Kartikeya instantly regrouped his flanks. Devised concentric circles which pushed everyone else out. The battlefield gasped.

Just him and Taraka now in the centre.

The demon invoked black magic again but, wonder of wonders, the child turned out to be equally adept at occult. If Taraka became clouds, Kartikeya became thunder. If he turned into fire, the other turned into water. Light against darkness. Elephant against lion. Serpent against hawk. With sorcery failing to faze the boy, Taraka now grabbed his sword. His blade was glaring at Kartikeya's lance. As they battled, dust flew. The particles soared high to envelop them both. That thick cloud was concealing their combat. Not revealing who was winning and who was losing. Only the clanging of metals was proclaiming the ferocity of that duel. Gradually, the sword seemed to be whimpering. Sounding less and less savage. More and more silent. When the haze parted, the Creator's words had come true. Kartikeya had driven his lance through Taraka's heart. The infant stood bedecked with six heads and twelve arms, manifesting in all his glory. The devas pounced again and smote the daityas.

The peacock was dancing. The rooster was flying high. Brahma's heart leapt with joy, but the next moment it sank again.

35

SHIVA BECOMES TRIPURARI

The Creator had watched Kartikeya's lance suck the life out of Taraka. One more demon had been eliminated. Disorder had ended. Order had returned. It was utterly perfect. Joyously clichéd.

And yet he was morose because the daitya had bred.

Brahma laughed. The irony! One more of so many ironies that were constantly attaching themselves to the very nucleus of his cosmos. He knew how vital procreation was for his Brahmanda. He had gone through such pangs of uncertainty before the process had finally established itself. Such doubts about whether his universe could keep perpetuating. And here he was now, lamenting that Taraka had reproduced. But not without reason. Like the five elements, creation, too, had become a blessing and a curse. Not every being born was a wholesome one. Not every new heart that ticked was pure. And evil appeared to be proliferating in larger numbers. It had made him sprout four heads. And it had made Taraka spawn three sons.

Vidyunmali, Viryavana and Tarakaksha.

A few moons later, the brothers were standing before the Creator and questioning him.

'Despite your blessing, our father was slaughtered,' Vidyunmali hissed. 'You blessed Hiranyaksha and Hiranyakashipu, but they died as well. Why do you offer death to those who come seeking life?'

'Not life,' Brahma countered. 'Eternal life. And that's not mine to give or for anyone to receive. What they obtained was only an approximation of immortality. The second-best option, which is never fully secure. It's their actions alone that brought about their end.'

'We three have also come for a boon, but I wonder if that's wise.'

'You need to propitiate me for that. Perform austerities.'

'Why tread that longer route?' they said, smirking. 'We are sons of Taraka. You do realise that no austerity is too daunting for us. We can gouge out more eyes than Vishnu did to please Shiva. Stay longer in water than the Prachetas and starve more resolutely than Parvati. You can peek into the future and see us achieving all that. Isn't your vantage point telling you that you are only delaying the inevitable?'

The Creator nodded. 'Yes. Better to end this now than a thousand years later. What do you wish for?'

'Three forts,' the brothers spoke in unison. 'The first wrought of gold. The second of silver and the third of iron. One for each of us and unassailable to all.'

'That's just another word for eternal life, which cannot be granted. Just as living beings must perish, an inanimate object must also be destroyed. I cannot make your forts invincible, but if you wish to keep them safe, set down the most impossible conditions you can think of.'

'Fine. The three forts must be airborne. And they can only be demolished when they align. And only by a single flaming arrow.'

'The forts shall keep moving in a circular path then,' Brahma said. 'Such shall be their orbits that they will come together in a single line every thousand years, when the Pushya star is in conjunction with the moon. They shall align then for a single moment.'

The trio agreed. Maya, the famed architect of the demons, was entrusted with the task, and soon three citadels were revolving in the sky. The one in gold was inhabited by Tarakaksha. The one in silver went to Viryavana, while Vidyunmali took the iron one.

They came to be called Tripura. The three abodes.

Gradually, a strange paradox began manifesting itself. The sons of Taraka were turning virtuous. Displaying a conduct most pious, as they performed rites and observed fasts. Venerated gods and befriended humans. Perhaps the fear of getting killed like other daityas was inspiring nobility within them. Soon, more demons began populating those forts. As the three abodes flourished, the devas started to panic. Fear began clutching their hearts about what was going on behind the walls of Tripura. Were the brothers as upright as they appeared or were they hatching a plot? What if they were turning their forts into garrisons and preparing to launch an attack? The gods took their doubts to Brahma.

'The daityas are surely gathering forces,' they snarled. 'These sons of Taraka are deceiving everyone.'

'What do you suggest?'

'Destruction. All three forts must be razed and the brothers killed so that—'

'That's unfair,' the Creator cut them short. 'They have done nothing to merit such a fate. I will not allow conjecture to get the better of us.'

The voices grew louder, but Brahma stood firm. He was not going to lift a finger. The devas spoke to Shiva and he, too, refused on similar grounds. But Vishnu appeared more receptive.

'I understand your fears,' he consoled them. 'But our hands are truly tied until the demons in Tripura cause real harm.'

'Why wait?' the gods demanded. 'They are daityas. Bestial by nature. Even if they are making efforts to be righteous, they cannot overcome the darkness within them. It will forever keep digging its fangs into their souls. Better to wipe them out.'

'But if they have truly reformed, assaulting them would be wrong. Very wrong. It's a delicate situation, and we will have to fish for a solution.'

The Preserver raised his hand and out came an entity from the depths of the ocean. A hairless being dressed in white called Arihant.

'What is your bidding, lord?'

'Go to Tripura. If you find the demons there leading righteous lives, try steering them towards the path of sin. Propagate a religion that deliberately negates the Vedas. Teach them that heaven and hell are but figments of the imagination. That virtue goes unrewarded and vice is never punished. Beguile every mind and every heart. If, despite your enticements, they do not stray, we shall leave them untouched. But if they heed your word and abandon virtue, we will have cause for action.'

Arihant reached the citadels and put Vishnu's plan into action. Initially, he found the demons impervious to his teachings. The three forts had become centres of a Vedic lifestyle, and the daityas had turned themselves into ideal beings. Arihant was about to give up when suddenly the tide turned. His lies began to take root. Spurt branches and bear flowers. In no time his immoral scriptures had permeated every soul in Tripura. The chaos lying dormant within the demons erupted now, demolishing the fragile edifice that they had themselves created. The brothers were raging. Challenging the triumvirate. The gods hastened to Kailash.

'That utopia was a lie,' Vishnu told Shiva. 'We have to decimate Tripura.'

'But it won't be easy,' Brahma reminded them. 'The sons of Taraka can only be killed when the three forts align under the Pushya star. It will happen tomorrow, but only for a moment. And they must be struck with a single flaming arrow.'

Shiva smiled. 'Gather everyone. I'll tell you how we shall do it.'

The next day, as the citadels began orbiting towards each other, Indra's army attacked. Many demons were slaughtered but Shukracharya kept reviving them. Soon, the battle tilted. Taraka's sons were crushing the divine army, when they suddenly froze.

A vision.

A cosmic vision was looming above the horizon. An image of miraculous proportions. Shiva was charging towards them astride a flying chariot. The vehicle's body was blazing gold, as if all the fire in Brahmanda had solidified into it. Brahma was helming the chariot while Surya and Chandra had become its wheels and the four Vedas had become its horses. Mount Meru had curled itself to become Pinaka, Shiva's bow. The Vasuki serpent was his bowstring and Vishnu was his arrow. Vayu was propelling the shaft and Agni was powering its tip.

Pushya ascended. The Tripura converged.

Shiva launched the flaming arrow and watched as it pierced the three forts at once. The citadels were burning. Bursting like a meteor shower. In that shimmering haze, new names were announced now for the Destroyer as he took a pinch of that ash and smeared it across his forehead in three horizontal lines.

He, who had wielded the Pinaka, had become Pinaki.

He, who had destroyed the Tripura, had become Tripurari.

36

ANDHAKA LUSTS FOR PARVATI

A strange incandescence from Kailash was blinding the sun. Incubating the mountain with such warmth that its flowers were unfurling and its fruits were ripening. Even its ice was glistening like the whitest of fires. Surya knew that the glow was not his. It was beaming from the god seated there. Beaming from every pore of his body. Beatifying everything it touched.

The aura of Mahadeva.

It was enthralling Parvati, too, as she watched that light making love to the elements around. She wanted to hold that radiance. Collect it and make it a part of herself. Tiptoeing behind her husband, she laughed and cupped her palms over the Destroyer's eyes.

Darkness. Total darkness now.

Had Shiva's eyes been illuminating Brahmanda? Had her fingers blocked that hallowed source? Parvati pulled her hands away, but touching Mahadeva's eyes had made them sweat. A drop trickled to the ground and suddenly a roar pierced Kailash. That sweat was bubbling. Proliferating like a fertilised egg. Parvati gaped as the drop gave rise to a male child. He was black. He was blind.

'What being is this?' she shrieked.

'Our son, Parvati.'

'Son?'

'Born of us right now as your body touched mine.'

'But he's blind.'

'Yes. An entity of darkness since he was conceived the moment you covered my eyes. That action robbed his vision and scarred his skin.'

'He growls like an ill omen. What shall we do with him?'

'A daitya has been appeasing me for several years for a son,' Shiva replied. 'This shall be his reward.'

Soon, the demon was joyously receiving the fruit of his penance. Finding enough love in his heart to foster the child, he never told him about his real parents and named him in keeping with his blindness. A name that did not mock his handicap but celebrated his indifference towards it.

Andhaka.

Years later, with the daitya's death, Andhaka now became lord of the demons. But the other daityas were not pleased. Not only because their new master could not see but also because he was not one of them. Not demonic but divine. Hatched from the water of Parvati and the fire of Shiva. Commanded by the old daitya to never reveal Andhaka's true parentage to him, the demons were simmering in silence. Hardly noticing that, although genetically opposed, the daitya's teachings had already corrupted Andhaka. To complicate matters, Prahlad was now laying claim to their throne.

'The demons have strayed far, Andhaka,' he warned. 'Their souls must be placed on the path of Lord Vishnu and the thread pulling them back would be too fragile if you do it. They disown you. They tell me that the smell of your blood repels them. They shall never heed you. Let me take over your father's seat.'

Andhaka could hear the pity in Prahlad's tone. Sense the anger in the daityas around. He immediately retired to the forest and began invoking the Creator. He chopped his flesh and burned his blood. Ripped his hair and hacked his bones. So unparalleled were his austerities that soon a shadow began creeping over Brahmanda. Like a drop of ink diffusing through it, that darkness was shrouding everything. Thickening around the cosmos like a layer of black slime. Brahma panicked.

'Stop!' he yelled as he manifested. 'You are smothering us all.'

'Your words gladden me. Do you see now the darkness that I am buried under?'

'But you have always risen above it, Andhaka. Those with eyes merely see, but you have trained yourself to observe. You are far superior.'

'I thought so too, but others are questioning my worth. Measuring every other faculty I possess against the single one that I don't. Their hearts are murkier than my blindness and I no longer wish to remain flawed. I seek two boons. First, give me my sight.'

'And the second one? Don't ask for immortality, for those born must die just as those dead must be reborn.'

'Then I shall lay down a condition which alone can cause my death.'

'Speak.'

Andhaka smirked. 'I have heard that you were punished once because you desired a woman whom you should not have desired.'

Brahma remained quiet. The wound on top of his heads was suddenly throbbing after all these years.

'I wish for the same. Let me die only when I try to attain the unattainable. When my lust for a woman is most inappropriate.'

The Creator sprinkled water, irrigating his vision and granting him the provision. Thus endowed, Andhaka let loose pandemonium. Thwarted Prahlad's proposal and dominated the daityas. They were trembling before him now as he began trouncing the gods. Extending his reign from one realm to another. Finally able to see all that the universe contained, Andhaka was only coveting. Seizing whatever he liked. And Prahlad was watching how nurture had again displaced nature.

'I was born from vice but I chose virtue.' He sighed to himself. 'If only you knew of whom you were born and what you have become.'

Years passed when, one day, a sudden doubt wriggled inside Andhaka. 'Am I supreme yet?' he asked his minister. 'Unparalleled in every way?'

'Almost.'

'Almost? What do I lack?'

'A woman, lord. The most ravishing one in all Brahmanda who shall elevate your splendour. But she's married to an ascetic.'

'What's her name?

'Parvati. Consort of Shiva.'

The minister began to catalogue the goddess's charms. The arch of her eyebrows. The ambrosia of her lips. The curve of her bosom. The scent of her skin. Hardly aware that the demon was so improperly describing his own mother, Andhaka began to salivate. His eyes were now yearning to see this marvel of nature.

'A yogi has no use for such beauty,' he declared. 'Go and command him to hand over his wife.'

The messengers stormed Kailash. Shiva heard them and smiled.

'Tell your master to come and take Parvati himself.'

Andhaka immediately laid siege with his army. Finding the goddess alone in a cavern, he charged in and stood still. His tongue had frozen. His heart was hammering out her name.

Parvati ... Parvati ... Parvati ...

His eyes were groping her violently. Gazing at how her body epitomised all that was exquisite. Unaware that he was mentally disrobing his own mother. Unconscious that he was fulfilling the condition for his death.

When my lust for a woman is most inappropriate ...

Andhaka advanced but Parvati turned the cave dark to confound him. The universe gaped in horror at a son trying to violate his mother. At Adishakti battling her own offspring. Wondering what cycle of cause and effect had brought such shame to pass. As Andhaka was about to grasp her, Parvati generated seven dazzling rays of light from her flesh. Seven mother goddesses were materialising before him.

The Saptamatrikas.

War erupted and the goddesses began massacring the demons. As countless daityas dropped dead, Shukracharya invoked the Mritasanjivani. Seeing this, an enraged Shiva opened his mouth. Stretched his jaws wide and swallowed Shukracharya alive. With their guru no longer present, the demons collapsed. All but Andhaka. He had been standing immune to every attack so far. Shiva's voice rumbled.

'You have been coveting your own mother, my child. Parvati is your mother and I am your father.'

Andhaka recoiled.

Parvati is your mother ...

The realisation instantly nullified the boon that had been shielding him.

'You are my parents?'

'We are.'

'Then why did you reject me? Because I was blind?'

'No,' the Destroyer replied as he impaled him on his trishul. 'Because you still are.'

As death began to overpower Andhaka, Brahma appeared next to him.

'What irony is this! All your life you mourned that no one ever saw beyond your body, Andhaka. But you too failed to go beyond Parvati's body to see who she truly was. You lusted after your mother just as I lusted after my daughter and we both had to suffer the wrath of Mahadeva.'

Andhaka realised his folly now and begged for forgiveness. The Destroyer healed him and made him one of his ganas at Kailash.

'Mercy! Mercy!'

The voice was coming from inside Shiva. The trapped Shukracharya was pleading to be freed. The god relented again and liberated him through his genital. Out came the guru in a drop of semen, and since then sperm began to be called Shukra.

37

BHRINGI CHALLENGES PARVATI

'Bhringi. I am Bhringi, lord.'

The sage was standing before Shiva with a vessel half-filled with milk.

'I venerate you, Mahadeva. You are the Atman. Parabrahman. Those who are ignorant say you destroy. They fail to see that you renew. Make rebirth possible. I have come with a request, lord. Will you agree?'

'Speak.'

'I wish to circumambulate you just as a thousand universes whirl around you in ecstasy. You are the cosmic pivot. The centre of every existence, including mine. May I?'

'You may. It shall please me.'

As Bhringi took his first step, a female voice accosted him.

'Wait!'

It was Parvati. Approaching them, she sat down next to Shiva.

'Brahmanda does not comprise him alone. It's a union of Purusha and Prakriti. Shiva and Shakti. We are the two halves of that composite whole. You cannot acknowledge one without the other.'

But Bhringi's devotion was oblivious to everyone else. The sanctum he had erected in his heart housed a single god. Only Mahadeva. Not Vishnu. Not Brahma. He glanced at Parvati.

And certainly not her ...

'Forgive me,' he said as he shook his head. 'I cannot worship anyone else. I am a Shaiva.'

'And I am Adishakti.'

'I shall only circumambulate him.'

'It shall be both or neither.'

Bhringi began walking. Bypassing the goddess and encircling only Shiva. Parvati inched closer to her husband, but the sage kept avoiding her. She slid even nearer and he still kept evading her. The goddess got up and perched herself on Shiva's lap.

'What now?'

Bhringi smiled and vanished. Parvati stared. He was neither behind her nor in front of her. Neither below nor above. She was wondering if he had bowed out in defeat when suddenly a humming noise assailed her senses.

A honeybee.

Hovering near her face. Threatening to sting her eyes. Flying rapturously only around the Destroyer like a planet revolving around the sun. Parvati glared. Bhringi's elliptical motion was mocking her. Shiva could feel her blood boiling. Her wrath foaming. Ready to spill over any moment now. The Destroyer closed his eyes.

There was only one thing to be done.

The bee paused. Something was happening. Its path was getting blocked. The gap between Shiva and Parvati was narrowing. The light between their bodies was tapering. The bee peered to see if she was leaning closer to him only to gasp in awe. Something incredible was taking place. The two bodies were becoming one. Shiva and Shakti were dissolving into each other. Their flesh and bones were fusing. Their souls were blending. Bhringi was witnessing that divine amalgamation that had once enlightened Brahma.

The Ardhanarishwara. Fountain of all creation. Two spheres of the universe melding into a whole.

Bhringi scowled. Instead of kneeling before the vision, he was filling with envy. Resenting the oneness of Shivangi with Shiva. Watching her laugh at him and wanting to silence her again. Morphing into a worm now,

Bhringi did the unimaginable. He began to gnaw. Nibble right through the flesh of the Ardhanarishwara to tear them asunder.

Parvati snapped. Detaching herself from the Destroyer, she pronounced a terrible curse.

'Your zeal has crossed all bounds, Bhringi. You exalt one aspect of the cosmos but remain intolerant of the other. Instead of celebrating the assimilation of this divine duality, you see a paradox that you cannot resolve. You are a fool to assume that you can isolate Shiva from Shakti. Blind to the cardinal truth that we are but one. Since you deny the Sacred Feminine that suckles Brahmanda, I curse you that you will lose all your flesh, for that is inherited from the mother. You shall be left only with bones, for they come from the father.'

No sooner had she uttered those words than Bhringi was reduced to a skeleton. With all his muscle gone, he could no longer stand erect. Finally, Shiva took pity and blessed him with a third leg.

Thus he would remain, forever propped on three limbs.

38

CHURNING OF THE OCEAN

Nothing was more renowned about Sage Durvasa than his temper. Legends whispered in fearful tones that Brahma and Shiva once had such a savage argument that the latter's fury had erupted, threatening to burn Brahmanda. Realising how vicious that energy was, Shiva had deposited it in the womb of Anusuya, wife of Atri. Born out of this caustic emotion, the sage's temper was perpetually on fire. And that had earned him his fitting name.

Durvasa. One who is difficult to live with.

Once, the sage came across a nymph wearing an exquisite garland of vaijayanti, symbolising good fortune. He had never seen such flowers. Inhaled such a fragrance. Taking the garland from her, Durvasa placed it around himself and began strutting through the universe. As he neared the gates of heaven, he saw Indra astride his elephant. Feeling a sudden spurt of generosity, Durvasa offered him the garland. The Devaraja hauled it up with his spear, but instead of adorning himself, he placed it around his elephant's head. Alas, the aroma of the flowers overpowered the animal and it tossed the garland to the ground.

'Wretched fool,' the sage bellowed at the god. 'How dare you mock my gift? Have the devas stopped venerating saints?'

Indra leapt down and touched his feet.

'I meant no disrespect, Holy One. This garland of vaijayanti can only be worn by someone who has transcended all ego. I know I have not done that.'

But the sage was quaking with fury.

'Your plea will not undo your act. This kingship of Swargaloka has filled you with conceit. Seated high on that elephant, you look down upon everyone. Not anymore. I curse you that, just as you have disowned these flowers, good fortune too shall disown you.'

The words clung to the Devaraja now and began sucking the life out of him. As Indra began to waste away, so did the grandeur of his loka. Gold lost its sheen and gems gave up their sparkle. Trees turned barren and weapons were no longer potent. Nothing was thriving. Every element was decomposing. Realising that heaven had turned powerless, the demons invaded. Led by Prahlad's grandson, Bali, they annexed Swargaloka and established their rule. Indra and the gods were now standing crestfallen before Vishnu. The Preserver sighed.

'Durvasa's curse is irreversible.'

'The asuras are emitting flames like never before. What can we do?' Varuna implored.

'If they have fire, you have water.'

Everyone saw what Vishnu was pointing at. That raging leviathan. Those heaving waves, as if a beast were breathing in and breathing out.

'You are forgetting that the very universe that fills us with darkness also offers light. The solution is all around us. We must churn this Ocean of Milk.'

'Churn Ksheersagar?' Indra frowned. 'What will that yield, Sri Hari?'

'Lakshmi. The goddess of wealth and fortune. Of all that is auspicious. Once she rises from these waters, Swargaloka will be yours again.'

But their faces were appearing more terrified now.

'The ocean!' Agni shuddered. 'This boundless stretch of water that hardly begins or ends. Even if all the devas unite, we shall fall short of completing this task.'

The Preserver nodded. 'I know that. I shall call a truce with the demons. You will join hands with them and do this together.'

'Join hands with the asuras?' Vayu flared.

'Yes. Only your combined effort will draw up the ratnas.'

'Ratnas?'

'The riches lying in the womb of Ksheersagar. Each of them symbolising dharma, artha or kama. They shall not only fortify heaven but also benefit the whole universe.'

'The demons will never agree. Nothing will make them aid us in any enterprise.'

'Not even to procure amrita?'

Amrita ...

That word! That one word! It changed everything. Latched on to every tongue.

'Amrita? We shall acquire amrita?'

'Yes,' Vishnu smiled. 'The ocean will yield many ratnas but none more miraculous than amrita. The nectar that will turn anyone who sips it immortal. Once the demons are informed, they will readily participate.'

'But they will also demand their portion of amrita,' Indra hissed. 'Are you asking us to share the elixir with them?'

'Ideally you should. Daityas and danavas are not only your half-brothers but they will also constitute half of the force required to draw up amrita. But for the sake of Brahmanda, we cannot let them become immortal. Besides, Mahadeva has already blessed them with Mritasanjivani, making them practically deathless. I shall ensure that they do not lay hands on the nectar.'

Thus assured, the gods approached Bali with the proposal. The demon king was a gentle soul and promptly agreed.

'How can I not heed the word of Sri Hari? We would be honoured to cooperate.'

The day dawned. Ksheersagar was seeing what it had never seen before. Devas and asuras were standing together. The blood in their veins was acknowledging their common pedigree today. That spark of Brahma. That seed of Daksha. But their faces were like the water around them. Welcoming but laced with invisible salt.

'Churning needs a rod and a rope,' Yama said. 'But this is an ocean. What tools can measure up to these mammoth proportions?'

All eyes turned towards Vishnu.

'I shall uproot Mount Mandara and place it as the churning pole,' he replied. 'And the serpent, Vasuki, shall be your rope.'

Soon, the mountain was resting above the heart of the ocean and the serpent was wrapped around it three-and-a-half times, like Kundalini around a spine. The demons grabbed its head while the gods held on to its tail. The churning began only to instantly halt. Something was amiss. Mandara was getting dislodged. Not anchored to the ocean floor, the mountain was floundering. As all faces crumbled, they saw Shiva smiling at the Preserver.

'It's time.'

Vishnu morphed. His body was transforming before their very eyes. Budding new limbs and a new head. Sprouting a gigantic upturned shell. The god had become an amphibian. A giant tortoise.

'Hail another avatar,' Brahma eulogised. 'Kurma Avatar.'

Diving into Ksheersagar, the tortoise steadied the mountain on its back. With Mandara propped atop firmly now, churning resumed in earnest. The gods were pulling Vasuki's tail and the demons were pulling its head. The mountain was rotating clockwise and anticlockwise. Gandharvas, yakshas and nagas appeared to witness this cosmic event. This great ocean being churned with this massive mountain. Everything divine was on one side and everything demonic was on the other. The Preserver himself had incarnated to cradle this colossal process. Never had anyone seen such scale. Such magnitude. Seen the devas and asuras working towards a common goal. Giving birth to an occurrence so epic that it would forever resonate through every yuga.

Ksheersagar was bubbling now.

The motion of Mandara was generating high energy down its core. That kinesis was radiating outwards, forcing the waters to move in a spiral motion. A giant whirlpool was spinning as the ocean frothed and foamed. Vasuki's body had begun scraping against the mountain. That vortex was turning violent. Scouring that expanse of water. As the force gushed through the spine of the ocean, it began sucking up what was lying below.

'Look!' they screamed.

The ratnas were surfacing like cream floating to the top of milk.

'Kalpavriksha,' Brahma identified.

The wish-fulfilling tree.

'Airavata.'

The five-headed elephant.

'Uchchaishrava.'

The seven-headed horse.

'Kamadhenu.'

The cow of plenty.

'Kaustubh.'

The jewel of consciousness.

'Varuni.'

The deity of wine.

'Rambha and Menaka.'

Apsaras divine.

'Parijat.'

The ever-flowering tree.

'Panchajanya.'

The celestial conch-shell.

'Sharanga.'

The mighty bow.

'Jyeshtha.'

The deity of misfortune.

'Lakshmi.'

Sri incarnate.

The universe rejoiced. Wealth had arrived. Fortune had surfaced. Lotuses were blooming and coins were clinking. White elephants were sprinkling water. The ten directions were singing Sri Sukta. Suddenly, the brine started to boil. Foul fumes were thickening into a fog. That miasma was spreading all around, darkening the sky. Scorching the air. Had their churning awakened a sea monster?

'Halahal,' the Creator identified. 'Poison.'

'Poison?' the gods screamed. 'Sri Hari never told us anything about poison.'

Brahma smiled. 'Didn't he say that where there's light, there's darkness too? That's rising up now.'

Oozing from the middle of Ksheersagar, as if a wound was festering. Coating that water with toxic scum. The loins of the ocean were discharging a venom so vile that it was threatening to dissolve Brahmanda.

'This deluge will devour all creation.' Indra shuddered. 'We must contain it.'

'There's only one vessel that can do that,' Brahma said and pointed.

They looked. Shiva was wading through Ksheersagar. The poison was swirling all around him. Conspiring to spill over to the shore. He bent and joined his palms underwater.

'The halahal,' Bali screamed. 'It's shrinking.'

Lo and behold! The venom was imploding. Rushing into his palms as if being pulled by an invisible osmosis. Filtering off the ocean water and collecting in his grasp. That sea of toxin had contracted into a mere fistful. They watched with wonder as Shiva raised his hands and drank. He whose wrath had spewed Durvasa was swallowing this poison now to save them all. As the halahal trickled down, a terrified Parvati placed her hand on his throat. The action chained the venom right there, staining his throat blue.

'Neelkanth!' the gathering chorused with tears in their eyes. 'Neelkanth!'

The Blue-Throated One.

The gods and demons heaved one last time. Their wrists were aching. Their fists were slipping. Vasuki was tightening as if it would crack Mandara. Its body was bleeding. Its skin was peeling. As they wrenched the serpent in one final tug, Ksheersagar birthed again. A being emerged now, bearing a golden vessel.

'Dhanvantari,' Brahma announced. 'Lord of Ayurveda.'

'And that vessel?' they asked.

'Amrita.'

39

VISHNU BECOMES MOHINI

Water had broken and nectar had emerged. The final ratna.

Amrita. The Deathless.

As Dhanvantari stepped on the shore, the gods and demons swarmed around him. Their gaze was fastened to the vessel in his hands.

'Today is a blessed day,' the Creator said. 'Ksheersagar has yielded all its bounty and time has now come to—'

Suddenly, an uproar ate up his words. The asuras had snatched the vessel from Dhanvantari. The incredible scent wafting from it had driven their senses wild. Their bodies were craving to relish this ratna and turn undying. Also, suspicious that the devas would refuse to share it, they had seized the nectar for themselves. As their king, Bali, hung his head in shame, the gods stood aghast. Watched the vessel pass from one demon to another. Any moment now, they were going to tip it into their mouths.

Laughter.

Silken peals fluttering like a butterfly.

As if wings of gauze were brushing against their skin.

Lotus in her hair. Discs in her ears. Shells around her throat.

A woman, like no woman the asuras had ever seen, was walking towards them. Her eyes were disrobing them. Her lips were throbbing to touch their flesh. Her arms were writhing to coil around their chests. Her hips were swaying to the beat of their hearts. Arousing such pangs in the asuras now that they were forgetting the amrita they were holding. Unaware that they were staring at an illusion. An ethereal apparition. At Vishnu who had surfaced from the ocean in this beguiling female avatar.

The enchantress, Mohini.

Walking into their midst, she tapped daintily on the rim of the vessel. Her fingers were generating a narcotic sound.

'You are such simpletons!'

'Why do you say that?' the demons asked.

'The bulk of amrita has settled at the bottom. A mass, rich and thick. What's floating on top here is only liquid.'

'What should we do then?'

'Let the gods have this liquid. Once they are done, you shall get to feast on the real nectar below.'

She simpered as they handed her the vessel. The devas were taking a sip each now. Experiencing a wild alchemy as that elixir touched their tongues. Flowed through their flesh. Immortalised them cell by cell, while the asuras stood gazing at Mohini. Their eyes still entranced by that face. Their senses still lulled by her anklets. None of them noticing that almost all the amrita had been consumed.

None but one.

The demon, Swarbhanu. His eyes were on the nectar rather than Mohini. Observing the movement of that vessel. He realised now that it was appearing much lighter. Its contents vastly diminished. Possibly only a fraction of amrita was remaining. With his whole clan standing mesmerised, he knew any protest would be futile. There was only one thing to be done.

Deceive the deceiver.

Tiptoeing through the gathering, Swarbhanu sneaked into the queue of devas and stood silently at the end of the line. Glancing now and then at the vessel as it slowly inched towards him.

Closer ... Closer ... Closer ... Closer ...

His race had been betrayed. It was time to think about himself.

Closer ... Closer ... Closer ...

That heady aroma again. It was storming his senses once more.

Closer ... Closer ...

Asking him to open his mouth.

Closer ...

Mohini was raising the vessel before his face now. Swarbhanu's eyes filled with tears at the sight of that ambrosia. His tongue was trembling as it dripped into his mouth. His insides were exulting as it saturated his throat. His mind was beginning to wonder how something so sweet could emerge from something so saline.

'Asura! Asura!'

Surya was shrieking. Pushing him away. Chandra leapt and snatched the vessel from Mohini's hands.

'It's Swarbhanu. He has drunk the nectar.'

Chaos erupted. The devas charged. The demon began to flee, when suddenly his limbs froze. He could hear a familiar sound. A deadly whirring of metal just before it decapitated him.

Sudarshana ...

Vishnu was no longer Mohini. He had ripped off that avatar to behead the asura. He watched now as Swarbhanu's blood stained the ocean. Watched his head and body floating away from each other. Suddenly, the demon's eyes snapped open. His head soared into the sky while his body stood up on the shore.

'Impossible,' Indra yelled.

'It's amrita!' Brahma sighed. 'He cannot be killed now. Neither by Vishnu nor Shiva.'

The severed head was fuming. The arms below were pointing at Surya and Chandra.

'You both have brought this upon me and now you, too, shall suffer. Yama may be your son, Surya, but you shall die. And Mahadeva may have healed you, Chandra, but you shall darken.'

The head hovered menacingly over the two gods.

'Henceforth, whenever I please, my head shall devour the sun and my torso shall cover the moon. You shall be blotted out of the sky. Unable to share your light just as you have refused to share amrita. The entire Brahmanda shall remain dark until I release you again. My head shall be called Rahu and my torso, Ketu. And they shall keep eclipsing you both till the end of time.'

As he vanished, Lakshmi clasped Vishnu's hand. Garlanded him and named him Vanamali. She had become his consort now and the devas soon regained Swargaloka. Days later, Shiva felt a yearning to behold Mohini again. Reaching Vaikuntha, he stood before the Preserver.

'Show me that avatar once more. Your only female avatar. The most bewitching in all Brahmanda.'

As soon as Vishnu transformed, Shiva stood spellbound. Mohini had ignited his ardour. Induced bhoga. His semen was dripping. Crystallising into ores of gold and silver. Longing for that divine form, Shiva embraced her. When his rapture broke, he found himself clinging to Vishnu. The Preserver smiled.

'We were always one, Mahadeva. Hari and Hara have become Harihara again.'

'And Mohini will become Mohan soon.' Shiva closed his eyes.

40

KADRU AND VINATA PLACE A BET

One of the many who were ecstatic at the churning of the ocean was Kadru. Daughter of Daksha, she, too, had married Kashyapa and received a boon to beget a thousand sons. Kadru had spawned one thousand serpents, making her the mother of the naga race. Her eldest son, Sheshnaga, had become the floating bed for Vishnu on the Ocean of Milk. And now her younger son, Vasuki, had acted as the Preserver's churning rope for Ksheersagar and acquired immense merit.

Kadru was, therefore, jubilant. But not her sister, Vinata.

Despite being siblings, a silent feud had been simmering between them for the longest time. Also married to Kashyapa, Vinata had requested for only two sons who would surpass Kadru's thousand. In time, she had brought forth two eggs, but they had displayed no signs of hatching. Losing her patience, Vinata had smashed one of them prematurely and stared in horror at the male embryo, nestling in a crimson glow, only half-formed. His face and torso had developed but below dangled a lump of red flesh. Raging at his mother, the deformed son, Aruna, had uttered a terrible curse.

'You shall soon be enslaved by your sister, Kadru. Your bondage shall end only if you permit the other egg to hatch on its own.'

Ages had passed since then, but the second egg had still not stirred. Shown no indications of life. Vinata sat gazing at it now like she had been doing for all these years. Her fingers were itching to break open this one, too, but Aruna's words were resounding inside her. She brushed her tears away as Kadru arrived.

'Did you hear about the churning and what my Vasuki did?' she gloated.

'I did. Such a noble gesture.'

'It's a blessing to have such sons who serve Sri Hari. You would know, Vinata, if you had a son, too.'

'Perhaps I would.'

'They are the only treasures that make a mother smile.'

'I hear fourteen treasures arose from the bottom of the ocean, too?'

'Indeed. One of them is right there,' Kadru pointed far above. 'The seven-headed steed, Uchchaishrava.'

'What beauty,' Vinata exclaimed. 'Pristine white from head to tail.'

'Not the tail. That's black.'

'Black? It's white. Every inch of it.'

'Surely black.'

'Obviously white.'

The sisters kept bickering. With neither of them ready to buckle, they turned it into a bet and decided to investigate at dawn. The loser would have to become the winner's slave. As soon as Kadru's sons heard about this wager, they flicked their tongues in dismay.

'What have you done, mother? You are going to lose.'

'Lose?'

'We have seen Uchchaishrava. It's white. All white. Every bristle on its tail.'

Kadru shrank. Suddenly, all the colours seemed to be seeping away from everything around her. Brahmanda was turning into one brutal monochrome.

White ...

She shook her head. She was not going to let that colour win. She was not going to become her sister's servant.

'White can be black,' she smirked.

'What do you mean, mother?'

'It's simple. Tomorrow morning, I want all of you to coil around that horse's tail. Wrap your black bodies in such a way that not a single white hair is visible. Vinata will never see through our deception and I shall win.'

While some of her sons agreed, many refused to comply. An infuriated Kadru cursed them that their descendants would burn to death in a ceremony in Kali Yuga. The next day, both the sisters stood behind Uchchaishrava. The tail appeared wholly black because of the numerous serpents entwining it. Unaware of their trickery, Vinata accepted defeat and became Kadru's slave.

Aruna's words had come true.

Five hundred years later, a cracking sound echoed through the cosmos. Vinata's second egg had hatched. Golden light oozed from the shell, as if it had been incubating another sun. But what burst forth was a hybrid. A magnificent hybrid that was half-bird and half-human. Red wings were fanning out from his gilded body. Talons were pronouncing him Nagari, or enemy of the nagas. Mightier than the thousand sons of Kadru, as promised by Kashyapa.

He was Garuda. The humanoid bird.

Upon becoming aware of his mother's slavery, he immediately demanded her release. The serpents agreed but on one condition.

'Vinata became our maid when the ocean yielded amrita. But none of us has tasted that nectar. Bring us amrita and we shall set your mother free.'

Garuda agreed, only to find out how daunting that task was. The gods had taken multiple precautions to secure the remaining elixir. A ring of fire encircled the vessel and killer blades rotated at the entrance to its lair. Two serpents also lay waiting to strike anyone who dared to enter. Garuda laughed.

'Venom is guarding amrita?'

The Nagari surmounted every obstacle. He showered the waters of all the rivers to douse that circle of flames. He reduced his size to sneak through the blades and then trampled the snakes to death. Flying back with the vessel now, Garuda froze.

Vishnu was standing in his way.

The Preserver had been observing him for a while. Aware of why he was stealing amrita and pleased that he had not partaken any of it, Vishnu not only allowed him to pass but also blessed him with a boon. Flying further, Garuda came across Indra. The Devaraja hurled his Vajra at him but that mighty weapon could only shed a single golden feather from his body. Recognising his prowess, Indra also moved out of his way but only after they had both bartered promises.

'I assure you that you will be able to carry away the amrita before the snakes consume it,' Garuda said.

'And I declare that henceforth the nagas shall be your food,' the Devaraja gave his word.

Reaching Kadru's abode, Garuda deliberately placed the vessel on the ground.

'Here's what you desired. Now release my mother.'

The serpents let Vinata go. As soon as they began slithering towards the elixir, Indra swooped in. Clutched the vessel and soared high. But as he fled, some of the amrita spilled on the grass below, where it lay glistening like dew. The snakes began licking those sharp blades and ended up slitting their tongues. As a result, the tongue of every serpent would hereafter be forked. And since they had ingested a bit of amrita, the nagas also developed an iota of immortality. They could now shed their old skin for a new one.

Kadru looked at Vinata and scowled. 'Your son tricked us.'

'Just as your sons deceived me. It's unfortunate that, like Diti and Aditi, we too have no love for each other. Their children are perpetually at war and now our sons have also become eternal foes.'

'But my sons are superior,' Kadru taunted. 'My Vasuki became Sri Hari's tool and my Sheshnaga carries him over Ksheersagar.'

'I, too, shall be carrying him,' Garuda proclaimed. 'He has blessed me with a boon.'

'What boon?' his mother asked.

'Sri Hari has made me his mount.'

Vinata glanced at Kadru. Vinata was smiling.

41

GANESHA COMES TO LIFE

Parvati was counting her tears.

Kartikeya's conquest of Taraka had made her supremely proud. But the more he battled now, the less she celebrated as she hardly got to see him anymore. The commander of the gods was occupied in unending warfare. His arrival had awakened the mother inside Parvati and his absence now filled her with longing. With surging maternal love and no one to shower it on. What could she do since Brahmanda had claimed her son?

A second son ...

She flinched. Had someone whispered in her ears? But she was all alone. Had the words come from inside her then? Her own voice? Had her own thoughts come wafting like a feather and stroked her heart? Parvati smiled. Was this how the cosmos got things done, she wondered. Turning everyone into its own instrument? Implanting ideas that would sprout into actions? She sat down. Another son would surely fulfil her motherly pangs. Not only receive love from her but also offer it in return. But Shiva was absent from Kailash at the moment. The mahayogi had also not been showing any interest in fathering another child after Kartikeya. As Parvati began to prepare for her bath, a plan began to take shape.

Mahadeva generated Kartikeya ...

I can do the same ...

Having smeared turmeric paste all over her body, she began rubbing it off now. Lumping the flakes into a ball of dough, she started moulding it into a child's body. Head. Torso. Arms and legs. Eyes and ears. The orb was acquiring form just as a foetus would have inside her. Gestating not in her womb but in her palms. She closed her eyes to blow life into him but paused.

Will Mahadeva accept him?

She nodded.

I love Kartikeya ... Mahadeva will love this one too ...

Parvati breathed. Her doll was breathing now.

'Mother!'

'My son!'

'What's my name, mother?' asked the boy.

'Our followers here are called ganas. So, you shall be Ganesha. Ganapati. Master of the ganas.'

She clasped him and did not let go. Moments later, she handed him a staff.

'I will be taking a bath now. Stand guard, son, and let no one enter.'

'You have my word.'

Walking inside, Parvati began thinking of Shiva. Wondering what he would say when he saw this beautiful child. Unaware that the Destroyer had already set foot in Kailash. That he was striding towards her chamber now, only to be stopped by Ganesha.

'Who goes there?'

'Who stands there?'

'I am Ganesha. Son of Parvati.'

'I am Mahadeva. Lord of Parvati. Let me pass.'

'My mother is taking a bath and has commanded me to prevent anyone from entering. You will have to wait.'

'Time waits for me but I wait for none. I am Mahakaal. No part of Brahmanda is inaccessible to me.'

'This chamber is, as long as I am here.'

'If you are truly the son of Parvati, then that makes me your father. Don't you know the meaning of obedience?'

'I am obeying my mother's words by barring your way. You may be my father but right now my mother's bidding outweighs yours.'

'My trident will pierce you.'

'My staff will pound you.'

Shiva stood confounded. The entire universe trembled before him, but this boy was unfazed. He was brandishing his staff as if that could spar with his trishul. Repeating the goddess's words like a mantra. Just as Bhringi had bowed only before Shiva, Ganesha was chanting only Parvati's name. The ganas pleaded with him but in vain. Narada also tried but failed. The Saptarishi descended to recount the scriptures but to no avail. Even Brahma and Vishnu attempted to coerce him but nothing worked. The boy was routing devas and repelling danavas.

'Looks like everyone is weaker than my resolve today,' Ganesha laughed.

'Enough!' Shiva's eyes were bloodshot now. 'You dishonour your mother with your defiance. Such blind devotion can only do more harm than good. Either I shall meet Parvati or you shall meet Yama.'

'My mother has blessed me today. My life will return even if someone takes it.'

The Destroyer flung his trident. Scratching three fiery lines in the air, it charged at the boy. He raised his staff but the trishul tore through it and severed Ganesha's head.

'Mothe—'

The death cry was deafening. Everyone stood hushed now. Only Parvati's footsteps were goring that silence as she staggered out to see. The trident, crusted with flesh. Dripping with blood.

Ganapati, lying dead at the feet of the ganas.

Parvati was Adishakti and she was seething now. Parvati was Prakriti and she was howling now. Brahmanda was quaking. Threatening to peel into ribbons. Sixty-four Yoginis were rising from the goddess's body to tear everything down. The oceans were vaporising. The mountains were detonating. Realms were teetering on the verge of extinction. As the cosmos screamed in horror, Shiva folded his hands.

'Calm down, Parvati. You are endangering us all.'

'What have you done?'

'It's not him,' Kashyapa came forward. 'It's me. My curse.'

'Your curse?'

'Yes. Long ago, my son, Surya, had tried to kill the asuras, Mali and Sumali. They were devotees of Mahadeva and had prayed to him for help. Mahadeva had struck Surya down, plunging the world into darkness. Enraged at my son's pain, I had cursed Mahadeva that one day he would decapitate his own son. It has come to pass.'

'Is that what my Ganesha was?' Parvati thundered. 'A tool to accomplish a curse? I generated him from myself, Mahadeva. My own body. You have not killed him. You have killed me. Watch now as my corpse collapses over Brahmanda.'

'You cannot do that. You cannot demolish what you yourself are.'

'Why not? I had done that as Sati and I shall do it again now as Parvati. You made Markandeya immortal because he deified you, but you took Ganesha's life because he defied you. You pardoned our son, Andhaka, who sought to dishonour me. Then how could you kill our son, Ganesha, who sought to defend me? You will save me now only if you save my child. Bring him back to life the way your Mritasanjivani does. Bring him back to life the way you revived Daksha.'

'But Daksha was revived with the head of a ram,' Brahma said.

Shiva glanced at his ganas. 'That shall be the solution once more. Bring me the head of the first animal you encounter lying towards the northern direction.'

'The direction of wisdom?'

'Yes. That alone shall resurrect Ganesha. But the animal must be willing.'

Vishnu nodded. 'It will be. Just as Kashyapa's curse has come true, the boon given to Gajasura shall also be fulfilled now.'

'Gajasura?' Brahma gasped. 'That elephant in whose stomach Mahadeva had once resided?'

'Indeed. Mahadeva had granted Gajasura that his head shall be forever worshipped. That head will now adorn Ganapati.'

Not long after, the ganas returned with Gajasura's head. As soon as Shiva affixed it, Ganesha touched Parvati tenderly with his trunk.

'Mother!'

Adishakti melted. As her chaos quietened, Brahma blessed the child.

'Hallowed are you, Ganapati. First, your mother brought you to life and now your father has done the same.'

Mahadeva declared, 'Henceforth, Ganesha shall be the cardinal deity. God of all beginnings. The first to be invoked. He tried obstructing my path but he shall be Vighnesha. One who removes hurdles from the paths of others. He shall be Gajanana. The Elephant-Faced. And he will be Vinayaka. The Leader Supreme.'

42

DURGA SLAYS MAHISHASURA

'Tell me, O Mighty One. Tell me, how you were born.'

The demon laughed. 'I am a descendant of Daksha.'

'The Prajapati?'

'Yes. Just as Daksha's daughter, Diti, gave birth to daityas, his other daughter, Danu, begot danavas, a wildly demonic race. Once, two danava brothers, Rambha and Karambha, resolved to perform austerities for the boon of invincibility. Rambha stood inside flames to appease Agni, while Karambha meditated under water to please Varuna. Both were invoking the two primordial elements. But Indra!'

'The Devaraja? What did he do?'

'What that coward always does. Petrified that the danava brothers would kick him out of heaven, he immediately targeted both. He entered the water as a crocodile and chewed up Karambha to death. Then, he penetrated the inferno to murder Rambha but was attacked by Agni. The fire god had been gratified with the demon's devotion and could not see him getting killed.'

'Two devas fighting over a danava's life!'

'Indeed. And Agni prevailed. But as soon as Indra fled, Rambha grabbed an axe. The news of Karambha's death had shattered him and he decided to sacrifice himself. Seizing his hair, he was about to chop off his head when Agni held his hand.'

'So, the fire god saved him twice.'

'True. Agni also offered him a boon to avenge his brother's death. Rambha asked for a son. An indomitable danava who would go on to become the master of Brahmanda. Agni blessed him that he could beget a son with the female of any species.'

'Any species?'

'Yes. Demonic or divine. Animal or human. And it came true when Rambha fell in love with a Mahishi. A she-buffalo. The creature yielded to his passion and they mated to bring forth a son.'

'You, Mighty One! Mahishasura. Part-buffalo and part-danava.'

'Fathered by Rambha. Blessed by Agni. But I need one more boon now.'

Thus, recounting the story of his birth to a herd of buffaloes, Mahishasura made his way towards the wilderness to appease Brahma. Years later, the Creator was standing before him. Gazing fondly at his face that so closely resembled Rambha.

'Your father was my great-grandson. Agni has already endowed you, Mahishasura. You are born to rule. What more do you wish for?'

'To be deathless. Agni has granted me victory over Brahmanda but not over my mortality. That's the ultimate triumph. What good would my conquests be if I am not alive to savour them?'

'Immortality is out of the question.'

'I know that.' The danava cracked his knuckles. 'I am seeking an alternative. Bestow on me the boon that no one can kill me except a woman.'

'Woman? Why a woman?'

'Isn't it obvious? Out of all your creations, she's the weakest. Her body is frail and her heart, feeble. She's the least likely to be a threat to anyone. Even my father did not need a woman to beget me. Grant me what I am asking for and I shall be practically immortal.'

Brahma smiled and nodded. Soon, the inevitable began to occur. Mahishasura seized Patalaloka and then Bhuloka and finally Swargaloka. His horns were goring gods and humans. His hooves were trampling every corner of the universe. As the stench of death swelled, the celestial assembly gathered.

'A woman,' the Creator said. 'We need a devi. The warrior form of Adishakti. Mahishasura is twice blessed, just as his father was twice saved. He has boons from both me and Agni.'

The fire god nodded. 'And he has abused them like so many asuras before him. My boon has played out. It's time now for yours to come true.'

'Gather around then. We shall give rise to the female warrior from our collective aura. A confluence of our energies. Distillation of our primeval powers.'

The devas stood in a circle and opened their mouths. From those dark cavities blazed shafts of light. Brilliant light, as if their divinity was emanating. The beams were colliding. Merging into a network in the centre of the circle. Creating a smouldering supernova that was slowly transfiguring. Acquiring a feminine shape. High forehead. Manifold limbs. Golden complexion. The devas were pouring themselves into that effulgence. Rays from each of them were transporting their very best to her like multiple umbilical cords. Shiva was moulding her face and Vishnu her arms. Indra her waist and Varuna her thighs. Dharma her hips and Brahma her feet. Finally, Vayu gave her ears and Agni created her eyes.

All the gods had manifested in a single goddess.

They named her Durga. The Defender.

Vishnu gave her his chakra and Shiva, his trishul. Indra gave her his Vajra and Vayu, his bow. From Varuna she received his conch and from Yama, his staff. Also wielding a sword, a mace and a spear, the ten-armed goddess rode into battle on a roaring lion. The combat went on for nine days. Mahishasura kept changing his forms and Durga kept trouncing them all.

On the tenth day, the devi pinned him down. Thrust her spear into him again and again, and watched him bleed to death.

43

PARVATI BECOMES GAURI

Parvati was the child of the Himalayas. Of the mountain monarch, Himavanta, whose skin was white as ice. But Parvati's complexion was not like the snow that crowned those peaks; it was like the soil that cradled them. Not like the dawn that would light up Kailash but the dusk that made it look ethereal. And yet, Shiva was laughing.

'Kali.'

'Kali?' She glared. 'Did you call me Kali?'

The Destroyer was still laughing but Parvati had taken it to heart. Not because she felt any less when she peered into her reflection in the water. Not because she feared that her Mahadeva's love for her was waning. But only because she embodied Prakriti. Mother Nature, who prided herself in every form. Who loved being the most spectacular part of Brahmanda and loathed any description that misjudged her resplendence.

'So, you think you can call me names because you are Karpuragauram? White as camphor?'

Shiva was silent. She stood up.

'I shall be back. I shall make sure that you never ridicule me again.'

Before her husband could respond, Parvati had left Kailash. Reaching the plains, she began to invoke Brahma. The word 'Kali' was sticking to her heart like a thorn and she was seeking the Creator to prise it out. Soon, Brahma materialised before her.

'Why such austerities? You don't need them to summon me.'

'I know that but I am the seeker here. I would rather earn my reward than seize it off your tongue. Then you won't mock me.'

'Has someone been mocking you?'

'Mahadeva. He called me Kali. I want you to make me Gauri.'

The Creator laughed. 'You are nature herself. Venerable in every aspect. Every hue. They are all you and you are all them.'

'I wonder if Mahadeva agrees. Will you do it or not?'

Brahma sprinkled water on her, and lo and behold, her body began to shed cells as if it was thawing. Her skin was sloughing off. The dark colour was draining away. Those cells were accumulating in a heap, leaving behind the whitest of complexions. Parvati had become Gauri. She was staring at her limbs when she gasped. The miracle had not yet ended. Those dark cells were throbbing. Coalescing to acquire a new form of their own. Telling Parvati that they did not need her body. That they were coming together to create a new one. A new devi.

Black skin. Dark hair. Red eyes.

A while later, Parvati was walking up to Shiva. Her body was now whiter than the icy forehead of Kailash. She was watching how he was gazing at her. She knew he was going to ask how she had so utterly transformed.

'Where's Kaushiki?' the Destroyer enquired.

'Kaushiki?' She frowned. 'How do you know about Kaushiki?'

'Isn't that what Brahmadeva has named her? The dark one who has risen from your skin?'

'Yes. Since she emerged from my cells, or kosha, he has named her Kaushiki.'

'Quite apt. But for me, she will always be Kali.'

Parvati trembled. She was hearing that name again and again now. Was her brain repeating it or was Kailash echoing it?

Kali ... Kali ... Kali ...

Pounding the insides of her whitewashed body.

Kali ... Kali ... Kali ...

Shiva's words were chiming in, too.

She will always be Kali ...

She ...

The goddess recoiled.

She ...

'Not me. You were not calling me Kali.' Parvati's voice buckled under the weight of her epiphany. 'You were calling her Kali. That dark form which was a part of me. You wanted me to generate her.'

'Yes. The other facet of you. The fierce facet of you. The grey ash that I smear on myself blends the hues of both Gauri and Kali. It's time she manifested. There's work to be done.'

'Work?'

'There are demons only she can slay.'

'She's ferocious.'

Shiva embraced Parvati. 'Kali denotes the supreme unmanifest. The darkest recesses of the womb from which leaps forth the light of life. The black in which merge all the colours of the universe. She denotes the unencumbered. The unconscious. The untamed. The Kundalini that lies coiled within all of us. She is Mahakali. The feminine aspect of Mahakaal. Of time transcendental. Just as you domesticate, she will destroy. Consume all that is chaotic. Dare everyone to confront what they are concealing. You calm me, Parvati, and I will have to calm Kali.'

She looked as the Destroyer nodded. 'A lot.'

44

SHUMBHA, NISHUMBHA AND RAKTABIJA

Hardly had the universe hailed the advent of Kali when a new terror loomed large.

A twin terror.

Demon brothers Shumbha and Nishumbha were tearing Brahmanda apart limb by limb. Subjugating every realm. Another pair of asuras called Chand and Mund had become their generals. Those two would leave at dawn every day and return by dusk with blood congealed on their swords. Entrails hanging from their jaws. Narrating exploits involving death and dread that would make Shumbha and Nishumbha laugh.

But not today.

Today, Chand and Mund were only talking about her. Her eyes black as venom. Her lips red as embers. Hair like a moonless night and limbs like sinuous snakes.

'Durga,' they chorused.

'The one who slew Mahishasura?' Shumbha and Nishumbha asked. 'Is she that intoxicating?'

'That and more. You both, who now possess all that is precious in this universe, must possess her too. We hear that she was sculpted from the aura of all the gods. A union of their vital forces. Make her your own and you shall humble the devas like never before.'

The brothers immediately despatched a messenger named Sugriva who read out their proposal before Durga.

'Do you accept, O Divine One?'

The goddess smiled. 'I am flattered. But there's the matter of my vow.'

'Vow?'

'Yes. I have sworn that I shall only accept him who can overthrow me in battle.'

'Battle?' Sugriva gasped. 'Are you demanding combat?'

'I am.'

'Speak with caution, Divine One. They will come. And they will not spare you because you are a woman.'

'But Shumbha denotes one who doubts himself,' Durga simpered. 'And Nishumbha denotes one who doubts others. With so much doubt filled inside them, will they truly fight?'

'My lords have conquered the whole of Brahmanda. Shamed those very gods who have created you. You may have killed Mahishasura, but you will not last before these two brothers.'

'That settles the matter then. If they defeat me, I shall garland them on the battlefield itself.'

Hearing her words from Sugriva's mouth, Shumbha glanced at Nishumba.

'A spirited woman. I am aroused.'

'What should we do, brother?'

'What should be done with a female like her. Shame her. Bend her spine with our fingertip. She wants war. Send Dhumralochana. Let's see if she can tackle him first.'

As soon as dawn broke, the daitya, Dhumralochana, invaded with a force of sixty thousand. Seeing his army advance, Durga let out a roar. Such was the fire in that cry that it instantly reduced Dhumralochana to ashes. The goddess's lion leapt and devoured every demon.

'Intriguing,' Shumbha hissed as Dhumralochana's remains reached him. 'Looks like the woman is in heat. This is wilder than I had imagined.'

'What now?' Nishumba yelled.

'Chand and Mund. They will drag her here like a slave.'

The next day, both commanders began battling valiantly. They were invoking every ounce of their skill. Every trick in their arsenal. And yet, a voice was scratching their insides today that this foe was unconquerable. That their end had arrived. The voice was getting louder and louder as the day wore on. As their army breathed its last. As Kali sprung from Durga now and decapitated both of them. As the heads of Chand and Mund rolled, Brahmanda screamed out a new name for the goddess.

Chamunda ... Chamunda ... Chamunda ...

The voice was resounding through the cosmos. Grating the ears of Shumbha and Nishumbha.

'Enough!' the brothers thundered. 'She wants to fight us. She will.'

The next day, Shumbha and Nishumbha marched towards the mountains where Durga had stationed herself. The battle raged as few battles had raged before. The brothers were displaying how they had crushed every loka. The goddess was revealing why she was Mahishasuramardini. By dusk, Durga was triumphing. Using Vishnu's chakra, she splintered the shield of Nishumbha. Before he could react, she dug Shiva's trident into his heart.

Shivering with fury, Shumbha mocked, 'Do you have anything of your own? Your weapons are borrowed. Your might is borrowed. Your body is borrowed. Everything you possess has been tailored by the devas. Why should I fight you?'

The goddess laughed. Brahmanda laughed.

'How ignorant you are, Shumbha! I am Brahma. I am Vishnu. I am Mahadeva.'

The demon stared as Durga's form magnified to embody every deity of the universe. Not only Brahma, Vishnu and Mahesh but also Brahmani, Vaishnavi and Maheshwari. She was Parabrahman. She was Parashakti. The omni-form stretching from one end of the universe to the other. Shumbha turned to flee but the goddess pounced. Forcing him to the ground, she cleaved his body into two. As he lay dying, Durga rammed her foot in his face.

'Looks like there won't be a wedding after all.'

But the asura was sniggering. Pointing at someone. As his life floated out, his words reached the goddess.

'What about him? The more you kill him, the more alive he is.'

She turned to look. The last demon was standing before her. Sole survivor of the carnage. Durga lunged and chopped a portion of his arm. But what occult was this? As soon as his blood fell on the ground, it gave rise to another one like him. The goddess gashed him once more and it happened once again. Again and again and again. Every time a drop of his blood touched the earth, it was seeding a replica. Germinating more and more of him.

'Who are you?' Durga glared.

'Raktabija. My own blood breeds me.'

She could hear Shumbha's voice deriding her again.

The more you kill him, the more alive he is ...

The battlefield was teeming now with hundreds of Raktabijas. Durga kept combating them all but she knew this would never end. The asura's blood was his elixir and was reproducing countless clones. The goddess closed her eyes. There was only one way out. Only one being who could counteract him. Her forehead quivered and out came the devi again. Durga could hear the clanking of skulls. See the swish of that blade. Feel the fire of her rage.

Kali had reappeared.

Whirling furiously, she began slashing every Raktabija. Their blood was descending drop by drop. Inching to touch the earth and spawn more replicas, when suddenly something fanned out. Something had appeared between the blood and the ground. Something red. Soft and fleshy. Uncoiling like the hood of a massive serpent. Kali had unfurled her tongue and was scooping up all that blood before it could hit the earth. Her sword sliced again. As the Raktabijas bled once more, her tongue swooped again, lapping it up. She was devouring every drop now. Encompassing the whole ground. Turning their blood barren. It went on and on and the replicas began to dwindle. The more Kali was drinking, the fewer Raktabijas were

standing. The battlefield was becoming emptier. Her tongue was turning redder. Thick with clotted blood as only one stood before her now. The last Raktabija. The true Raktabija. Kali's sword swung. Her tongue flicked again and she gulped one last time.

Shiva was watching. Shiva was smiling.

Then he frowned. The butchering of Raktabija had infected Kali with bloodlust and she was now killing more and more beings. Slurping more and more blood. Her tongue was lolling as if she wanted to suck the universe dry. Bring about a mahapralaya.

Shiva manifested. He was watching her lost in her own violent frenzy. He had once pacified Narasimha and it was time now to pacify Kali. The god sprawled himself in the path of the goddess. Smacking her lips and jangling her garland of skulls, Kali had turned blind to everything.

The next moment she froze, biting her tongue. She had stepped on her husband.

45

NACHIKETA TRAVELS TO HELL

Swaha was yearning to embrace Agni again.

Not only because she adored her husband but also because of Brahma's decree. The fire god burnt the offerings made by humans in yagnas but Swaha was the cosmic conduit who transported them to the devas. The Sacred Feminine who alone could ensure that the gods stayed nourished and men earned merit. The loving wife who would become one with Agni whenever the word 'Swaha' was chanted in a yagna. She was waiting now for King Vajashrava to do the same. His altar was ablaze. The offerings had arrived. Vajashrava began to make oblations.

'Om Swaha! I offer to Vishnu.'

'Om Swaha! I offer to Shiva.'

'And me, father? Whom will you offer me to?'

The king turned to find his adolescent son eyeing him curiously.

'Do not intrude, Nachiketa,' Vajashrava caressed his face. 'It will mar the rituals and anger the gods.'

He picked up another set of offerings.

'Om Swaha! I offer to Indra.'

'Om Swaha! I offer to Vayu.'

'Om Swaha! I offer to Varuna.'

'But me, father? Won't you offer me to anyone?' Nachiketa persisted.

'I told you to stay away.' The king struck his arm. 'Do not disturb me until I complete the yagna.'

He began pouring the oblations again.

'Om Swaha! I offer to Surya.'

'Om Swaha! I offer to Chandra.'

'Me too, father.' Nachiketa planted himself on Vajashrava's lap now. 'Offer me to someone too.'

'I will.' The king seized him furiously by the hair. 'I offer you to Yama. Go to hell.'

The boy stood up.

'If that's your will, I shall obey.'

Vajashrava watched as Nachiketa prepared a bundle. Bid everyone farewell and began to walk away. He rushed and grasped his son.

'Where are you going?'

'To Naraka as you have ordained.'

'I spoke in anger, my cherub. Forgive me. I have conquered many emotions but not rage. My words mean nothing.'

'They mean everything to a son for they have been uttered by a father. They became a command the moment they were spoken. If I don't follow them, I shall be sinning and end up in Naraka. Isn't it better that I go to hell to carry out your will instead of being cast there for disobeying you?'

Vajashrava stood transfixed. Nachiketa touched his feet.

'Bless me, father. Bless me so that I can make you proud.'

'But no one can enter Naraka alive,' the king shrieked.

'Maybe I will,' the boy smiled.

Vajashrava pleaded again and again but, like Dhruva, Nachiketa was unshakeable. Soon, he was descending through the seven regions of the netherworld. The bowels of Brahmanda infested by demons. Crossing Atala, Vitala, Sutala, Talatala, Mahatala, Rasatala and Patala, he finally stood before Naraka.

The domain of Yama.

He was watching the chaos. Hearing the cacophony. Of the multitude of sinners who were being dragged down through those infernal gates. Some were clinging to walls, too terrified to enter. Some were clawing their way out, their nails cracking and bleeding. They were howling. They were biting. They were scratching. They were writhing. But Naraka was sucking them all into its maws. All but Nachiketa. Every time he was trying to pass through, the gates were turning impervious to his live body. He was attempting to flout a cardinal law and Naraka was refusing to be his accomplice. Determined to fulfil his father's command, the boy now decided to wait for Yama. For three days he kept watching the excreta of Brahmanda being dumped into Naraka. On the fourth day, he turned as a voice addressed him.

'Who are you?'

Complexion like storm clouds. A garland of fire. Draped in red and yellow. Carrying a mace and a noose. Nachiketa knew that he was in the presence of Death incarnate.

'I bow before you, Yamaraja.' He folded his hands.

As he narrated the events that had brought him here, Yama stood fascinated. He had never encountered such filial love. Such a sense of duty. Such a singular paradox that so noble a soul was eager to walk into hell. The boy was waiting for his reply now. There was no terror on his face. Just truth in his eyes. Yama gestured.

'Come.'

'Are you letting me inside?'

'I am.'

'But what about the rule that no living being can set foot in Naraka?'

The god smiled. 'I think the universe wants me to bend its rules for you like it did for Markandeya.'

The gates opened and Nachiketa entered. All the horrors that he had heard about hell were playing out before his eyes. Sinners were being flung into boiling oil. Dismembered with jagged saws. Some were being impaled. Others were being torched. Some were being poisoned. Others were being hung. Everyone was melding into a soup of bodies for Naraka to consume. Flesh was bleeding. Flesh was burning. The dead were begging to die.

'You have done your father's bidding,' Yama lauded him. 'I am pleased with you and grant you three boons.'

'Three boons?' Nachiketa exclaimed.

'For the three days that you waited for me. For the three days that you did not abandon your quest. What do you wish for?'

'As my first boon, grant me the welfare of my father.'

'Granted.'

'As my second boon, show me the path towards attaining heaven. I ask this not only for myself but for everyone on Earth. I shall guide them once I return so that they can escape these agonies of hell.'

'Granted.' The god of death smiled. 'Now the last one.'

'As my last boon, answer a simple question. What comes after death?'

Yama froze. A moment later, he found his voice.

'Do not ask me that, boy. It remains a mystery even to the gods. Ask for anything else. The throne of Indra. The riches of Patala. The nymphs of Swarga. Imagine any pleasure you can think of and multiply that a thousand times. You can have it all.'

But Nachiketa was adamant. 'All these are material things that come to an end. I am keen to know what lies beyond the end. Do we fall off the edge or do we begin all over again?'

'Those are secrets that cannot be divulged.'

'But you said Brahmanda wanted you to bend its rules for me?'

Yama sighed. Seeing that Nachiketa had chosen the eternal over the ephemeral, he finally enlightened him with the knowledge of atman. That it was unborn and undying. That it was like a warrior while the body was its chariot, the senses its horses and the mind its reins. That a soul galloping after desires was forever enmeshed in a loop of birth and death. But a soul that broke free realised the Supreme Self. Attained moksha.

When Nachiketa returned to his father's palace, crowds thronged to hail the only person alive who had been to Naraka and back. The first true seeker on Earth.

'Tell us about a torture you saw being meted out there,' one of them requested.

'I saw some sinners being made to embrace fiery female statues. Their flesh was melting bit by bit.'

The gathering shuddered. 'What sin had they committed?'

'They had dishonoured women.'

46

GANESHA AND KARTIKEYA RACE

Shiva and Parvati were arguing aloud.

'But Kartikeya is the elder one.'

'But Ganesha is the mature one.'

The knot was all tangled up. Refusing to untie itself.

'What about birth?'

'What about worth?'

The couple was wondering now if they had begun to take sides.

'Kartikeya will not like it.'

'And Ganesha will hardly fight it.'

They fell silent. The Destroyer nodded.

'There's only one way out.'

'What way is that?'

'What Brahmadeva and Sri Hari had done.'

He sent for both the sons. As they stood with folded hands, Shiva spoke.

'We have been thinking about your marriages. Your mother made a householder out of me and it's time for you both to take that path.'

Ganesha lowered his eyes, while Kartikeya smiled.

'But we are unable to decide who should marry first. Being the elder one, you are entitled by birth, Kartikeya, but Ganesha is the cardinal deity.'

The younger one continued to gaze at the ground, while the elder one turned somewhat sullen now.

'There's only one way to resolve this. You both must race.'

'Race, father?'

'Yes. Tomorrow, in the presence of all the gods, you shall participate in a race. The winner shall wed first.'

Ganesha took a step back.

'Why make a spectacle out of this, father? Brother Kartikeya is your firstborn. He deserves to marry before me. We don't need a race.'

Kartikeya laughed. 'We don't need your charity either, Ganesha. Birth is an accident but worth is an achievement. I would rather marry because I have proven to be better and not because I happen to be older. Father's proposal is quite fair. I do not object and neither should you. Unless you are afraid.'

'Afraid?'

'Perhaps you fear that my peacock will outrun your rat.'

'I fear nothing,' the elephant god replied. 'My only concern was that a contest often stirs up the darkest of emotions. Fractures relationships. One sometimes loses oneself in order to win. But if you feel you are above all that, we can certainly race.'

He pointed at his mount.

'And that's a mouse. Not a rat.'

The next day seemed to dawn faster, as if the sun was burning with excitement. So were the other gods who were assembling at Kailash. They had heard how humans on Earth made roosters fight and horses race. Long ago, they had watched Brahma and Vishnu sprinting against each other to locate the ends of a fiery pillar. Today, they were about to savour that once again. That bliss of standing on the fringes and watching others perform. That wild rush of adrenaline without having to exert themselves an inch. Parvati announced the rules now.

'Both contestants must make three rounds of the Earth. Three complete circles. They shall use their mounts and not hinder each other's passage. The one who finishes first shall be declared the winner.'

The gathering cheered as the race commenced. Cheered louder as Kartikeya's peacock took majestically to the skies. Soared above the planet and began charting its course. The bird's plumes of blue, green and gold were twinkling like stars. Its call was vibrating throughout that void. The young god seemed to have merged with his mount now, as if a glorious hybrid was encircling Bhuloka. Leaving behind a trail as if he was erecting a pathway to victory for generations to admire.

'Ganesha!' Vishnu exclaimed. 'Look at Ganesha!'

The elephant god had still not left Kailash. And it seemed as if he had no intention of doing so. The devas stared in confusion.

Has he not comprehended the rules?

Has he accepted defeat watching Kartikeya take off?

What is our cardinal deity up to?

Seated on his mount, he was circumambulating Shiva and Parvati. Not even looking at the sky where his brother had vanished. His mouse was taking one sluggish step after another as the god's weight bore down upon it. Moments after he completed his third revolution around the couple, they heard a rustle of feathers. Kartikeya had returned. Confident that he was the undisputed victor.

'Ganesha wins,' Shiva proclaimed. 'He shall marry first.'

A hush fell over Kailash. The gods were glancing at each other. Parvati was standing, perplexed. Only Vishnu and Brahma were nodding and smiling. Kartikeya leapt off his bird.

'Ganesha? I covered the entire circuit thrice. He did not even take part in the race.'

'He did and finished before you.'

'What do you mean, father?'

'He encircled me and Parvati. For a child, his parents are his world. His father denotes the sky and his mother denotes the earth. Together, they constitute his universe. You took the physical path. He chose the mystical one. Your dimension was material. His was spiritual. You both invoked the same truth but you were all body, which always takes longer. He was all mind, which is invariably shorter.'

'True,' Vishnu agreed. 'One does not need to wander through Brahmanda to gain wisdom. One can do so rooted to a single spot.'

As enlightenment flooded the assembly, they began chanting Ganesha's name. Hoisted him on their shoulders. Showered him with flowers. Parvati's heart was bursting with joy but she was gazing at her elder one. Watching the discontent that was swirling through his face. She gathered him in her arms but Kartikeya wrenched himself free.

'This is foul,' he shrieked at his father. 'You are unfair.'

'I am not. You both are equally dear to me. You come from me and signify my destructive aspect. Your brother comes from Parvati and symbolises her creative aspect. You are the two halves that complete us.'

'You lie. Perhaps you still carry the guilt that you had beheaded Ganesha and this is how you are seeking absolution.'

'You are wrong.'

'Am I? Ganesha has cheated to win the race like Father Brahma had cheated that day. How can you curse one but celebrate the other?'

Shiva did not reply but the Creator spoke.

'I had acted deceitfully, son. Ganesha has done no such thing. He has merely followed what the Vedas prescribe. By condemning his action, you are condemning the scriptures. Challenging the sacred wisdom of Brahmanda. Don't grudge your little brother his victory. Rejoice that he has proved that he truly deserves to be the cardinal deity.'

Ganesha soon married Riddhi and Siddhi but Kartikeya was nowhere to be seen. He migrated to the south and vowed never to return to Kailash.

47

SURYA FALLS FROM THE SKY

The asura king Sukeshi was deeply devoted to Shiva. Despite his demonic birth, he had a tender heart that drove him, now and then, to try and foster peace with the devas. Delighted with the monarch, Shiva had blessed him with a city in the sky. A paradise beyond belief. Such was the charm of this airborne citadel that clouds floating by would pause to gaze in wonder. Birds would circle it joyously all day and gods would envy it in their dreams all night.

Once, Sukeshi ventured into the Magadh forest in Bhuloka and found himself in the company of sages. He realised that he was standing in the presence of profound knowledge. A stream of wisdom was inviting him to cup his hands and drink deep. Ask those questions to which he craved answers. The king bowed.

'What path leads to salvation, O Learned Ones?'

'Dharma.'

'How does one practice dharma?'

'By knowing your Self and surrendering to the Almighty.'

'And what are the properties of dharma?'

'It has ten properties. Truth. Non-violence. Charity. Forgiveness. Restraint. Compassion. Cleanliness. Austerities. Love. And not stealing from others. These ten organs animate dharma. Hence, it's called Dashanga.'

Thus illuminated, Sukeshi returned and shared this wisdom with his subjects. The asuras not only embraced it but also began practising it. The tenets had opened their eyes to new possibilities. Beautiful possibilities. Inspired by their king, they started mending their ways.

The gods were stunned!

The last time this had happened was when the Tripura had come into existence. The sons of Taraka had tried to carve a moral path, but Sukeshi's demons were venturing further. They had begun revering dharma as their highest principle. The Vedas as their deities. Such was the glow of virtue in that aerial city now that it began to dazzle like a nova. Illuminate Brahmanda. Its light was even obscuring the sun. Reducing him to a star.

Surya turned livid.

The only quality that made him divine was his brilliance. Anything blazing brighter was intolerable to him. And a colony of demons outshining him was no less than sacrilege. Blind to the fact that the city was radiating goodness, all he could think about was how it was surpassing him. All he feared, like his brother Indra, was how he might lose all esteem. Surya glared at the citadel and, lo and behold, it began to fall down. Plunge towards the Earth as if suddenly overwhelmed by gravity. Finding themselves in danger, Sukeshi instantly invoked Shiva. When the Destroyer realised what was going on, he glanced furiously at the sun. Now Surya, too, began to fall from the sky.

Catastrophe!

With Surya collapsing, there would be no agency to provide heat and light. No energy to nourish life. The Saptarishi advised the deva to land in Kashi. While he bathed in the Varuna and Asi rivers, the sages appealed to Shiva.

'You had once restored Chandra. Pray, reinstate Surya.'

The sun had been humbled by now. Reminded how trivial he was compared to the Parabrahman. How misplaced his desire was to be superlative. Shiva relented.

The elements cheered as both Surya and Sukeshi's city glinted in the sky once more.

48

BHASMASURA CHASES SHIVA

Like so many demons in Brahmanda, Vrikasura was a devotee of Shiva. When Narada learnt about this, the trouble-maker hastened to test his faith.

'No one can call himself Mahadeva's devotee until he performs austerities for him,' the Devarshi claimed. 'You shall be truly blessed only when you receive a boon from the lord.'

Eager to demonstrate his worth, Vrikasura reached Kailash and began invoking Shiva. When the god did not manifest even after hundreds of years, he turned to rituals highly demonic. For six days he kept hacking parts of his body and offering them as oblations. The more his flesh was decreasing, the more his fervour was increasing. With still no sign of the Destroyer, he now dangled the sword above his neck. As the blade was about to swing, Shiva clasped his arm, healing his body.

'What do you seek, Vrikasura, that you are paying the price with your blood?'

'A gift, lord. A gift no other being has. A gift that shall exalt me to the highest rank of your believers.'

'Ask.'

'Make my flesh magical. Grant me the boon that any living creature on whose head I place my hands would be instantly reduced to ashes.'

'But that's so violent. How can such a boon elevate you as a great devotee of mine?'

'The fact that you have granted me such a terrible boon shall prove that you truly adore me.'

'Fine. I bless you, Vrikasura. Since you can now reduce anyone to bhasma, I rename you as Bhasmasura.'

No sooner had the god spoken than anklets began to tinkle nearby. Parvati was walking down the slope. Searching for Shiva. One glimpse of the goddess and Bhasmasura stood enraptured. He had never laid eyes on anyone so ravishing. The demon appeared to have fallen into a trance. Appeared to have forgotten that he was gazing at Adishakti herself. His every sense now was thirsting for the nectar of her body but his mind was whispering that she was married. That he could not have her until her husband was dead.

Until Mahadeva was dead ...

Bhasmasura smirked. He was going to claim his first victim. Use the god's boon against the god himself. Destroy the Destroyer.

As he inched closer, Shiva took a step back. He realised what was going on. The asura was no longer in awe of him but his wife. No longer folding his hands but wanting to place them on his head. Shiva spun and fled. His knew that his boon was all-pervasive and would not spare even him. That even the Parabrahman would have to play by its own rules or the universe would lose all meaning. The only way to survive now was to distance himself from Bhasmasura. The god kept running. Traversing all ten directions. But whenever he would look back, the demon was right behind. His flesh, burning with lust, was craving to burn Shiva. The Destroyer was getting tired. His legs were refusing to carry him anymore. With the last shred of strength now, he dashed towards the only place that could save him.

Vaikuntha.

Storming inside, he found Vishnu smiling.

'I know everything, Mahadeva. Why did you have to turn him into Bhasmasura? Why must you grant every wish of your devotees? Even gods cannot afford to have such generous souls. You are truly Bholenath.'

'And you are Sri Hari. Protect this Hara.'

Vishnu vanished. In his place now stood a woman. That same woman. That same maya that had enticed the demons when they had seized amrita. That female avatar that had filled Shiva with desire. As soon as she appeared before Bhasmasura, he forgot everything. Parvati. Mahadeva. His boon. Himself.

'Who are you?'

'Mohini.'

The asura spoke no more. As his eyes drank in that illusion, she grasped his hand.

'Come. Dance with me.'

He followed. He no longer had any will of his own. He was no longer Bhasmasura but a puppet, yoked to her exquisite fingers. Tethered to her choreography to be animated solely by her command. He was swaying when she was swaying and pausing when she was pausing. He did not know his body anymore. Did not know his limbs for they had all turned into extensions of her mind. He had relinquished every control and become her mirror image. Replicating her every stance. Every move. Twirling on his feet the way she did. Jutting out his hips the way she did. Leaning his torso the way she did. Placing his hand on his head the way she did.

Mohini laughed as she whirled now around that pile of ash.

49

CHANDRA COMMITS ADULTERY

The nakshatras were twinkling half-heartedly again. Someone had snatched their light once more. Someone they had begun to loathe. Someone their husband had begun to love.

'Tara,' Pushya scowled.

'Brihaspati's wife,' sobbed Swati.

Megha's eyes blazed. 'This is sacrilege! Brihaspati is the guru of the gods. How can Chandradeva fall for his guru's wife?'

'He's besotted.' Vishakha gnashed her teeth. 'Besotted since the day he saw her at our yagna.'

Rohini turned red. 'Ketu eclipses only him but this Tara has eclipsed all twenty-seven of us.'

They looked at her. 'Now you know how it feels, Rohini. Not long ago, Chandradeva had eyes only for you. You would soak in his love all day while the rest of us would lie parched. Now he has found someone else. Just as he waxes and wanes, so does his heart.'

'He will not wait for long,' Poorva warned. 'He will want her body and Tara will not stop him.'

Their fears swiftly came true. Brahmanda was soon quivering with the news that Chandra and Tara had eloped. Someone's husband had fled with someone's wife. Never had such an anomaly dared to occur before. Many began spouting the vows of matrimony, while others began questioning if they had any value. A livid Brihaspati demanded his wife back, but the moon god flatly refused. He even mocked that the guru was unworthy of possessing such a beauty and should find someone more befitting his appearance.

'Tara finds nothing illicit about our bond,' Chandra told Brihaspati's messenger. 'The guru strives more to be a hermit than a husband. He needs her more for his rituals than for himself. Sangya left Surya because his presence was too hot, but Tara has abandoned her husband because he's too cold. Because her bed was too cold. But I have warmed it now. If she goes back, both of them will suffer.'

The guru kept sending envoys for days and they kept returning empty-handed. Only one option now remained. A war for Tara.

They named it the Tarakamaya War.

Gods and demons began choosing sides. While the devas rallied behind Brihaspati, the asuras pledged allegiance to Chandra. The gathering of these forces became a sight to behold. One half of the universe was endorsing law, while the other was rooting for love. As the war raged, Shiva hurled his Pashupatastra at the moon, who retaliated with his Somastra. The weapons were about to collide when Brahma intervened.

'How dare you, Chandra?' the Creator thundered. 'You are but a drop of water and Mahadeva is the ocean himself. The one who had rekindled you when all your light was gone. Has your lust for Tara turned you into a daitya? Don't you recognise this very forehead that provides you refuge?'

The moon god fell to his knees. The war was over.

'Return Brihaspati's wife and Mahadeva will forgive you,' Brahma declared.

Chandra nodded. The ranks parted as Tara now entered the battlefield. Her anklets were spearing that silence. Her feet were turning red. Sinking into the blood of those who had died for her.

'Will you accept her, Brihaspati?'

'I will, Param Pita,' the guru replied. 'A bad fruit need not always be thrown away. She may not be pure anymore, but she's pious. Her presence is vital for my rites and I accept her back.'

'Will you accept this too?'

It was Tara. She was raising the cloth over her belly to reveal the swelling. Caressing it as if she was caressing a flower.

'You say I am yours. Will this be yours too?'

The gods and demons stared. Chandra's face had darkened. Brihaspati's gaze seemed nailed to that pregnant belly.

'Whose child are you carrying?'

'My child.'

'But have I fathered it or the moon?'

'I refuse to answer.'

The guru pressed her again, but she did not speak. The gods commanded her, but she remained silent. The demons threatened her, but she stood her ground. Suddenly, a voice wafted from inside of her.

'Whose child am I, mother?'

Tara clutched her womb.

'Whose child am I?'

Her fingers were failing to smother that voice.

'You may deny your husband, mother. Your lover. You may deny the devas and the asuras. But will you deny me? Your unborn?'

She trembled.

'Will you, mother?'

'I cannot. You are my moonbeam.'

'Moonbeam, mother?'

'Yes.' She glanced at the father now. 'A ray of Chandra's light.'

The battlefield fell silent again. They were looking at this woman surrounded by men. This mother towering before them.

Tara asked Brihaspati once more, 'Do you accept me with it?'

'Never. It shall never be mine.'

'It will have to be,' Indra asserted. 'It may not be your seed but it now grows inside your wife. That makes you the father. You must raise it as your own.'

'Is that the law?'

'That is the law.'

'I curse it then.' Brihaspati struck his sword with fury. 'I curse this child in the presence of everyone here that it shall be a neuter. Neither male nor female. Just like his father remains neither half nor full in the sky. Just like his mother now is neither Chandra's nor mine.'

Tara smiled. The child soon took birth and was named Budh. Realising the nature of the guru's curse, Budh asked Tara what path was to be taken.

'You simply be.' She smiled again. 'Life will come your way.'

50

THE VAMANA AVATAR

Aditi was lying on the ground.

The mother of Indra was shedding tears for him. For all her adityas. That salt water seemed unending, as if an ocean was surging behind her eyes. The demons had once again usurped heaven with the help of Shukracharya. Their chief, Bali, had become king, while Indra had been overthrown. He was now wandering through the cosmos along with his brothers. Eating what they could find and resting where they could lie. Hence, Aditi had also begun shunning food and sleeping on the ground. Kashyapa had been observing her for days. He had barely said a word but today he broke his silence.

'I can't see you mourning like this. What does your heart long for?'

'A mother's heart is tied to her children. You know what our sons are going through. How can I smile when my adityas no longer laugh?'

'Then start praying to Vishnu. Give up all food and consume only milk for the month of Phalguna. Summon all your senses and meditate upon his name alone. If you can keep the austerities going, you may be able to bring comfort to our sons.'

The Devamata began carrying out the rituals unwaveringly. Diti had once performed austerities to ravage Indra. Aditi was doing so to restore him. Soon, her eyes opened to behold that celestial shade of blue.

'I also want what you do,' the Preserver said. 'But Bali is no tyrant. He reveres me. He convinced the asuras to help us churn the ocean only because I had sent him word. Like Prahlad, he's another beautiful example that even the demonic can be divine. And he's generous, too. Nobody returns from his presence empty-handed. If he had been born with a layer of gold on his body, he would have ripped it off for charity. Bali has endeared himself to me.'

'But he has captured Indraloka. Replaced benign forces of the universe with demonic ones. He may be a saint but his asuras are not. They are tearing down all that is virtuous and he's not stopping them. How can someone so wise be so blind?'

'He's Diti's descendant. He's your blood, too.'

'Indeed. My blood, too. That only makes it easier. No one can say that I am favouring my sons because Bali is also my own. This is not about pedigree but principle. Not about race but righteousness.'

Vishnu nodded. 'I shall tackle him.'

'Not you,' Aditi folded her hands. 'I want one of my sons to have that honour. Pray, grant me this boon.'

'But your adityas are too weak right now, Devamata. Neither Indra nor the rest can stand against Bali.'

Her face fell. The Preserver was watching her silently. He took the bowl of milk she was holding.

'Since I must grant you what you wish for, here's what we shall do. My next avatar shall now take birth from your womb.'

Aditi gasped.

'Thus, when I defeat Bali, it shall be your son who would have done it.'

Not a word fell from her mouth. Her womb was suddenly filling with inexplicable weight. Pulling her down to the ground. Her eyes closed with ecstasy. Vishnu had vanished but she knew he was there. Growing inside her. Filling her with the light of a thousand blue jewels. Borrowing her body to create his own. Her flesh and blood were now preserving him who preserved them all. When he finally took birth in the month of Bhadrapada, trees began to shed flowers. Yellow flowers. Brahma gave him a copper pot, while Shiva gave him a rudraksha garland. Brihaspati gifted him a sacred thread, while Kashyapa gave him a waist chain. Surya handed him a parasol, Chandra a wooden staff and the Saptarishi a ring of grass. The boy was exactly fifty-two fingers high and never grew any taller.

He was Vamana. The Dwarf. Vishnu's first avatar now in Treta Yuga.

Soon, Bali organised the grandest Ashwamedha Yagna ever. A pillar of fire was rising from his altar. Gandharvas were strumming and apsaras were dancing. The entire legion of daityas and danavas was attending. Their horse had returned unchallenged after cantering through the universe. Its head held high was to be severed now. Just as Shukracharya raised his sword, he paused. He was listening.

Footsteps.

They turned to look.

The Vamana.

Parasol in one hand and staff in the other. Sandalwood paste on his forehead and white thread around his torso. That tiny frame was appearing even tinier before the demons.

As he strode closer, Shukracharya whispered to Bali, 'Something seems amiss.'

'Why?'

'What's a Brahmin doing here? We never invited any.'

'Is he one of the four Kumaras of Brahmadeva?'

'No. This is someone else. Beware. He has a strange aura.'

'He surely does.'

'The gods may have sent him to deceive us.'

'What should I do?'

'Nothing. Promise him nothing. Decline whatever he asks for.'

Bali smiled. 'You are asking me to go against myself. How can I do that, Asuracharya?'

The dwarf was standing before him now. As Bali folded his hands, he blessed him.

'May you live long, O King. Not many rulers in Brahmanda have had the might to conduct an Ashwamedha Yagna. You are truly exceptional.'

'I am nothing, Venerated One. You are being too generous.'

'Not as much as you are. I hear that while your grandfather, Prahlad, embodied devotion, you are the very spirit of charity. You refuse nothing to anyone.'

'Who am I to refuse when the universe is willing?'

'Then will you grant me whatever I ask?'

A drop of sweat oozed from Shukracharya's forehead. Slid slowly down his face. The assembly seemed to have stopped breathing. Bali trembled.

'Tell me, Venerated One. What do you want?'

The gathering had turned motionless. Waiting for the Vamana's lips to move.

'Land.'

'Land?'

'Yes. All I want is some land.'

'How much?'

'As much as my three steps can measure.'

The assembly exhaled. Some were laughing, while others were pondering. Shukracharya was gazing at the dwarf's feet. Small feet like two lotus buds.

'Three steps?' Bali asked.

'Yes, O King.'

'Are you sure?'

'Absolutely.'

'But that's hardly anything to ask.'

'If one is not content with three paces of land then one shall never be content with anything,' the Vamana smiled. 'Just as the size of my body satisfies me, so will the land I am asking for.'

'But I can surely give you more than—'

Shukracharya cut in. 'If that's all he wants, why must we argue? Three steps it is, Holy One. Our sovereign grants it.'

'Does he?' The dwarf looked at Bali.

'I do. Where would you like to place your feet?'

He froze. They all froze. The Vamana was growing. His limbs were stretching. His torso was enlarging. His face was soaring behind the clouds and beyond. Proportions so cosmic that his body seemed to be expanding into a Brahmanda by itself. So gigantic that only the tip of his right toe was visible before them now. That foot was rising. Looming like a firmament of blue skin. The demons were quailing. Bali was gaping. And two words were paralysing Shukracharya.

Three steps ...

The dwarf had dwarfed the universe. Become Trivikrama. His voice came from the ether above.

'I place my first step here, O King.'

And he measured the entire Earth.

'I place my second step here, O King.'

And he covered all of heaven. Brahma bowed before his foot and washed it with water from his vessel.

'Where do I place my third step, O King?'

Bali was smiling. His eyes were brimming.

'My third step, O King?'

'You are not Vamana.'

'I am.'

'You are Lord Vishnu. The infinite one who's showing me how finite I am.'

'Where do I place my third step?'

'Brahmanda is your playground, lord. You have gathered the entire cosmos in the dust of your feet with just two steps and there's nothing left now. Only one place that I can humbly offer.'

The demon king bowed.

'Kindly place your third step on my head. Let me be consecrated by becoming the soil for Mahavishnu's foot.'

'He's tricking you, Bali,' Shukracharya screamed. 'Tricking you as Vamana just as he had tricked us as Mohini. Open your eyes.'

'I have opened my heart. Surrendered to him as how my forefather, Prahlad, had.'

The dwarf's foot descended. Light around Bali faded as that sole came

nearer. The blue sole was closing in as if the sky was falling. The asuras fled. They were certain that the Vamana was going to crush Bali. Certain that when that foot would rise again, they would find their king's bones sticking to it. But Bali was alive. The foot was not trampling him but pushing him down. Further and further down. All the way down the spine of the universe to deposit him in Sutala.

'You are truly beyond compare,' the Vamana marvelled. 'The three realms will forever remember that just as the demon Bala gave all of himself, the demon Bali gave me his all. I crown you monarch of this netherworld. Reside here and rule it well.'

Soon, Aditi was cooking a feast. Her sons had returned to heaven and Indra was Devaraja again. Brahma informed the gods now that he had turned the water in his vessel into a being.

'What is this water?' they asked.

'The Charanamrita of the Vamana. The water with which I rinsed Sri Hari's foot. That stream has become a beautiful woman.'

'What's her name, Param Pita?'

'Sanctified by the foot of Vishnu, she's Vishnupadi. But I like to call her Ganga.'

51

GANGA, LAKSHMI AND SARASWATI FIGHT

Ganga had enchanted the whole universe. She was white like a cascade of milk. As if a million moons had melted and dissolved into her water. Bubbling with more nectar than what had surfaced from Ksheersagar. Not offering immortality but salvation. Not eternal life but eternal liberation. But while Brahmanda had fallen in love with her, she herself had lost her heart to someone.

Vishnu.

But Ganga had a rival. The goddess of knowledge and music. She, too, draped herself in the whitest of robes. Surrounded herself with white swans and white lotuses. And she, too, had become enamoured of Vishnu.

Saraswati.

Once, Ganga was strolling through Vaikuntha when she found the Preserver all by himself. Her emotions began to ripple. Swell and spill over. Drenched with passion, she approached him and began to speak in amorous tones. Her eyelashes were fluttering. Her bosom was heaving. Her fingers were touching the skin of Vishnu. Her body was aching to merge with this blue ocean when Saraswati arrived. Watching Ganga, she instantly fathomed what was going on.

'You wretch!' Saraswati pulled her back. 'How dare you stand so close to Sri Hari? I have been noticing how you lust after him. Have you forgotten yourself? Forgotten that you came into being by the touch of his feet?'

'And you?' Ganga retorted. 'You are the deity of speech but look how vile your own tongue is.'

Vishnu tried to calm the two but in vain. Ganga's fury was at high tide, while Saraswati was shrieking like a broken veena. The Preserver had never seen goddesses brawling like this. Never known divinity to be this dissonant. Ganga to be so uncontrollable and Saraswati, so unwise. He immediately walked out of Vaikuntha but that only flared their tempers as both began blaming each other for his exit. Saraswati lunged now and yanked Ganga's hair. Horrified at this spectacle, Lakshmi intervened. She tried separating the two but Saraswati thought that she was favouring Ganga. Insane with rage, she laid a curse upon Lakshmi. Hearing this, Ganga also heaped a curse on Saraswati, who cursed her right back.

Soon, Vishnu returned to hear how ugly that squabble had turned. He called the three of them.

'What did you curse Lakshmi with, Saraswati?'

'That she would have to live on Earth in the form of a plant.'

The Preserver looked at his consort.

'It shall happen. A part of you will soon grow on Earth as the sacred tulsi plant. But grieve not for I, too, shall appear as a stone called shaligram and we shall be together.'

He turned towards Saraswati again.

'What curse did you lay upon Ganga?'

'I cursed her that she shall flow on Earth and carry the bones of the dead.'

'That, too, will come to pass.' Vishnu gazed at Ganga. 'You shall soon drink the sins of mankind and they shall venerate you. Call you mother. But you also burst with fury today, Ganga, and cursed Saraswati. What did you utter?'

'My curse is that she, too, shall become a river in Bhuloka.'

'She shall. Because Saraswati physically abused you, she will turn into a river before you do. She will become the consort of Brahmadeva now, but a part of her shall flow on Earth as a stream that will vanish one day.'

52

VRINDA CURSES VISHNU

Parvati was watching Shiva age.

Silver hair was hanging from his head like stalactites in the caves of Kailash. His face was hiding behind wrinkles. His frame was losing sinew. Even the moon and the serpent were no longer visible.

'Why, lord? Why are you altering your appearance?'

'For Indra.'

'Indra?'

'He has been yearning to see me. He is reaching here today in the company of Brihaspati. I shall be waiting.'

'What will you do?'

'What I do with all my devotees. Test his faith. Wring his heart to see how much devotion drips from it. See if he can recognise me despite my transformation.'

As soon as Shiva seated himself at the base of the mountain, he saw them approach. The king of the gods and the guru of the gods. Indra's gaze was scanning the peaks of Kailash. Barely noticing what was present right before him. He tripped over Shiva.

'Forgive me, O Sage,' Indra cried out. 'I did not see you. Are you hurt?'

Shiva closed his eyes.

'I asked if I hurt you.'

Eyes still closed.

'Are you deaf? Can you not hear me?'

Still closed.

'No one treats me with such contempt,' the Devaraja fumed.

Stepping back, he hurled his Vajra. The thunderbolt came scorching through the air but suddenly froze. Paused in terror just an inch from the meditating figure. Then it bent into a curve as if bowing before him and vanished. Shiva's eyes were opening. His forehead was throbbing. His fingers were crushing a flower he was holding.

Then his third eye opened.

'Mahadeva!' Brihaspati squealed. 'It's Mahadeva.'

A beacon of fire was swelling inside the third eye. Becoming a conflagration. Detaching itself now to vaporise Indra.

'Mercy!'

The heat was scalding their bodies. As it erupted, the guru stood in its path.

'Mercy, Mahadeva.'

'Move,' Shiva thundered. 'The flames are for the one hiding behind you. The one whose faith is a lie. Whose presence taints my Kailash.'

'Your fury is valid, Mahadeva, but torching Indra will only put heaven in peril again. Bring the demons back. You swallowed halahal for the sake of creation. Don't render that act futile. Don't endanger everything that you saved that day.'

The inferno was still raging. Shiva's voice pierced through it.

'What about this blaze then that has risen from me? If not Indra, it will cremate the whole of Brahmanda.'

'I will take care of it. You drank the poison that oozed from Ksheersagar. Now those waters will drink this fire exuded by you.'

Brihaspati instantly redirected that flaming orb towards the Ocean of Milk. As soon as it penetrated that surface, the impact spawned a child. A male child who began wailing louder than the waves. The sound reached Brahma, who commanded Ksheersagar to nurture the infant.

'What shall I name him, Param Pita?' the ocean asked.

'Since your waters have cradled him, let him be called Jalandhar.'

The child soon came of age and married a beautiful woman named Vrinda. With his mind and might making him lord of the demons, Shukracharya now began inciting Jalandhar against the gods.

'Your wife's father was the daitya, Kalanemi. He was brutally killed by Vishnu.'

'But Vrinda is devoted to Narayana. She keeps telling me that even though her body belongs to me, her soul belongs to him.'

'I know. I have seen her fasting for him. Wearing yellow robes and chanting his name. There's something about Vishnu that even those who should loathe him end up falling in love. He prevented us from consuming amrita. Polluted our minds in the form of Mohini. Turned Swarbhanu into Rahu and Ketu. The devas even seized the best of the ratnas that emerged from the churning.'

'Did they really?'

'If you think I lie, ask Ksheersagar. Your parent stands witness to the elaborate ploy that was carried out on its shore that day. It shall tell you how the devas used us and then refused us.'

The ocean confirmed everything and then asked a question. 'What are you thinking of doing, Jalandhar?'

'I shall command the gods to return everything.'

'Don't do that. You are my son. When something is flung into my waters, I always send it back. I keep nothing for myself and you should do the same.'

But Jalandhar paid no heed. He despatched a messenger to heaven demanding the ratnas back. Claiming that they rightfully belonged to him since he was the son of Ksheersagar. Indra kicked the envoy out and war erupted. The devas battled valiantly but the asuras routed them all.

'I know why we lost,' Vayu sputtered. 'Because Sri Hari was nowhere to be seen.'

'True. Where is he? Why didn't he fight?' Yama queried.

The gods reached Vaikuntha but Lakshmi stopped them at the gates.

'He stayed away because I told him to.'

'You?' they exclaimed.

'Of course. Jalandhar is like my brother.'

'Brother?'

'He hails from Ksheersagar, like me. The same ocean flows in his veins as in mine. Sri Hari will not raise a hand against Jalandhar. It's enough that he slew Vrinda's father in the past.'

The gods gaped at each other in disbelief. The goddess they had pulled out of the waters to defend them was shielding their foe. Without the Preserver, they were doomed. Who would deliver them now?

'Mahadeva,' Narada asserted. 'The chakra refuses, but the trishul shall save us. And I know how.'

'How?' they asked.

'Exactly how Andhaka was foiled.'

The Devarshi reached Jalandhar's presence and began eulogising him.

'I bow before you, O Son of the Sea. It's uncanny how you rose from that bed of milk but bathed Swargaloka in blood.'

'Not as much as your devas have spilled,' the demon king retorted.

'You possess everything today but I am saddened for you. Everything and yet nothing.'

'Nothing?'

'Haven't you seen how all the rivers empty themselves into Ksheersagar? Just as an ocean needs those streams, a man needs a woman.'

'I know. I have my Vrinda.'

Narada smiled a beguiling smile. 'A monarch like you is worthy of the prettiest one.'

'Whom are you talking about?'

'Parvati.'

The Devarshi began extolling her charms. Describing the goddess in such deliberate detail that it seemed as if she was materialising before Jalandhar. As if every winsome part of her was manifesting itself. Her lips. Her eyes. Her navel. Her bosom. Andhaka, who had emerged from Parvati's water, had been bewitched by her. Now, Jalandhar, who had risen from Shiva's fire, was also burning with lust. Staring at that luscious body that his mind had sculpted. Clawing to grasp it and make it his own.

'I want her.'

'No. Never.'

Vrinda had entered the court and overheard every word of Narada's.

'Devi Parvati is married to Mahadeva himself. Even a single impure thought about her shall make you a sinner.'

'I thought you were a Vishnu devotee,' Jalandhar sneered. 'Why such concern for Shiva's consort?'

'My concern is for you alone, my love.'

But the demon king's hands were still groping the air before him. Still trying to fondle that fantasy. The next day, his forces invaded Kailash. His troops, clothed in blue, were surging up that mountain as if the ocean had flouted natural law to flow upwards. As they laid siege, Jalandhar searched for Parvati. On being informed that she was inside a grotto, the demon king smiled. He had thought of a ruse. An illusion so profane that no one had dared to employ it before.

Jalandhar turned himself into Shiva!

Entering the cave, he began advancing towards Parvati. His eyes were unblinking. His face was unyielding. And she was watching how this course of events that had begun with the disguise of Mahadeva had now arrived at this disguise of Jalandhar.

'I may not have a third eye,' she snarled. 'But I can see.'

'Then look.' He laughed. 'I am the child of the ocean. Water can take any shape it's poured into. If this form of Shiva pleases you then I can become this body for the rest of my life.'

'Can you become that heart?' Parvati asked and vanished.

As Jalandhar began hunting for her again, the Destroyer now confronted Vishnu.

'How can you sit here in Vaikuntha when the gods need you?'

'I am helpless, Mahadeva. My Lakshmi binds me. I cannot lay a hand on Jalandhar.'

'But you know that you have to lay hands on his wife.'

The Preserver closed his eyes.

'You know what you are destined to do, Sri Hari. You know that you are only delaying the inevitable. You know that it's Vrinda's purity that makes

Jalandhar indomitable. You know that Jalandhar derives his power not from his own body but from his wife's, which is chaste.'

As Vishnu stepped back, Shiva held him.

'You know that you have to dishonour her so we can decimate him.'

A tear was flowing down the Preserver's face. The Destroyer wiped it gently.

'You have always known that, Sri Hari. Known that, like me, you too would have to drink this poison for the sake of dharma.'

Vishnu nodded. 'I do. But Vrinda reveres me. Prays to me every day to safeguard her purity. What cosmic irony is this that I am ordained to defile her?'

'I, too, was destined to behead Ganesha. To repel Kartikeya. But our intentions will forever remain greater than our actions. Vrinda's chastity is protecting a canker that must be removed. We are gods. We are not blessed with the luxury of choice like humans. We must do what must be done. Jalandhar has turned himself into me to get Parvati. Now you must turn yourself into Jalandhar to have Vrinda.'

'I decapitated Bhrigu's wife.' Vishnu spoke as if in a trance. 'Now I must desecrate Jalandhar's wife.'

'Yes. And be cursed once again. Are we truly the masters of Brahmanda, Sri Hari, or its slaves?'

Vrinda woke up in alarm. A terrible nightmare had assailed her sleep. She had seen black snakes swarming over her body. A black lotus sprouting from her navel. Jalandhar had appeared standing before her, wreathed in black flowers. Looking at her as a black disc sliced her flesh. As her blood stained their bed. Rubbing her eyes now, Vrinda heard her husband's voice.

'Beloved!'

She got up. 'You are back, my love?'

'Yes.'

'And the war? Devi Parvati?'

'I retreated.'

'Retreated? But you have never done that before.'

'Sometimes one must do what one has never done, Vrinda. Parvati is alluring but the more I gazed at her, the more I remembered your face.

Your eyes. Your lips. I was wrong. She's nothing before you. She does not have your body or your soul.'

'I know nothing about souls.' She clasped him. 'Just the body I can see. To touch and be touched.'

She saw him open his arms wide.

'Come, Vrinda. Let's become one as all beings must eventually be. Let you and me not matter anymore because all is one and one is all.'

She was smelling that odour of the ocean on him. The scent of his skin that she loved so much. As they embraced, Jalandhar collapsed at Kailash. His strength was draining. A wound seemed to have suddenly sprung inside him and all his might was ebbing through it. The more Vrinda's pleasure was heightening, the more Jalandhar's pain was devouring him. As he turned brittle and crumbled, he let out a terrifying scream.

'Vrinda!'

That which had been encasing him had been breached. Shiva swung his trident now and pierced his heart. Jalandhar's essence was merging once more with the Destroyer. Returning to that third eye from where it had stemmed.

Suddenly, a heat wave was billowing through Kailash. Searing the ice. Melting the mountain. A temperature so savage that even the gods were beginning to blister.

'What's happening?' they yelled.

'She has found out,' Shiva replied. 'My third eye had opened for Indra that day but the one who burns is Vrinda.'

She was glaring at Vishnu. The flames she had invoked were consuming her now as she roared. 'You were my god, Narayana. You gave me this body and I would have given it back to you. But you deceived me. You ask your devotees to have faith in you but you had no faith in me. You separated me from the one I love and I curse you now. Curse you that during your avatar as Rama, your beloved, too, will be taken away from you. Just as you changed your form to lure someone's wife, your wife, too, shall be lured in the same way. You shall pine like how I pine. And you shall turn into stone like how your heart is.'

53

VISHNU IS BEHEADED

Vishnu was exhausted.

He had been battling a demon for sixteen thousand years and still not conquered him. His own celestial weapons seemed to be betraying him. He had blown on his Panchajanya conch but its sound had failed to set the asura on fire. He had hurled his Kaumodaki mace but it had been sucked into the demon's body and pitched back at him, pulverising his chariot. He had even launched his Sudarshana, but an invisible wall around the asura had sheltered him from that disc.

'Nothing can destroy me,' the demon was cackling. 'I have been blessed by a divine one. Only he who knows my secret can slay me.'

Weary, the Preserver returned to Vaikuntha. Resting his chin on his Sharanga bow, he fell into a deep sleep. As Yoga Nidra enveloped him, the gods led by Brahma entered his abode. All their divinity had failed before the asura and they had resolved now to conduct a yagna. Vishnu's presence was imperative, but he was fast asleep. Those lotus eyes had shut like petals at dusk. The devas tried everything but could not wake him up. Years of war had drained his body and it was refusing to be roused. As their patience wore thin, Brahma offered a ruse.

'He's sleeping on his bowstring. If that snaps, its sound will resonate throughout the cosmos. That should jolt him awake.'

The gods instantly changed themselves into termites and began nibbling at the string. Eating away as furiously as they could. It was turning thinner and thinner as they gnawed faster and faster. Thinner and thinner. Faster and faster. It was fraying now. Thinner and thinner. Faster and faster. Twisting and curling. Thinner and thinner. Faster and faster. Unravelling now. Thinner and thinner. Faster and faster. Trembling to be free. Thinner and thinner. Faster and faster. Still cradling the Preserver's face. Thinner and thinner. Faster and faster. Thinner and thinner. Faster and faster.

Twang!

As if a comet had crashed. Or a planet had exploded. Detaching from the bow, the string had snapped wildly. Lashing out, it severed Vishnu's head.

Silence.

His torso was oozing blood.

Silence.

His bowstring was turning red.

Silence.

His head was rolling away.

Silence.

His eyes were still closed.

Silence.

He whose chakra beheaded all was lying headless before them.

Brahmanda was standing catatonic. The devas were staring at the body of the Preserver. Sweat was gushing from their pores. Tears from their eyes. A single thought was shredding their souls.

What have we done?

A shadow fell before them now. Lakshmi was approaching. Stepping on Vishnu's blood and leaving red footprints. She stood gaping at her husband. Then she walked towards Brahma. Towards all the gods. As she raised her hands, they began to quake. But she folded them together.

'Forgive me.'

'Forgive you?' The Creator cowered. 'It's us. We have done the unthinkable.'

'Only because I made it possible.'

'You?'

She grasped Vishnu's limp hand. 'This asura is invincible because of a boon.'

'Yes. A divine boon which ...'

Brahma paused.

Divine boon ...

The words were suddenly echoing louder than the bowstring had.

'It was you, Devi?'

'Yes.' Lakshmi's grip tightened. 'I. Parashakti. The gods often lament about how you give away boons to asuras. How Mahadeva does the same. Not this time. This one is my doing. I was touched by how this demon was doing so much to propitiate me. How he was wondering every day if he had appeased me enough or if he should appease me some more.'

She let go of her husband's hand. She was gazing at something else. Something far away in another dimension of Brahmanda.

'That moment,' she whispered as if speaking only to herself. 'That moment when we grant a boon. There is something beatific about it. About that yes or no that can forever alter a life. That sows a new seed to bring forth a cycle of cause and effect. That's what I did that day and that's what is keeping this asura alive.'

'The secret?' Brahma asked. 'What's the secret of his death?'

'I had blessed him that he can only be killed by a god who bears the head of a horse.'

The gods gasped.

Head of a horse ...

Their eyes slanted slowly towards the decapitated Vishnu.

'That's why! That's why!'

Lakshmi nodded. 'Our universe is never random. It always looks after itself.'

'What now?'

'Get the head of a horse. Sri Hari shall be Hayagriva again. The Horse-Headed One who slew Madhu and Kaitabha at the very beginning of creation. That avatar will deliver us once more, following which Sri Hari shall regain his form.'

Not long after, Hayagriva was neighing aloud as the demon fell silent.

54

BHRIGU TESTS THE TRINITY

Once, all the sages of Brahmanda congregated to ponder upon seminal questions. The Saptarishi presided as the gathering began by compiling a list of superlatives. Which was the greatest Veda? Who was the noblest king? What was the worthiest virtue and which was the foulest sin? As they debated fiercely, a voice cut through.

'And god?'

It was Sage Bhrigu.

'Who's the greatest god? Brahma, Vishnu or Shiva?'

The cacophony died.

Greatest god?

Was that even a valid query? Could gods be measured against each other? Had Bhrigu just blasphemed?

'A statue cannot rate its sculptor,' the Saptarishi chorused. 'Gods are beyond assessment.'

'Are they?' Bhrigu asked. 'The Trimurti also function within this Prakriti. Since all the realms revere them, should we not declare who is the most venerable?'

'But how does one decide between Brahma, Vishnu and Shiva? The Creator, Preserver and Destroyer? Three aspects of the same Parabrahman?'

'Why not? All humans are birthed from the same divine seed and yet they are constantly graded. The four Vedas emerged from Brahmadeva but we are trying to rate them. If the Parabrahman chose to manifest in three distinct forms, surely those can also be ranked.'

The gathering clamoured some more and then the hoary sages spoke again.

'Since Maharishi Bhrigu has raised this query, he must seek its answer. Test the triumvirate and tell us who is the greatest.'

The sage set out. He first visited Brahmaloka and deliberately paid no obeisance to Brahma. Neither folded his hands nor dedicated a hymn. The Creator flared up and threatened to curse him. Bhrigu laughed.

'Mahadeva was right to condemn you. You shall never be worshipped the way other gods are.'

Bhrigu arrived at Kailash next but was denied entry. Shiva's ganas kept blocking his way. Making strange excuses and asking him to leave. Watching his anger mount, Nandi came forward now and whispered the actual reason. Their lord was making love to Parvati. The sage uttered a curse as he departed.

'Your Mahadeva shall now be worshipped more as a lingam than in his actual form.'

Traversing the cosmos, Bhrigu finally stood before Vishnu. The one who had beheaded his wife. Alas, the Preserver was lost in Yoga Nidra. The sage tried to awaken him but he would not stir. Bhrigu charged and kicked the god in the chest.

'How can you sleep when the universe lies awake in pain?'

Lakshmi glared. Sheshnaga hissed. But Vishnu got up and began pressing Bhrigu's foot tenderly.

'My apologies. Did my chest hurt you?'

'What?'

'I asked if my chest hurt your foot.'

'No, Narayana.'

'You have anointed me with your touch, Revered Sage,' the Preserver said. 'And you utter a cardinal truth. He, whose task is to preserve, cannot sleep too much. I thank you for opening my eyes. Your footprint now shall remain forever enshrined on my chest as a hallowed mark called Srivatsa.'

Bhrigu stood in silence. Tears were flowing down his face. His mind hummed and the assembly of sages seated on Earth heard every word he uttered.

'Not me, Narayana. You have opened my eyes. All our eyes. I, who had cursed you once, bless you now that you are truly the greatest.'

The Preserver shook his head.

'I am not. I, Brahmadeva and Mahadeva are forever equal. Three facets of this universe. It's the devotee who embraces one facet and proclaims that to be supreme. Alas, this often divides. Leads to more harm than good.'

'But the sage appears blind to that,' Lakshmi scowled. 'He once harboured daityas and is out now to grade devas.'

Bhrigu gasped. The goddess's eyes were flashing with rage.

'How dare you kick Sri Hari? And how dare you rank Brahma, Vishnu and Shiva? You have transgressed and your entire varna shall pay for it now. Henceforth, I will never visit the houses of Brahmins and they shall always remain poor.'

55

SUDYUMNA BECOMES A WOMAN

King Sudyumna had been ruling well, following the precepts of his father, Vaivasvata Manu. Once, he was out for a ride on his horse alone when he came across a forest below Mount Meru. One that he had never seen before. Everything here seemed soaked in a strange afterglow. The deeper he entered, the more wondrous it became. The sky looked red and the rivers hummed like maidens. The trees bore no fruits and the flowers held no pollen. Does sprinted past and sows slumbered on. Peahens danced and tigresses roared.

He slowed down.

His body was stirring. Throbbing as if it was filling with stardust. A strange alchemy had begun coursing through his veins. Moulding his flesh. Dissolving in his blood. Was that why something was suddenly flapping across his face? The more he was pushing it away, the more it was stinging his eyes. Sudyumna paused. It was now hanging in clumps from his head. He touched it gingerly. Fearfully. Then furiously. His fingers were clutching it. Clawing at it. Tearing tufts of it to gaze in disbelief.

Hair. Long hair was cascading all the way down to his waist.

Sudyumna yanked his reins so hard that he fell headlong to the ground. As he got up, his hands brushed against his bosom, sending a chill through his core.

Breasts ...

I have breasts ...

His body was sweating. His throat had gone dry. His fists were clenching. Refusing to touch any more of himself. Then his hands rose and began ripping off his garments. One by one. Layer upon layer. He was gazing at a brook ahead. That film of water seemed to be beckoning him as if it knew what was happening. As if it wanted him to see for himself. His legs were quailing but they finally inched forward. Step by step, they took him to the edge of that mirror.

Woman ...

The king was staring at his reflection.

I am turning into a woman ...

'Indeed, Sudyumna. So you are.'

The voice had come from behind him. He turned and collapsed.

'Mahadeva!'

That moon. That snake. That trident. That ash.

'What enchantment is this, lord?'

'It's this forest.'

'Forest?'

'Parvati and I often come here to make love and once a few sages stumbled upon us. To ensure that no male gaze falls upon her again when she's unclothed, I cast a spell. Any male who steps into this pleasure grove of ours shall turn female. He could be human or animal. Deva or danava. You, too, are becoming a woman now, Sudyumna. Feminine like everything else in this forest.'

The king gaped at his stallion, which had turned into a mare. The occult of this place was flooding him with dread. He grasped Shiva's feet.

'But I am a monarch. My subjects need me. I was ignorant to enter these woods. Pray, release me.'

'That won't be possible. My spell spares no one, but I shall amend it for you. You will not be a woman permanently but every other month.'

'Every other month?'

'Yes. For one month you shall be male and the next month, you shall be female. Thus, you will now be androgynous. Alternating between both genders. A singular icon of Ardhanarishwara.'

'But I am the grandchild of Surya,' Sudyumna protested. 'We value stability just as the sun is a constant in the sky.'

'Not anymore. Henceforth, you shall exist in a fluid state. As a woman, you will forget your life as a man, and when you turn into a man, you will be oblivious of your existence as a woman. In each phase, you shall forget your other self. As a man, you shall remain Sudyumna. As a woman, you shall now be Ila.'

'Ila?'

'Ila.'

'But what about ...'

His voice choked. Not only because Shiva had vanished but also because so had his baritone. The last shred of his manhood.

No longer Sudyumna ...

udyumna ...

dyumna ...

yumna ...

mna ...

na ...

a ...

la ...

Ila ...

She was walking out of the forest now. Wondering who she was. Why she was alone. Where she had come from and where she was going. Wondering why all the creatures around her seemed to be whispering about her. Twilight had now descended when she saw a being. A lustrous being.

'Who are you?' the being asked.

'Ila.'

'What are you doing here?'

'I am not sure. I don't remember much. Was I someone else before? Am I someone else now?'

'You mean you could be liminal? Both this and that?' the being laughed. 'I know that state.'

'Really? How?'

'My father also fluctuates. He waxes and wanes.'

'Chandra?'

'The eternal shape-shifter. You say you could be both this and that, while I am neither male nor female. Perhaps we can fulfil each other.'

'What's your name?'

'Budh.'

She stretched out her hand. 'Will you stay by my side?'

The being held her close. 'Always.'

Brahmanda watched as the moon and the sun became one.

56

URVASHI TRICKS PURURAVA

Budh and Ila gave birth to Pururava with whom now dawned the Chandravanshi dynasty. Such was his majesty that he soon completed multiple Ashwamedha Yagnas. Alas, too much splendour attracts trouble and three forces now decided to test the king. They were neither gods nor demons but the highest abstractions. Three goals of human life.

Artha. Kama. Dharma. Prosperity. Sensuality. Morality.

Curious to find out which of them Pururava revered the most, they assumed the form of human sages and arrived at his court. The king served them a royal repast and gifted them several offerings. But the subconscious mind often senses what the conscious mind cannot. And so it came to pass that, while Pururava's bounty appeared equally divided among the three, he had somehow been a little more generous towards Dharma. The goal that he valued the most. With morality thus ending up with more offerings, the other two instantly cursed the king.

'You shall lose your wealth,' Artha screamed.

'And you will become besotted with a nymph,' Kama roared.

The king fell at their feet but Dharma held his hand. 'You shall never stray from the path of righteousness.'

Days later, Pururava was journeying through a forest when piercing shrieks made him halt. The asura, Keshi, was abducting an apsara. The king trounced him and rescued the frightened being.

'What's your name?'

'Urvashi. I am a water nymph.'

Pururava froze. Kama's curse was chiming in his ears now. Standing before him in the most captivating form. His mind was urging him to look away. Throwing a lasso and pulling him back, but the king knew how fragile that knot was. His heart was already getting enmeshed in that auburn hair. Already pounding at the sight of that face. Voices inside him were screaming that he was falling under the spell of his own doom, but all Pururava wanted now was to hold this curse and make love to it.

News soon reached Indra that the king had saved one of his prized apsaras and he invited Pururava to celebrate. Celestial music played as the nymphs began to dance. Rambha, Menaka and Urvashi were pirouetting to lyrical strains. Their feet were making exquisite moves. Their fingers were sculpting visions in the air. Their bodies were swaying in perfect tandem as if they were not three but one. The act was nearing a crescendo when Urvashi suddenly fell out of step. She had been gazing at Pururava and had missed her beat. Indra's voice rumbled.

'I banish you from my loka. You shall live on Earth now for a period of one hundred years.'

Although distraught at being exiled, Urvashi embraced Pururava when he proposed marriage. But the water nymph knew that she could not remain tied to a human. That while she had descended on Earth for now, she would have to return to the skies once Indraloka reopened its doors to her. To ensure that the king would be unable to stop her, she laid down three conditions.

'I shall tether two sheep to my bed and you must ensure that they are never stolen. I must never see you naked except when we are making love, and I must always be served butter in my food. The day these conditions are breached, I shall go back to heaven.'

The couple began a blissful life but soon the gandharvas started pining for Urvashi. As soon as a hundred years elapsed, they began conspiring to get her back. Learning about her three conditions, the minstrels, led by

Vishvavasu, sneaked into her palace one night and stole the sheep from under her bed. Urvashi smiled. The moment she had been waiting for had arrived. It was time to loosen her bond with Earth. Time to carry out this charade.

'My sheep! My sheep!'

Her screams awoke Pururava. The king sprung at the thieves at once but alas, he did not have a single garment on his body. The crafty gandharvas instantly flashed a bolt of lightning, making the apsara see her husband in all his naked glory. And as they fled, they smashed every pot of butter in the palace.

The next day, Urvashi was back in Indraloka. But she descended again when Pururava began longing for children and bore him several sons.

57

SATYAVATI IS DECEIVED

The words of the sage had still not sunk in.

I wish to marry your daughter ...

King Gadhi was wondering what to reply. His daughter, Satyavati, possessed beauty that could make rulers forsake their crowns, warriors their swords and poets their quills to attain her love. But this poor sage had wandered in and was asking for her hand. Gadhi was itching to throw him out. Not only because he was a Chandravanshi monarch but also because Satyavati's hand was for a ruler who would become his powerful ally. Not for a hermit like this one standing before him.

'We are Kshatriyas,' the king finally replied. 'And you are a Brahmin.'

'Yes. I am Richika. Son of Sage Chyavana and a descendant of Maharishi Bhrigu. I have always loved Satyavati and wish to make her my wife now. Do we have your blessings?'

Gadhi smiled. He had found a way to decline without angering the holy man.

'I would be honoured, O Sage. But I have taken a vow that I shall wed my daughter only to him who can gift me a thousand horses.'

'I can do that.'

'A thousand horses?'

'Indeed.'

'Swift ones.'

'Absolutely.

'With white skin.'

'If that pleases you.'

'But black ears.'

'As you wish.'

The king smiled again. He was confident that no such breed existed in Brahmanda. But Richika was throbbing with love and began austerities to please Varuna. So pure was his plea that even the water god melted. He provided the horses and Satyavati now became the sage's wife. The princess not only embraced life with her husband but also found bliss in their frugal abode. Days after their nuptials, Richika began preparing for a yagna. A secret yagna.

'What's it for?' Satyavati was curious.

'For a son. An incomparable son. At the end of this ritual, I shall offer you a bowl of rice. Consume it and the seed shall be sown.'

The princess was jubilant. That a yagna could be so miraculous thrilled her to no end. Suddenly, another thought nibbled at her heart.

'Could you make a second bowl for my mother?'

'Your mother?'

'Yes. I am their only child and I know how lonely they are now. A son will not only keep their clan alive but also become a successor to the kingdom.'

The sage was fascinated. With a single request, Satyavati had fulfilled twin roles as a daughter and a princess. Secured not only her parents but also her people. But Gadhi's words clanged in his ears now and he expressed a doubt.

'Will your queen accept the offerings of a sadhu? Will your Kshatriya father acknowledge the prowess of your Brahmin husband?'

Satyavati assured him that they would, and Richika soon placed two bowls of rice before her at the end of the yagna.

'This earthen one is yours,' he instructed. 'The metal bowl is for the queen. I am leaving to visit a nearby village and shall be back by dusk.'

Satyavati immediately sent for her mother and revealed the magic that was lurking in those grains. So eager was she to share the concoction that she failed to notice the glint in the queen's eyes.

'I think the right thing to do would be to exchange our bowls, my child.'

'Exchange? Why, mother?'

'You say Richika conducted this yagna to procure a son. Naturally, your rice must be far superior to mine. You shall birth an extraordinary son but he will only go on to become a Brahmin like his father. His remarkable qualities shall be of no use to anyone as he will end up a sage. My son shall grow up to be king. Shouldn't he be the superlative one?'

'But a Brahmin also needs to possess exceptional traits.'

'A Brahmin only caters to his own family, while the fate of an entire realm rests on a king's shoulders. Which responsibility is the greater one?'

The queen thus kept reasoning and overwhelming her daughter. By the time Richika returned, the bowls had changed hands and their contents consumed. The sage bristled with rage.

'What have you done, Satyavati?'

'But my mother made sense. A ruler needs to be remarkable.'

'That's exactly how I had prepared the rice. Your mother's portion was in a metal bowl since it contained the ingredient for a Kshatriya. Infused with Rajas Guna to give birth to a valiant king. Yours was earthen for it was filled with Sattva Guna to produce a Brahmin. An enlightened soul. But you swapped the bowls and now the reverse shall happen.'

Satyavati was shattered. Pleading forgiveness, she begged her husband for a remedy, but Richika shook his head.

'Your mother's child shall rule but will eventually become a sage. That cannot be altered. In our case, I can only delay the inevitable by one generation. Our son shall be the Brahmin I desire, but his son will become a fierce warrior.'

He glanced up. 'A Brahmin in a king's house and a Kshatriya in a sage's house. What are the gods planning?'

In due course of time, the queen gave birth to Kaushika, while Satyavati brought forth Jamadagni. The universe was now waiting. Waiting to see who that warrior would be.

58

VISHWAMITRA ATTACKS VASHISHTHA

Kaushika soon proved to be an able king. His foes feared him and his people revered him. But his parents were still living in a state of dread. Richika's prophecy for him still lay buried in their hearts like a dagger.

He will rule but will eventually become a sage …

Immensely fond of hunting, Kaushika would often troop through forests with his men. One evening, the tired retinue arrived at the hermitage of Sage Vashishtha. Looking at the meagre surroundings, the king was astounded when Vashishtha treated them to a lavish spread. Such drinks that he had never tasted before and such food that had never come out of his royal kitchen. Towards the end, the sage even gifted them robes and riches. Kaushika could no longer contain his curiosity.

'I have never seen such bounty, Holy One. What treasure do you have here that shames even the wealthiest of rulers?'

Vashishtha smiled and pointed. 'There stands my treasure.'

Kaushika turned. He was looking at white hide. Pink udders. Benign eyes and shapely horns.

'A cow?'

'Not just any cow. You are standing in the presence of Kamadhenu.'

The king's eyes widened.

Kamadhenu ...
Bovine goddess ...
The cow of plenty that fulfilled every desire ...
He was gawking. Greed and envy were storming his face. Staggering towards the cow, Kaushika touched her gingerly. His heart was hammering. Sending the same message again and again.

I want her ...
He addressed Vashishtha once more but his tone had changed.

'You are a Brahmin with few needs. What use is this miraculous being to you? Hand her over to me. Let her provide for me and my people.'

The sage shook his head. 'I do not keep her for material gains but for spiritual ones. Kamadhenu serves a sacred purpose for the gods. For the souls of the dead. She is also vital to our rites and rituals.'

'How can you refuse me? I am your king.'

'Because I answer to the higher powers that made you king.'

Alas, Kaushika had turned deaf to every word. The hunter inside him had awakened and he was not leaving without this game. He offered Vashishtha coins and jewels, but the sage refused. He offered him a thousand cows but to no avail. He even added horses and elephants, but Vashishtha rejected them all. A furious Kaushika now commanded his men to seize Kamadhenu. No sooner did they advance than the cow began transforming. Her eyes became embers. Her horns turned massive and so did her hooves. Even her udders filled with milk now seemed drenched in blood. As the king stared in terror, warriors sprung from every pore of Kamadhenu and butchered his men.

Fleeing to save himself, Kaushika came across a pond in the forest and collapsed at its edge. The water was showing him the imperial sword he was carrying and whispering.

The power that knelt before the occult of Brahmanda ...
The water was showing him the pearls around his neck and whispering.
The wealth that knelt before the rags of Vashishtha ...
The water was showing him his face and whispering.
The monarch who knelt before the might of a monk ...
Kaushika flung everything away. Gashing his palm, he proclaimed

aloud, 'I, Kaushika, hereby renounce my kingship to become a sage. I am no longer a Kshatriya but a Brahmin. I shall strive now to emerge greater than Vashishtha. Greater than the man who routed me today.'

Blood began to collect in his palm as he closed his eyes to meditate. When they opened again, a thousand years had passed. That blood had turned to water. He was no longer Kaushika. Richika's words had come true.

He had become Sage Vishwamitra.

Eager to avenge himself using his newfound spiritual might, he immediately proceeded to the banks of River Saraswati where Vashishtha had set up hermitage. Glaring at the sage on the other side, Vishwamitra commanded the river, 'Bring Vashishtha to me so I can kill him. Carry him here using your powerful current.'

Saraswati refused and Vishwamitra began threatening her. Petrified of his rage, the river now sobbed before Vashishtha, revealing everything. The sage smiled.

'Looks like he'll always be more Kaushika than Vishwamitra,' he said. 'I shall ride your current. Take me to him.'

As soon as Vishwamitra saw Vashishtha approaching, he began to search for a weapon to slay him. Horror gripped Saraswati now. The ghastly realisation that she was about to become instrumental in the killing of a Brahmin was flooding her. She at once veered sharply and carried Vashishtha back to safety again. Like the cow, the river, too, had foiled Vishwamitra and he now laid a curse upon her.

'May your stream nourish only daityas and danavas.'

No sooner had he spoken than Saraswati turned red. Blood began bubbling through her waters, making her unfit for humans and animals. For rites and rituals. As the pestilence spread, men deserted her shore. Trees died on her banks and fish floated on her surface. Only demons thrived, drinking and bathing in that sludge. Thus, for a year, the river remained an outcast. A wound on Brahmanda's face that would not stop bleeding. Finally, Vashishtha journeyed to the very source of Saraswati and made her pure again. The blood flowed away and gave birth to a new stream.

Aruna. The Red One.

59

TRISHANKU FALLS FROM THE SKY

One of the wholesome fruits from the Suryavanshi family tree was called Trayaruni. As the ruler of Ayodhya, he was constantly striving towards all that was ideal so that his people would do the same. Alas, his son, Satyavrata, was a disgrace to his own name for he neither practised truth nor righteousness. Trayaruni had appointed Vashishtha as the royal priest and the sage had been watching how Satyavrata's vices were flowering. Time had come now to weed him out.

'You want me to banish the prince?' Trayaruni's voice darkened. 'My successor by law?'

'I see your pain,' Vashishtha soothed him. 'But a limb that rots must be severed. There's every indication that Satyavrata will turn out to be a reckless ruler.'

'But he's my son. The one who will save my soul from entering Naraka.'

'Better you languish in hell than letting your subjects suffer. What will you choose, O King?'

Trayaruni gave in and Satyavrata now began living with Chandalas on the margins of Ayodhya. The lowest social tier who disposed of human corpses. He would sleep next to burning pyres. Watch the dead attaining salvation. Suddenly, chaos erupted throughout the state. The king had passed away while grieving for his son and, without a monarch, the realm had turned inauspicious. Its earth had become barren and soon a drought descended. A twelve-year-long drought, as Satyavrata watched in silence. Something was sawing his insides now. Condemning him for blighting his land and his people. Filled with self-loathing, as he passed through the marketplace one day, a cry rang out.

'My son in exchange for food! Take my son but give us something to eat!'

A woman had knotted a rope around her son's neck to barter him for food. Never had the prince encountered such a sight. Could love so easily lose to hunger, he wondered. Could the stomach overpower the heart?

'How can you sell your own son?' Satyavrata wrenched the rope from her hand.

'Just as your father could disown you, O Prince,' she replied. 'We humans are often bereft of every choice. My husband is far away and I have many more sons to feed. Answer me before you judge me. Will you take care of our hunger?'

He ripped the noose with his hands. 'I will.'

Satyavrata had given his word, but where would he find food in this parched land? The earth had nothing but scabs on her back. Suddenly, he recalled that Vashishtha owned a large number of cows. Since the sage had got him banished, the prince was also certain that Vashishtha was partly responsible for Ayodhya's miseries. Raiding his barn now, Satyavrata stole a cow. Moments later, his axe was poised over the animal's neck. The metal was asking him if it should behead a creature that was venerated by Brahmanda.

The blade swung.

The prince consumed some of the meat himself and bundled up the rest for the woman's family. As he walked up to her door, they saw Vashishtha approaching.

Satyavrata laughed. 'Come closer, O Sage, see how my breath reeks of cow flesh. You are surely here to curse me.'

'I am.'

'Go ahead. I regret nothing, for only when one has nourished the body can one nurture the soul. I have merely followed natural law. Something must die for something else to live. I killed one life to save many lives, but in your eyes I have sinned.'

'You have, Satyavrata,' the sage affirmed. 'You are inverting what the scriptures say and your soul now bears the weight of three transgressions.'

'Three?'

'You stole and killed a cow. You ate her meat. And by this ungodly act, you have angered your father and your forefathers.'

The prince remained quiet. Vashishtha held out three fingers.

'Three sins, Satyavrata. Hence, from now on, you shall be called Trishanku. And you shall find no resting place in any of the three realms.'

As the sage left, Trishanku turned to see the woman shuddering at the sight of the cow flesh in his hands. Just then, her husband arrived and she recounted everything in a fearful tone. But the man gaped at the prince in awe.

'You put yourself in peril to keep my family alive. That intent alone earns you merit. Who has cursed you?'

'Sage Vashishtha.'

'Vashishtha?' The man frowned. His voice had echoed that name with ire. He touched Trishanku's head.

'I cannot dissolve his curse, but I can grant you a boon. Ask me anything. Anything.'

'I would like to ascend to heaven when I am old. And ascend in my mortal body.'

'Why so?'

'I have seen what happens to the human body after death while living with Chandalas. I find that unacceptable and would like to cross over along with my body.'

The man nodded. 'It shall be as you say.'

The prince folded his hands. 'What is your name, Holy One?'

'Vishwamitra.'

Years later, Trishanku saw his son, Harishchandra, become the king of Ayodhya and requested the sage to fulfil his boon. Vishwamitra commenced the yagna and soon Trishanku was ascending towards heaven in his physical body. Soaring higher than the sun and the moon. Piercing through every cloud. The gods instantly panicked. Never had the walls of their realm seemed so porous. Never had a human infiltrated Swargaloka in flesh and blood. Both men were breaching a cosmic rule and Indra now screamed in fury.

'What anarchy is this? Only a righteous soul can enter heaven and not the mortal body. And certainly not someone like Trishanku, who has sinned thrice. How can we bar demons from invading our loka if humans do the same? You are a sage who should be upholding the laws of Brahmanda and not flouting them.'

Vishwamitra laughed. 'And you are devas who forever keep everyone away from these higher realms.'

The Devaraja pointed. 'Look there. At the highest point of the universe twinkles Dhruva as a star. Placed by Sri Hari himself. No one can keep you away if you are worthy, but what you are doing is unworthy. You are attempting to prove that you are superior to Vashishtha. Stop right away or Trishanku shall fall from the sky just as his patriarch, Surya, had once fallen.'

But Vishwamitra carried on. Revelling in the sheer power of his yagna, he had turned oblivious to everything else. Trishanku was mounting dangerously close now. Nearing the gates of Swargaloka. The gods assembled at the threshold and began pushing him back. Human will was intruding but divine will was resisting. Trishanku was getting pushed and pulled. Rebounding like a coil of spring as he strained to cross over. Brahmanda was seeing what it had never seen. Seeing the resolve of a man threatening to gouge a hole in heaven. But the devas were prevailing now. Foiling every chant of Vishwamitra's. They heaved together for one final push and Trishanku began hurtling back towards Earth.

'Save me, O Sage!' he shrieked.

Plunging faster and faster.

'Save me!'

In the clutches of gravity again.

'Do something!'

As if his wings had melted.

'Help me!'

Suddenly, he paused mid-air. Right at the cusp of land and sky. Vishwamitra had uttered a mighty incantation that had suspended Trishanku at that critical point. The gods were still yelling that no one could play with the rules and the sage was still asserting that he was merely keeping his word. He even began conjuring a parallel Swargaloka for Trishanku when Indra stopped him and an agreement was reached.

'He can reside where he is,' the Devaraja permitted. 'But he shall dangle upside down.'

And there hung Trishanku. Stuck in limbo between heaven and Earth.

60

HARISHCHANDRA TRICKS VARUNA

A king whose name was resonating throughout Brahmanda now was Harishchandra. Son of Trishanku, he was not being extolled for his clan or his charm. Neither for his might nor his wealth. The universe had fallen in love with how he honoured his every word.

'It's the purest act of all,' Harishchandra had declared. 'One may give up one's life but never go back on one's pledge.'

However, the king was an unhappy man. He had a beautiful wife named Taramati but no son. No one to inherit his teachings or his throne. So, when Narada came visiting, Harishchandra's eyes shed copious tears.

'They say a father always finds himself renewed in his son, but my family tree no longer bears fruit. Will this solar race get forever eclipsed?'

'Looks like you need to water the tree. Pray to Varuna.'

Harishchandra's lips now began to constantly chant the Varuna mantra. Chanting while awake and even in his sleep.

Let us meditate on the reflection of water ...

O god of ocean blue ...

The tide finally turned and Varuna appeared.

'I know you ache for a son,' he said. 'And you shall have one if you accept my condition.'

'Anything. Anything you say.'

'You shall sacrifice the child in my name as soon as it's born.'

'Sacri...' Harishchandra choked. 'Sacrifice? I don't understand.'

'That's what I demand.'

'But why must you snatch what you have bestowed?'

'Do you agree or not?'

The king stood gaping at the god. Narada had claimed that Varuna's waters would fertilise his hopes but instead they were flooding them all. And yet, the prospect of being a father, even for a fleeting moment, was filling Harishchandra with bliss. Perhaps that one moment would last a lifetime, he mused, and agreed.

'I know you will keep your word,' Varuna smiled as he vanished.

In due course of time, Taramati bore a son. As the king held him in his arms, he felt as if an invisible thread was sprouting from him and attaching itself to his child. Telling Harishchandra that they were fastened forever now. That if anyone ripped this strand, he would die.

But my word ...

Harishchandra laid his son down to sleep.

But my son ...

He was rocking his cradle.

My son ...

Rocking faster now.

My son ...

'Your son,' he heard Varuna's voice behind him. 'The hour has come to sacrifice him.'

The king turned slowly. A thought was holding his hand now.

'Don't the scriptures say that a newborn is impure until he's ten days old? Do you want me to pollute the yagna by sacrificing him right away?'

The water god agreed. Ten days later, he was back again.

'I hear you have named your son Rohita. It's time now for his sacrifice.'

'But Rohita hasn't grown any teeth yet.' Harishchandra opened the infant's jaws. 'A living being can only be offered to gods if it has teeth. Grant him that period.'

Varuna vanished and returned when the prince turned six.

'But these are milk teeth,' the king argued. 'Let him cut proper teeth.'

The god was back again after a few years to find Harishchandra still procrastinating.

'You are demanding the son of a Kshatriya. Unless Rohita learns the art of warfare, he shall remain incomplete. Would such an offering please you? Let him study those skills.'

Years later, when Varuna returned once more, the prince was nowhere to be found. He had come to know of the god's intentions and fled to the forest. Roaming there for months, Rohita came across Sage Ajigarta, who was dwelling with his wife and three sons. Realising that the family was on the brink of starvation, a thought suddenly struck the prince. A sinister thought.

'I need a boy for a sacrifice,' Rohita told the family. 'Will you sell one of your sons to me?'

The prince waited, wondering if Ajigarta was going to curse him for making such a heinous offer. But the sage was quiet. He was considering his words. Conferring with his family. Rohita exhaled.

They think I am saving their lives ...

If only they knew that I am saving my own ...

He was watching what the need to survive could make humans do. How it had made him abandon his parents. How it was making this family now decide which of their three sons was dispensable.

'I shall not sell Shunahphuchha, my eldest,' Ajigarta stated.

'I shall never sell Shunahlangula, my youngest,' his wife asserted.

They fell silent. The decision had been made. Unspoken. Unmoved.

'It shall be me then. The middle one.'

'What's your name?' Rohita asked the boy.

'Shunahshepha.'

Soon, the people of Ayodhya were gathering to watch their prince return home. Ajigarta and Shunahshepha were right behind him. As Rohita advanced towards his father, Varuna barred his way.

'Enough! You belong to me.'

'I have brought a substitute, Divine One. He's agreed to take my place.'

'I will not accept that.'

'Not even if he's a Brahmin?'

Everyone froze. The water god's face was rippling.

'Brahmin?'

'Shunahshepha.' The prince pointed. 'Son of Sage Ajigarta.'

Varuna agreed. Four priests were invited and rituals for the sacrifice began. A vessel of water was placed to collect the boy's head. But when the moment arrived, the priests refused to bind Shunahshepha to the sacrificial post.

'He's a Brahmin child. Our hands will rot and fall,' they chorused.

'I'll do it.'

It was Ajigarta. The gathering gasped, but he was looking at the prince.

'I'll do it if you give me twice the amount you have promised.'

Rohita agreed and the father tied up his son. But who was going to wield the blade? Those terrified to bind him would hardly spill his blood. The sage came forward again.

'Make it thrice the amount and I shall hack my son's head.'

The prince nodded. Harishchandra trembled.

'Are you certain, O Sage?'

'I am only saving my other sons, O King. Like you are saving yours.'

As Ajigarta's fingers curled around the sword, many looked away in horror. A Brahmin was going to kill another Brahmin. A father was about to sacrifice his own son. What cause and effect had precipitated such a monstrous event? The crowd closed its eyes fearing that even watching this act would condemn them to hell. Shunahshepha was seeing the blade rise. Its shadow was grazing his face. He sent a silent prayer to Surya.

Tat savitur vrinimahe vayam devasya bhojanam ...

At once, the sword crumbled. His knots loosened. Sunlight was scorching that vessel of water as a cosmic voice roared.

'Fie, Harishchandra! Look what you have done. You refused to offer your son and now another father must slaughter his son. By refusing to honour your word, you have given rise to a void and now the universe is filling it. Sealing the crack that you have created. It's not Ajigarta who's beheading this child. Not Rohita either. It's you. Your hand will reek of his blood.'

The king fell to his knees. As he wailed hysterically, Varuna stepped forward.

'No one needs to die. I withdraw my demand. There shall be no sacrifice.'

One of the four priests now walked up to Shunahshepha and placed his hand over the boy's head.

'You are priceless. You need a father who realises your worth. I adopt you as my son.'

As they descended the steps of the altar, Harishchandra screamed, 'Forgive me, child. I failed to uphold my own principle. The sun god denounces me now for I have shamed my Suryavansh. The father in me displaced the ruler but never again.'

The priest turned.

'Never again?'

'Never. Henceforth, every resolve I make shall be dearer to me than my life. Dearer than everything else. To be fulfilled at any cost.'

'Any cost, O King?'

'Any cost.'

'We shall see,' the priest remarked. 'We shall see.'

As he walked away with Shunahshepha, the boy gazed at his new father.

'What's your name, Holy One?'

'Vishwamitra.'

61

HARISHCHANDRA IS TESTED

The universe truly enjoys measuring the spine of a man.

Why else would Harishchandra go hunting one day and hear the doleful cries of a woman? Why would he nock and begin to charge towards that sound? Why would his face turn more and more taut as that voice became more and more shrill? Little did the king know that a wicked spirit called Vighnaraja was producing those feminine noises to rankle a sage. As soon as it saw Harishchandra approaching, the spirit snickered.

I shall toy with both of them ...

Entering the king's body, Vighnaraja began hurling abuses at the meditating figure. The sage's eyes snapped open and all he saw was Harishchandra yelling at him. He had been carrying out intense austerities and those had come to nought now. Suddenly, a convulsion swept through Harishchandra. Vighnaraja had floated out of his body. As the king regained control of himself, he gazed in terror at the sadhu seated before him.

Vishwamitra ...

Harishchandra's faculties awoke with a jolt. He kept telling the sage that a spirit had usurped his body. Kept explaining that it was not him but that vile entity who had outraged his peace. Kept bowing and begging for forgiveness. But Vishwamitra was immune to his every word. The king finally folded his hands.

'I was once prepared to sacrifice another life to save my son. Perhaps that's why I stand guilty today for the actions of another. I kneel before Brahmanda. What must I do to absolve myself, O Revered One? Tell me and I shall obey.'

'Will you?' the sage mocked. 'Varunadeva is not likely to agree.'

Harishchandra fell at his feet. 'I am no longer that man. As Suryadeva is my witness, I take this pledge that I will grant you anything you ask for. You have my word. What do you want?'

'Your throne.'

'All yours.'

'Your wealth.'

'All yours.'

'Your Ayodhya.'

'All yours.'

The next morning, as Rahu eclipsed the sun, people gathered to see their monarch bidding farewell.

'I no longer rule over you. My crown now lies at the feet of Sage Vishwamitra. I, my wife, Taramati, and son, Rohita, have become commoners like all of you. Since we do not own this land anymore, the sage has asked us to leave. Pray, bless us that we may conduct the rest of our lives upholding our vow.'

Harishchandra raised his foot to take his first step but paused. A pair of folded hands had appeared beneath his sole. An old man was lying prostrate, beseeching him not to leave. As the king watched, all his subjects dropped to the ground one by one. Men, women and children were pleading with him not to abandon them. Harishchandra broke down but Vishwamitra laughed.

'Bravo! Nothing like tears to move an audience. You have no intention of leaving Ayodhya. You are staging emotions now to make your people stop you. What's the point of renouncing your kingdom when your heart is still clinging to it?'

'No, Revered One,' the king protested. 'I only ...'

'You are a hypocrite! You always were. You are inciting your subjects to revolt against me. To kill me right here so you can reclaim your throne. I curse you.'

As the sage raised his staff, the crowd whimpered in fear. Harishchandra clasped the hands of his wife and son.

'I am a Suryavanshi and I have given you my word. Ayodhya and her people belong to you now. We shall begin our lives anew somewhere else.'

They had hardly moved ten paces when Vishwamitra spoke once more.

'Hold on! You haven't paid me yet.'

'I don't understand.'

'Ah! He pretends again. By giving me your empire, you have performed an act of charity. Since I have accepted your charity, I have enabled you to earn merit. You need to pay me dakshina for that.'

Harishchandra spread out both his hands. 'But I have nothing left to give.'

'I must have my dakshina or I cannot receive your charity.'

Ayodhya watched as their king hung his head in shame. As their queen shed tears. Harishchandra spoke again.

'Kindly give me a few days.'

'A month. At the end of thirty days, you must pay me the dakshina or you shall be a blot on your solar clan.'

Suddenly, five bolts of lightning flashed in the sky as the Vishwadevas appeared. Guardians of the five directions. They instantly condemned the sage.

'Woe upon you, Vishwamitra. Is it not enough that you have seized everything from this noble man? How can you place yet another demand? How can you call him a blot when you are giving every hermit a bad name? He's no longer that soul who had tricked Varuna but you are still that thief who had tried to steal Kamadhenu.'

The gathering watched as the sage glared at the Vishwadevas and pronounced a curse. 'You five shall be born on Earth. Stripped of your divinity, you shall take birth as humans and endure every mortal weakness.'

The guardians vanished and so did the royal family. Journeying southward for days, the trio reached Kashi.

'This is hallowed land,' the king told Taramati. 'Mahadeva had come here with Brahma's skull stuck to his hand and Kashi had unburdened him. Suryadeva had sought refuge here after falling from the sky and Kashi had cleansed him. It shall release us, too, from our debt.'

The couple knocked on every door but found no work that would earn them money to pay the sage. To feed themselves or to buy a piece of new cloth. As the month came to an end, Vishwamitra appeared in their dreams that night.

'Your time ends tomorrow at sunset. Keep my dakshina ready.'

The next morning, Taramati clutched Harishchandra's hand and dragged him through Kashi. Stopping before a mansion, she pointed.

'This house belongs to an elderly man. He's looking to buy a maid.'

The king pulled his hand away. 'No, Tara.'

'Sell me to him.'

'No.'

'How will you pay the dakshina?'

'Not by selling you like cattle.'

'I am willing.'

'I am not. How can I live apart from you?'

'You must. This debt is the only thing that still chains us to our past. We must start afresh. Do it or I shall kill myself.'

'Tara!' He collapsed. 'Tara!'

'The star burns, O King. The star burns.'

The transaction soon completed itself. Harishchandra stood in silence when he received the amount. In silence, when the queen told him that Rohita would live with her. In silence, when he found Vishwamitra by the ghats and placed all the coins in his hand.

'This is only half,' the sage said.

'Half?'

'The dakshina must always be proportional to the charity you do. What you have paid is just half of that amount.'

'This is all I have, Revered One.'

'How did you get this?'

'My wife. I sold my wife.'

'Then you can sell yourself, too, and give me the rest,' Vishwamitra smiled.

The king nodded. 'I will. But to whom?'

'To him.'

The sage was pointing at a man. His skin was dark. His whiskers darker. A filthy cloth was wrapped around his loins and a revolting smell was coming from his body.

'He needs a servant,' the sage said.

'Who is he?'

'A Chandala.'

Harishchandra felt the word knifing through his flesh.

Chandala ...

Those who disposed of human corpses ...

His senses were now identifying that stench coating the man's skin.

That of the dead ...

The king shuddered. 'Not his servant. My clan will denounce me. My son will become a pariah. I would rather be your slave.'

'Will you?' Vishwamitra asked.

'From this very moment.'

'I accept. Now that I own you, here's my command. I want you to sell yourself to this Chandala and pay me the rest of the dakshina.'

'Revered One ...'

'You have lost your right to refuse. Your father, Trishanku, had lived with Chandalas and now you shall work for one.'

The Kshatriya stood frozen between the Brahmin and the Chandala. Then, lifting his fingers, he rubbed the mark of the sun from his forehead.

'I will, Master.'

Harishchandra now found himself slaving at one of the cremation ghats of Kashi. Burning the dead for a fixed sum of money. Wielding an axe to keep dogs and jackals away. Watching how, no matter the caste, all bodies turned into the same ash. Watching how men would shield their faces whenever he crossed their path.

Like the moon was doing right now.

It had gone behind a cloud and the night had darkened. A single corpse had been burning for a while now and the flames had died. The king bent down to collect the bones.

'My son.'

A woman's voice was calling out.

'My son.'

'Who is it?' Harishchandra turned.

'I have come to cremate my son,' the shadow sobbed.

'Do you have the fee?'

'Fee?'

'The dead can burn in Kashi only if they pay a fee. One-third of it goes to the king. One-third to the Chandala I serve, and one-third to me. The men here have put a price on salvation.'

'But I have no money.'

'Then I can do nothing.'

He saw the shadow stagger towards him and place her dead one at his feet.

'My child is no more. What do I do with his body?'

'My heart goes out to you but I am helpless.' Harishchandra picked up the corpse. 'Take him back.'

The moon emerged, illuminating Kashi again.

'Rohita! My Rohita!' His eyes fell on the woman. 'Tara!'

His arms were quaking under the weight of his dead son. His lips were caressing that cold face as if they could blow life into him.

'Our Rohita is dead, O King,' she wailed.

'Dead?'

'Bitten by a snake.'

'My Rohita?'

'You could not cremate your father for he hangs between heaven and earth. But you can cremate your son.'

'No, Tara.'

'No?'

'I cannot.'

'Why not?'

'I cannot unless you pay the fee.'

'But I told you I have nothing,' she shrieked.

'I must have the fee.'

'Have you too become like Vishwamitra? Does nothing matter to you but your fee? How can you refuse to carry out the rites of your own son?'

'How can I betray the master I serve? I have given him my word.'

'Your word!' She lashed out like a cobra. 'Look where your word has brought us. I hardly care if my body rots when I am gone. Crows can peck at my flesh and dogs can suck on my guts. But not my son. You can surely break your word for our Rohita.'

'I had done that once.' Tears gushed down Harishchandra's face. 'And I am still paying the price. Understand me, Tara. Forgive me. Curse me if you want. Spit on me and never look at me. But do not let me turn weak again, Tara. Take him away. Kashi is watching. The gods are watching. The dead are watching. How can I sin in their presence? How can I shame my clan once more?'

His eyes were flooding, but hers were flaming. 'Your clan lies dead, O King. Your Rohita lies dead. I, too, shall live no more.'

The queen grabbed the axe from his waist. The blade was looming above her neck when she heard her name.

'Taramati!'

She paused.

'Taramati!'

She turned.

'Taramati!'

She looked. Vishwamitra was calling out to her. He was standing next to her husband and the Chandala. And Rohita was running towards her.

'My son!'

As she clutched him, Vishwamitra embraced Harishchandra.

'You are truly singular. I was certain that I would defeat you, but I was wrong. Like Dhruva, you remained unwavering on this path. Emerged greater with every trial I put you through. Testing you any further would be a sin. I give you back everything I took. You are, once again, the monarch of Ayodhya.'

'A monarch who's now an outcast,' the king said, glancing at the Chandala.

But that man was laughing. A glow was radiating from his body and enveloping him. The next moment, that shell of light cracked to reveal Yama. His thumb touched Harishchandra's forehead and recreated the mark of the sun.

'You will always be Suryavanshi and your name shall now epitomise truth and integrity.'

Dawn was breaking on the ghat. The king gazed at Vishwamitra again.

'Would you grant something else if I asked, Revered One?'

'Tell me.

'The five Vishwadevas. Kindly lift your curse.'

'I cannot revoke it,' the sage answered. 'But I shall minimise its duration. Born as humans, they shall live on Earth for a brief period and will be liberated again.'

Those five guardians would go on to take birth as Upapandavas in the Dwapar Yuga. The five sons of Draupadi who would be killed by Ashwathama at the end of the Mahabharata War.

62

SAGARA LOSES HIS SONS

Six generations after Harishchandra, the solar throne embraced a king named Subahu. Married to Yadavi, he began his reign by walking that lustrous path carved by the Suryavanshi monarchs. Alas, even the sun bows before the night and Subahu soon turned ignoble. Too fragile now to uphold the virtues of his clan, he crumbled and so did his regime. People revolted. Foes gathered. The king lost everything and fled with Yadavi. Resting under a tree in the wilderness now, he heard two birds conversing.

'Come. We must fly away from here.'

'Why?'

'That's Subahu, the sinner. Even his shadow should not fall on you.'

A spasm of guilt so racked the king's heart that it instantly sucked the life out of him. Yadavi broke twigs and branches and piled them atop each other. Climbing on the pyre with her husband's corpse, she set it on fire.

'Don't!'

A sage was rushing towards her. Face frantic. Arms outstretched.

'Stay away,' the queen warned.

'Don't do this.'

'Who are you?'

'Aurva. I know you are Yadavi. Don't do this.'

'My king is no more. My land is not mine. Why must my life go on?'

'Because your life now carries another life.'

The queen froze inside that blazing circle. The flames had begun licking Subahu's body. Letting go of her husband's hand, Yadavi touched her belly.

'Life?'

'Yes. You are with child.'

'You lie.'

'I don't. I can see the ray of Suryavansh beaming inside you.'

The fire was creeping towards her now. Eyeing her live flesh. Her juicy foetus.

'A prince, O Queen.'

Scalding her thighs now.

'Your only heir.'

Eating the skin of her stomach.

'A son cremates his mother. Why are you cremating your son?'

Yadavi leapt. As Aurva steadied her, she broke down.

'Even if I am with child, what if he grows up to be another Subahu? What if history condemns me for bringing him to life?'

'History shall celebrate you,' the sage assured her. 'Nobility often skips a generation and I can see that your son shall possess every quality that his father lacked.'

Reaching his hermitage, Aurva asked his wife to tend to the pregnant queen. But alas, the woman grew convinced that the sage had been unfaithful and that Yadavi was carrying his seed. Blind with rage, she began to secretly add a drop of poison called gara to the queen's food. Began to wait for the foetus to perish but, nine months later, Yadavi delivered a cherub of a boy. Glaring silently at his wife, Aurva christened the infant prince.

'I can see that you have been born with gara. I name you Sagara.'

The poison had neither affected the child's body nor his mind. Under the sage's tutelage, Sagara now emerged worthy of his bloodline. Valiant yet virtuous. Academic yet pragmatic. The sun watched as, with the passage of time, the prince trounced his enemies and marched triumphantly back into Ayodhya. Seated on the solar throne, he took two wives, Keshini and Sumati, and asked Aurva to bless his lineage. The sage smiled.

'Both your wives shall bear sons. One will have a single son but the other shall beget sixty thousand. Take your pick.'

Keshini chose the former, and Sumati went for the latter. Ayodhya was soon rejoicing as the wailing of infants filled her air. Alas, Keshini's son, Asamanja, grew into a savage man and had to be banished from the land. His son, Anshuman, assumed his father's mantle as Sagara now called for an Ashwamedha Yagna.

'Our royal horse shall trot freely throughout Bhuloka,' he explained. 'Every territory it enters will either accept our sovereignty or battle with us to prove otherwise. Who among you is willing to walk behind the steed to defend it?'

'We are,' the sixty thousand sons of Sumati chorused. Anshuman folded his hands.

'And I shall stay here with you, grandfather, and help perform the rituals.'

On the appointed day, all of Sagara's sons left with the horse as the king sat down by the ceremonial fire with Anshuman. Awaiting their return after which the animal would be sacrificed. Oblivious that Indra had once more begun shuddering in heaven.

Ashwamedha Yagna ...

Distant memories were terrorising the Devaraja's mind.

Just like Prithu ... Just like Bali ...

That same fear was crawling down his spine again.

Will Sagara too turn Chakravarti?

He watched. He waited. The princes had now reached the seashore with the horse and were taking rest. As soon as they fell asleep, Indra abducted the animal.

'Come,' he led it away. 'I have something in mind for you.'

Soon, Sagara's sons were looking around in panic. Diving into the sea. Digging up the land. Questioning each of the five elements. Losing an Ashwamedha steed was no less than sacrilege. The yagna would fail and their clan would be doomed. Wandering frantically, they entered the netherworld and one of them screamed joyously.

'There!'

They had found it. Tethered next to what looked like a hermitage. As they neared, another one pointed.

'It's Sage Kapila's abode.'

The rapture turned into rage. Unaware that Indra had deliberately planted the horse there, the princes became convinced that Kapila was the thief. Storming inside, they began vandalising his hermitage. They pulled down his roof and trampled his plants. Urinated on his food and smeared dung on his sanctum. As the walls around them crashed, they saw Kapila seated in padmasana. The chaos had jolted him out of his meditation. The princes began abusing him. Flinging their sandals at him.

The sage closed his eyes.

And opened them again.

Days later, Sagara gazed expectantly as Anshuman entered the hall. The princes had still not returned with the horse and the king had sent his grandson to look for them. Anshuman was standing now with his fist clenched. His fingers black. His face white.

'What news of your uncles?' Sagara asked.

The gathering shrank back as Anshuman opened his fist to reveal a handful of ash.

'Charred.'

'What?'

'Charred. All sixty thousand of them.'

'Charred?'

'Sage Kapila glared at them and a wave of fire from his eyes consumed them all.'

The assembly turned catatonic. The king's tongue trembled.

'But why? What did they do?'

As Anshuman narrated the events, Sagara stuttered with horror. 'Such a violent end never liberates the dead. The souls of my sons must be trapped in agony.'

'They are, grandfather. They are begging for peace. Begging to be delivered. My ears bled as I stood there for I could hear all sixty thousand of them howling in pain.'

The queens fainted. The king stared at the ash. At the irony that while one sage had saved him from burning, another had burnt his sons alive.

'What now, Anshuman? How do we offer your uncles salvation?'

'I pleaded with Sage Kapila and he revealed it to me. Ganga.'

'Ganga?'

'The river goddess who exists in heaven. The sage affirmed that her waters alone can absolve these souls.'

Sagara doused the yagna's flames. Staggering towards the window, he gazed at the sky.

'But how do we bring down Ganga?'

63

BHAGIRATH BRINGS DOWN GANGA

Sagara had tried.

His grandson, Anshuman, had tried.

Anshuman's son, Dilip, had tried.

Three generations of Suryavanshis had laid down their lives chanting that name. Three descendants of that orb of fire had perished invoking that stream of water. Their mouths had dried up propitiating that nectar. Their bodies had crumbled at the altar of that one word.

Ganga.

Now Dilip's son, Bhagirath, was attempting to carry out the task. He had been meditating for a thousand years. His body was static but his mind was in relentless motion. Uttering incantations with every heartbeat as if his heart would stop if he did. Like his forefathers, he, too, did not know if the undertaking would succeed. If the river would deign to descend. But he was doing it because it had to be done. The sole purpose of his birth. The only quest of his clan.

He quivered. Drops of water had suddenly landed on his skin. Was she here?

Ganga?

'Open your eyes, Bhagirath.'

He looked. Brahma was sprinkling his face.

'The grit of your dynasty has won us all. Your ancestors never gave up and it culminates with you now. It's time. The inevitable must happen.'

Bhagirath could hear a sound as if a stream was suddenly rippling by him. Ganga was approaching. Pure. Hallowed. Untouched. Whiter than the whitest. A flood of benevolence that the Earth would clasp and never let go.

'Ganga,' the Creator addressed her. 'The words of Saraswati must come true now. You shall descend to Bhuloka. Liberate not only the sons of Sagara but every mortal who sins. There shall be multitudes and they will keep flocking to your shore. Immersing themselves in your womb as your waters encase them. Thus nourished, they shall be birthed anew. Rinsed and restored. Absolved of everything. They shall also bring their dead to you and you shall offer them salvation.'

'But I am pristine,' the river said. 'Will my waters not get tainted when I cleanse so many? Will those sins that I absorb not gather inside me and make me a sinner too?'

'No, Ganga. You are Vishnupadi. Sanctified by the foot of Vishnu. You shall remain the purest even when you touch the vilest. Even when you drink their chaos and make them whole again.'

'They await you, mother,' Bhagirath fell at her feet. 'Sixty thousand of them. Still shrieking. Still burning. That fire refuses to die. Your water alone will wash away their pain.'

'I can't.'

Brahma glared at her. 'This is your charge, Ganga. How can you refuse? Your descent shall push new life into Bhuloka's veins.'

'It will grind her to dust.'

'What do you mean?'

'When I descend from heaven, my pace will be torrential. Falling from such a height, my impact will be devastating. My waters will crash over Bhuloka and tear her asunder. Split her right through the axis.'

Brahma and Bhagirath stood silent. Their minds were imagining that horror. Wondering if Ganga was deliberately painting that picture to avoid entry into Earth. But she spoke again.

'There's only one solution. Mahadeva.'

'Mahadeva?'

'He alone can break my fall. Sustain the ferocity of my volume. If he agrees, I shall precipitate on his head and flow into Bhuloka.'

Instructed by the Creator, Bhagirath now began appeasing Shiva. When he finally manifested, he smiled hearing the king's plea.

'I took the venom that flowed from below. I can surely take this nectar that flows from above.'

The earth watched as Shiva now stood on the edge of Kailash. Opened the knot of his matted hair and let the tresses fan out like a giant receptacle. The firmament was rumbling. Shuddering as if nearing orgasm. The waters exploded. Squirted by the sky, Ganga plunged ruthlessly. A wave of white foam like liquid lightning. Her acceleration was multiplying a hundred times as she came closer. Closer. Closer. Cascading faster. Gathering kinesis. That enormous reservoir was emptying all of herself as she closed in on the Destroyer's head. The universe quaked. She had made impact. That deluge was bouncing high like a titanic wave crashing against a mountain. Splitting into a million drops. Many tributaries. Spilling over, she now found herself chained by Shiva's locks. Quelled on all sides. The more water was pouring from above, the more it was getting enmeshed below. Soon, that stream ceased. Ganga no longer existed in heaven. All of her was now captive inside the labyrinth of Shiva's hair.

Sourced from Brahma. Beatified by Vishnu. Now cradled by Shiva.

The man whose forefather had been fed poison in the womb had compelled her. The god who had swallowed poison for Brahmanda had contained her. The river that would now suck poison from the souls of men was calling Shiva by a new name.

'I bow before you, O Gangadhar. Pray, release me so I may carry out my bidding.'

Bhagirath wept as he saw Ganga liberating his ancestors. Wept again when she told him that she would now also be called Bhagirathi.

64

SARASWATI BATTLES VISHNU

'Tell me, lord.'

But Brahma was wondering. Whether to respond or to refrain.

'You are toying with me with your silence, lord. Do reply.'

But not a sound was emerging from the Creator's four mouths.

'Are you baffled, lord? Surely you who have spawned this cosmos can answer a simple query.'

But the Creator only smiled, hoping that would somehow substitute the need for words. She shook her head.

'Let me ask you again. Who among us three principal goddesses is the most glorious? Me, Lakshmi or Parvati?'

'Why must we compare, Saraswati?' Brahma finally said. 'Bhrigu had also attempted a ranking of the male trinity and that did not end well for him.'

'And you fear that this might not end well for you?'

'I am only asserting that all three of you are dimensions of Shakti. Progenitors of Prakriti. Creation needs knowledge, which makes you my consort. Preservation requires means, which makes Lakshmi Sri Hari's consort. And destruction demands power, which makes Parvati Mahadeva's consort. You three are the hallowed feminine who make us divine. The maternal component of Brahmanda that nourishes life. There's no contest here.'

'And yet I can smell an answer on the tips of your tongues,' Saraswati inched closer.

'You are mistaken,' he backed away.

'You thought of a name as soon as I posed the question.'

'I did not.'

'Tell me your choice, my lord.'

'Stop it.'

'Tell me.'

'But ...'

'Tell me.'

'If I must choose, it's Lakshmi.'

Saraswati fell silent. The next day, she was nowhere to be found. Brahma searched every high and every low but to no avail. The devi had abandoned the deva. Days later, all the gods descended upon Bhuloka. The Creator was performing a yagna and they were congregating to bless the ritual. The altar had been designed as a seven-pointed star with each limb being occupied by a Saptarishi. Water had been brought from Ganga's shore and flowers from Indra's garden. Agni was kindling the pit and Vayu was feeding the flames. Vishnu was blowing his conch and Shiva was rattling his damru. Narada had begun to chant a hymn when he froze.

A veena was reverberating. Devouring every other sound. Saraswati had appeared before them in a manner they had never seen. She was plucking those strings as if she was pulling the entrails of a beast. The veena was howling in pain. Growling with rage. Her fingers were bleeding. Her eyes were blazing. Every loka had begun trembling with the vibrations of that lyre. She had turned her instrument into a weapon. Her music into ill omen. Suddenly, Brahmanda twanged as if someone had snapped its spine. A string on her veena had violently ruptured.

'Pray, stop, Saraswati,' Brahma pleaded. 'Listen to me.'

'Listen to you, when you continue to disgrace me? First in private and now in public? I see Sri Hari here seated with Lakshmi. Mahadeva with

Parvati. Indra with Indrani. Agni with Swaha. But not you. You refuse to acknowledge your consort.'

'I looked everywhere but couldn't find you. I was hopeful that you would return today and you have. Join me now. Hold my hand so we may commence the yagna.'

'But I am here to destroy the yagna,' Saraswati snarled.

The gods gasped. The Creator frowned. 'Destroy?'

'Yes. I am not Sati who leapt into fire because she was not invited. I am Saraswati who will set the yagna on fire.'

'We are carrying out this ritual for the good of the universe,' Brahma countered. 'And I know that you, too, have always desired the same. Do not let your anger towards me cloud your compassion towards others.'

'You chose her over me.' The goddess pointed at Lakshmi. 'Wealth over wisdom. Prosperity over creativity. The material over the spiritual. I want to see now if all that can safeguard your yagna.'

'They don't need to as long as I am present,' a voice echoed.

The devas looked. Saraswati looked. It was Vishnu.

'You have allowed chaos into your veena and it now taints your ragas. Taints the very melody of creation. Taints that ocean of knowledge that resides within you. You are endangering a ritual that has the noblest of intentions and I cannot allow it. You can demolish this yagna only if you demolish me.'

The goddess flared like a volcano. Her garment was turning black. Her lotus was turning black. Her swan was turning black. She was inverting her own form. As Saraswati and Vishnu stood facing each other, the universe began to pray. Deva was challenging devi. Purusha was challenging Prakriti. The two halves of Brahmanda were now at war. Saraswati charged at once by generating Maya Shakti as a massive inferno, but Vishnu doused it. She then gave rise to Kapalika Shakti, but the Preserver thwarted it. Summoning terrible powers, she now brought forth Kalika Shakti, but Vishnu foiled it too. The goddess was quaking. Her eyes were bloodshot. Her hair was wild. Her swan was screeching. Her lotus was wilting. As the gathering watched, Saraswati began to morph. Turn into water. Her body was melting like a

figurine of ice. Becoming a giant whirlpool. Carving an enormous basin in the ground that she was filling to the brim.

'What is she doing?' Parvati asked.

'Turning into a river,' Brahma replied. 'She could not burn the yagna and now wants to drown it.'

The goddess was no longer there. Only a stream that was lunging savagely towards the altar. Peeling the skin of Bhuloka. Pounding stones to dust. Becoming more and more ferocious as if blood was bubbling through the veins of Earth. Carrying a current so livid that it was threatening to suck the yagna into its lowest depths. Vishnu began to walk towards it.

'Can Sri Hari calm her?' Lakshmi asked.

Shiva nodded. 'Like how I calmed Ganga. Like how I calmed Kali.'

The Preserver lay down in the path of the river. He had taken the reclining posture of Anantashayna, but he was not sleeping. He was watching. Watching that water accelerating. Watching Saraswati surging towards him in all her liquid fury. Closer now. The stream was deluging. Closer now. Thundering like a wave. Closer now. Spilling over the banks. Closer now. Tearing more of the earth. Closer now. Lakshmi quailed. The gods flinched. Inches away from Vishnu, the river swerved. Turned sharply towards the right. Gouging a hole in the ground, it began plunging into the netherworld. Vanishing into the bowels of Brahmanda. The devas breathed. The yagna gazed. Saraswati was draining herself away. The goddess had surrendered before the god.

'So, deva bridles devi again,' Parvati glanced at Shiva.

The Destroyer offered her a flower. 'Devi, too, curbed Mahishasura. Devi, too, curbed Raktabija. Deva also bridled another deva when I as Sharabh calmed Sri Hari as Narasimha. When Sri Hari calmed my Rudra Tandava. It is never about deva or devi. It is forever about counteracting any poison that threatens the cosmos. And poison has no gender.'

65

THE PARASHURAMA AVATAR

Which one?

Sage Jamadagni was observing his sons. Those five sturdy lads toiling in his hermitage. More precious to him than anything in the world. And yet, that same thorn was tormenting him again.

Which one?

He was again recalling what his mother, Satyavati, had told him long ago. How she had consumed the wrong rice portion and what his father, Richika, had subsequently prophesied.

I can only delay the inevitable by one generation ... Our son shall be the Brahmin I want ...

Jamadagni had indeed grown up to be that noble sage. His abode had become a sanctuary for many seeking light. Seeking to unravel life. But Richika had also made another forecast.

His son will be a fierce warrior ...

And so Jamadagni was watching his sons. Wondering who among these five was destined to be that warrior. Whose blood was more Kshatriya than Brahmana. Whose eyes were reflecting more passion than piety.

Which one? Which one?

Wondering if the body could betray the soul it was hiding.

Which one?

Meanwhile, at a river nearby, his wife, Renuka, was filling her vessel. Not only was she devoted to her family but also utterly loyal to Jamadagni. So potent was her chastity that the pitcher she had fashioned to carry water every day was made of unbaked clay. Held together simply by the might of her purity. As she turned towards the bank now, a pair of male gandharvas rode across the sky. Their bodies were limber. Their smiles luring. Renuka's eyes met theirs for a moment and something tightened inside her. Something thawed. Something she had never known before.

Crash!

Her vessel was in pieces. That which had weakened her flesh had weakened the clay. Her fingers were now struggling to shape that pitcher once more but in vain. As all of it dissolved in the river, she knew.

He has come to know ...

She kept sitting by the water all day. When she finally returned at dusk, Jamadagni stood in her way.

'Your clothes are stained with clay, Renuka.'

'They are.'

'I was thirsty.'

'Perhaps, I was too.'

The sage called out to his five sons. 'Your mother has lost her sanctity. I command you to cut off her head. Do it without trembling.'

'Father!'

'A single blow.'

The four elder ones fell to their knees. 'If she has sinned, why do you ask us to sin as well? How can we kill the woman who gave us life and—'

They recoiled. Renuka's head was rolling. Her torso was writhing on the ground as her life spurted away. The youngest one was holding aloft his axe, or parashu, caked with her blood.

'Rama,' they screamed. 'What have you done?'

'Obeyed father.'

Jamadagni glared at the four of them now. As his eyes turned red, they turned into statues. All their horror had crystallised into stone. He turned and wrenched the axe from Rama.

'It's you. The Brahmakshatriya whose birth was postponed. Who has sprung now from that violent recipe of my father. Only you could have beheaded your mother without remorse. Only you can stand here so calm despite this gore. You sicken me. You frighten me. Your axe has tasted blood. It will keep craving for more and you will keep feeding it. I should throw it away. I should hack you with it. But you have carried out my command without questioning me. Such reverence towards a father is exemplary. The others failed and I have punished them. But what do I do with you? I offer you two boons. Ask anything you want.'

He folded his hands. 'Bring my mother back to life. And turn my brothers human.'

The sage stood dazed for a moment. Then he reanimated his family and placed the parashu back in his son's hand.

'I was wrong to fear you, Rama. Your body is savage but not your soul. Your axe has a conscience. It will slaughter many but only those who imperil dharma. It will drink blood like Mahakali but only of the depraved. It will be your chakra. Your Vajra. So inseparable from you that I shall now fuse its name with yours. I shall give you a new name, Rama.'

And he became Parashurama. Another hallowed avatar of Vishnu.

Years later, when Parashurama was away at Mahendra Parvat, a Haihaya king called Kartavirya Arjuna arrived at Jamadagni's hermitage with his retinue. To the common eye, he was a man, but in reality, he was the human incarnation of the Sudarshana. Not long ago, the chakra had grown proud of its might and begun clamouring to be worshipped like Vishnu. To humble his weapon, the Preserver had brought about its birth on Earth as Kartavirya Arjuna. Like the edges on the disc, he too possessed a thousand arms which had earned him the sobriquet, Sahastrarjuna. As Jamadagni's family laid out an array of food before the king, he saw that the sage owned a divine cow that fulfilled every need. Overcome with jealousy, Kartavirya began to demand the animal.

'My arrows have been powered by Agnideva himself,' he hissed. 'Each is tipped with flames that can turn your hut into a pyre.'

'The pyre is where we are all headed, O King,' Jamadagni retorted. 'Why must the river fear the sea?'

Kartavirya unleashed his army. Like a pack of dogs, they began to maul those who had been feeding them. As the sage stood helpless, the king seized the cow. Soon after, a furious Parashurama tore through Kartavirya's fort. Dismembering his arms one by one, he placed his parashu over his throat.

'It's time, Sudarshana,' the avatar said. 'You must be beheaded now as you behead others.'

Vishnu's axe sliced Vishnu's disc and Parashurama returned with the cow. But alas, the bloodbath had not yet ended. In his absence again, the sons of Kartavirya stormed his hermitage and butchered everyone. Killed Jamadagni by stabbing him twenty-one times. Retaliating once more, Parashurama put all the descendants of Kartavirya to death. Standing before that pile of corpses, he touched the blade to his forehead.

'I, Parashurama, take a vow that every Kshatriya who oppresses others shall become fodder for my axe.'

True to his word, he began a genocide now that Bhuloka had never seen. His parashu had become a tool of doom and it purged Earth of vile kings twenty-one times. The same number of times that Jamadagni's body had been slashed. At the end of these killings, the axe had spewed so much blood that it filled up five lakes. This turned a vast area red, which came to be known as Shyamanta Panchaka. Land of the Five Red Lakes. This red would soon turn redder when another carnage would occur at the same place in Dwapar Yuga. A carnage following an odious spectacle where the purity of another woman would be questioned.

The Mahabharata War.

66

GAUTAMA CREATES A RIVER

Sage Gautama was gazing at the land below and the sky above.

Both halves had become dry. Neither were clouds drifting nor rivers flowing. Only a drought was spreading like a plague. Like the tongue of Kali, sucking every drop of water. As life around him began turning into dust, Gautama invoked Varuna.

'Bhuloka is dying. Why have you forsaken us?'

'I am helpless.' The water deity sighed. 'Indra is the god of rains. I cannot intervene if he is withholding his grace.'

'Can't the soil give us what the sky will not?'

Varuna nodded. Soon, Gautama's hermitage at Brahmagiri was blessed with a lake that carried an endless supply of water. Hundreds began flocking to its shore and filling themselves to the brim. Gautama and his wife, Ahilya, made arrangements as their land turned into a settlement. A single reservoir had bound together countless lives. Countless homes. Thus, twenty-four years elapsed but the drought persisted. Standing by the edge of their lake, the sage smiled.

'It's a bliss to see everyone so content here.'

'Indeed,' Ahilya agreed. 'I hope none of them leaves. We can all thrive together.'

'We surely shall. Civilisations have always sprung by rivers and this shall be the same. Once they ...'

He paused. The sky was drizzling. Its blue was turning black. Clouds were swelling up. Lightning and thunder tore them open and a torrent swept the drought away. Jealous of all the merit Gautama was earning by sheltering so many, Indra had suddenly released rain. With the lake no longer needed, the families began to leave. Gautama and Ahilya watched like a pair of old birds as their nests turned empty one by one. All by themselves now, they looked at their deserted oasis.

Had it all been a mirage?

'Why didn't you stop them?' she asked.

'It's natural law,' he replied. 'Those who come must also go. We were wrong to believe that we could hold on to them.'

Only a group of hermits lingered on, terrified that Gautama might curse them if they tried to depart.

'He must surely be displeased with everyone abandoning him,' one of them whispered. 'We are the last ones. All his wrath will fall upon us.'

'What do we do?' the others queried.

'I have thought of something. I know it will work.'

The next day, Gautama spotted a feeble cow grazing in his fields. Devouring all his barley. As he yelled at the animal, the hermits joined in.

'She will not budge like that,' they said. 'You will have to shove her out.'

The sage walked up to the cow and poked her with a blade of grass.

'Move.'

The animal collapsed, dead. Before Gautama could realise what had happened, the hermits crowded around the lifeless body.

'What have you done?'

'You have killed a cow!'

'This is a disgrace for all Brahmins!'

'How could you do that?'

Gautama stood confounded. Unaware that this was a trick devised by the hermits, he tried defending himself. 'I barely touched her. This makes no sense.'

But the hermits were shaking their heads.

'This is sacrilege. You have tainted yourself and your clan. Tainted this place now that bears the weight of a dead cow. We can no longer live here or we shall be ostracised.'

The sage nodded. 'That's true. You can leave whenever you wish. But do tell me, how do I make amends?'

'Pray to Shiva,' the hermits urged and bolted.

Gautama began meditating upon a lingam and soon the Destroyer manifested.

'You ride the venerable Nandi, Mahadeva,' he said, lowering his eyes. 'Will you forgive me who has killed a cow?'

Shiva smiled and plucked a strand of hair from his head. 'Take this, Gautama.'

'It's wet.'

'Yes. Flushed with the remnants of Ganga. Place it next to the animal and all will be well.'

'But my sin, Mahadeva?'

'All will be well.'

As soon as the sage placed the hair next to the cow, a stream issued from it. Jets of water were surging from the strand and carving a basin. As the fountain gushed, it spilled over the carcass and brought her back to life.

'You are alive!' Gautama raved, embracing the animal.

'I am but an illusion,' she said.

As that waterbed stretched further and further, the cow revealed how the hermits had deceived him. Filling his palms with water from that stream, the sage laid a curse upon them. 'Those hermits will be reborn as cheats and liars and herald the onset of Kali Yuga.'

Unlike Ganga, which was watering the north, this river coursed south. Brought down by Gautama, it was called Gautami Ganga, but acquired a beautiful mononym.

Godavari.

One who grants water.

67

VISHNU TRICKS MURA

One of the danavas in the lineage of Danu was called Mura. And like so many daityas, he, too, was trying to extract a boon from Brahma. Asking the Creator to grant that he could put anyone to death by the mere touch of his hand.

'Why must you demons invert everything?' Brahma queried. 'Touch is a beautiful thing. It arouses. It comforts. It even listens and observes. Makes the body feel adored. Why make it a tool of doom?'

'Because I wish to be mightier than the mightiest. Pray, infuse my flesh with this power.'

'What if I grant you that whatever you touch shall turn into gold? Solid gold. Think about that. Such a wondrous ability! Humans on Earth might even make an idiom out of it. They are good at doing that. They may call it the Mura's touch.'

'But I would starve,' the danava countered. 'Even the food I touch will turn into gold. So will my water and my wine.'

Brahma smiled. 'You are wiser than I thought. Have it your way.'

A jubilant Mura now embarked upon a touching spree. His hands were sucking the life out of every creature they were landing on. Man and beast. Deva and daitya. Snuffing them out one after the other. Leaving behind a trail of death as he arrived at the palace gates of a king called Raghu.

'I hear you are quite the duellist,' the danava smirked. 'How about a round or two with me?'

Raghu was no stranger to Mura's boon. Tales of his tactile terror had reached every circle of Brahmanda by now. The king instantly found a way out.

'I am but a mortal. What will you acquire by vanquishing me? Go and fight Yamaraja.'

'Why Yamaraja?'

'Death conquers everyone. So, imagine conquering death himself. What a feat that will be! Your name will be glorified till the very end of time.'

The danava fell in love with that thought. As soon as news spread that he was charging towards hell, Yama leapt on his buffalo and fled to Vaikuntha.

'What do I do?' he queried, trembling before Vishnu.

'Nothing. Send him to me.'

Mura was soon challenging the god of death but he had his answer ready.

'I can duel with you only if my master permits.'

'Master? You have a master?'

'Indeed. Sri Hari.'

'Then I shall tackle him first and then come for you.'

Yama grinned. 'I will be waiting.'

Soon, the danava was standing before Vishnu, daring the Preserver to fight.

'Let's end this quick,' he beckoned. 'Your slave awaits me in Yamaloka.'

'Gladly,' Vishnu uttered. 'But why are you so terrified, Mura?'

'Me? Terrified? Never.'

'But your heart,' the god pointed.

'My heart?'

'It's pounding so hard that I can hear it all the way from here.'

'But I hear nothing.'

'Impossible. It's hammering in panic. You are clearly a coward.'

'I am not. I don't hear anything.'

'Then you have obviously got used to that noise. It happens when one keeps hearing the same sound again and again. That means your heart keeps palpitating like that all the time. It's forever frightened. Why, Mura? Why are you in a constant state of fear?'

'I am not!'

'But your heart ...'

'What heart? What heart?'

Mura's hand furiously clutched his own chest. Vishnu was laughing. The three realms were laughing. As the demon collapsed, dead, Brahma appeared and bowed.

'You have done it again, Sri Hari. Thwarted another threat. Acquired another name. From this day onwards, you shall also be worshipped as Murari. The one who slew Mura.'

'Touch!' Vishnu smiled. 'Such a beautiful thing.'

68

NARADA GETS A NEW FACE

'And I foiled them! Foiled them all!'

Narada's antics were making Shiva laugh. Those facial contortions. Exaggerated actions. The Devarshi had not stopped chattering about himself since his arrival at Kailash. Telling the Destroyer how he had begun meditating at the foot of the mountain. How Indra had panicked and despatched nymphs to ruin his austerities. And how he had risen above every temptation.

'Enticing me is harder than blowing out the sun,' Narada whooped. 'I must compose a lyric in my honour. About how I degraded the Devaraja himself.'

Shiva watched as he continued to gloat. He was tempted to tell Narada that it was he who had enabled him to thwart Indra. That his yogic powers which infused Kailash had shielded the Devarshi from flames of lust. But he let Narada savour his illusion.

'Quite a tale,' the Destroyer remarked. 'I suggest that you don't share it with anyone else.'

But Narada was itching to spread his exultation all over Brahmanda. He was soon standing before Brahma and repeating every word. The Creator also saw through the fantasy and tended the same advice.

'Incredible, but keep it to yourself.'

Alas, dazzled by himself, the Devarshi was convinced that both Shiva
and Brahma had turned jealous of him. He recounted his feat before
Vishnu now and even invented details to further magnify his triumph. The
god clapped. The god cheered. And as Narada left, the god grinned.

'Aham Brahmasmi?'

Heading out of Vaikuntha, Narada soon came across an enchanting
city. It was floating on clouds and decked with rainbows. A mighty army
was guarding a palace of gold. Everyone was celebrating the swayamvara
of their king's daughter today. Wading through that carnival, the Devarshi
entered the court to find countless rows of young men. Each one had
arrived, chasing that knot. Musicians were playing and dancers were
twirling. Attendants were showering flowers and the ruler was handing out
gifts. But Narada had suddenly turned blind to everything around him. He
was only gazing at that face. Her face.

I love her ...

In a trice, Narada was back in Vaikuntha and lying at the Preserver's
feet.

'The princess?' Vishnu asked. 'You wish to marry that princess?'

'More than anything else.'

'Go ahead. It's a swayamvara and you are eligible.'

'Not eligible. I want to be undefeatable. And only you can do that.'

'Tell me how.'

'Make me as captivating as you. Your limbs. Your body. Turn me into
Hari.'

The blue finger rose and touched the Devarshi. 'So be it!'

Transporting himself back to the palace, Narada took his place among
the suitors. The princess was walking by his row now, holding that circle
of flowers. Lifting her gaze and then dropping it. Glancing at them one by
one. The soft tread of her feet belying the storm in her heart. Narada sat up.
Her anklets were ringing louder. She was coming closer.

Closer. Closer. Closer.

Her fragrance was tickling his senses now. She was standing right
before him. Looking at his face. Looking long and hard. Not moving away.

Gazing as if she had never seen anyone like him. The Devarshi was barely breathing. Time seemed to be barely ticking. Her fingers tightened. Her bosom heaved. Her lips curved. She was smiling. Smiling at him like she had not smiled at anyone else here. Narada leapt to his feet.

She loves what she's seeing ...

She's smiling ...

Smiling ...

Laughing ...

Laughing?

Laughing???

The princess was laughing so hard that Narada was sure she would explode. But she was no longer alone. The entire court had joined her. Everyone was cackling with a strange glee. Pointing at him. Making faces. The cacophony was mounting. The princess was rolling on the ground now. Her body was quaking and her eyes watering. So intense was her mirth that the garland had slipped from her hands. The Devarshi inched closer and picked it up. She was muttering something. Two words were struggling to pass through those convulsions of laughter.

'Your ... face ...'

My face?

Narada spun towards a large vessel of water behind him and looked.

My face ...

Hardly divine.

My face ...

A sublime body but the face of a monkey.

'Narayana!'

Suddenly everything around him was dissolving. The princess. The king. The suitors. The court. The entire city was fading into nothingness. Only Vishnu was standing before him.

'Maya.' The Devarshi ripped that circle of flowers. 'Your maya again.'

'It has been a while, Narada. Wasn't it right after Brahmadeva lost his fifth head that you encountered maya? No wonder you have forgotten all about it.'

'But I was truly in love with her. Does love mean nothing?'

'Love means everything but attachment is vile. Love is selfless but attachment is selfish. Love liberates but attachment binds.'

'Why, Narayana? Why disgrace me so much?'

'Because you had the hubris to believe that you were beyond maya. It was Mahadeva who had countered Indra's ploy but you failed to see that. You convinced yourself that you were immune to desire. That's why I had to remind you that even you could stray from your path. Succumb to this matrix of delusion. Fall prey to the very maya that you thought you had conquered.'

'But a monkey?'

'Of course! You desired to look like Hari, and another meaning of that word is monkey. A monkey is also a mimic. It has nothing of its own and merely imitates. Similarly, you and everyone else in the universe do nothing on your own. Like pieces of glass, you merely reflect us. Play out our thoughts. Our actions. Our will. You are but puppets stringed to this theatre of Brahmanda, just as Brahmadeva, Mahadeva and I are stringed to the Parabrahman.'

Narada folded his hands.

'I have erred. I accept that you command our reality, but your maya could have been less brutal. You toyed with my emotions and I shall curse you for it. Bhrigu has cursed you that you shall take human births and Vrinda has cursed you that, as Lord Rama, you will be separated from your wife. You gave me the face of a monkey and I curse you now that, once separated, you won't be reunited with your wife unless a monkey comes to your aid.'

The Preserver laughed. 'You still don't understand, Narada. It's not you who curses me. Nor is it Bhrigu, nor Vrinda. There's no You. No He or She. Only Me. It's all my doing.'

As Vishnu vanished, the Devarshi heard his voice again.

'It's I who curse myself.'

69

NIMI LOSES HIS BODY

One of the wiser souls in this yuga was King Nimi. He once commenced a yagna that would last a thousand years. Nimi requested Vashishtha to conduct the ceremony but the sage was already occupied with Indra's Parashakti Yagna. He informed the king that he would be able to come only after five hundred years.

Alas, the tongue often muddles the brain. Different minds decode the same words differently. Nimi thought that the sage had refused his offer, while Vashishtha thought the king was going to wait for him.

Five hundred years came and went.

Vashishtha now arrived at Nimi's yagna to discover that it was already in progress with Sage Gautama presiding. Confounded, embarrassed and finally enraged, he laid a curse upon the unfortunate king.

'You will no longer possess your body.'

His words took immediate effect as Nimi's spirit floated out of his physical self. The horrified gathering began to plead with Vashishtha. The subjects were wailing. The ministers were urging. Everyone was standing with folded hands, but not the king. Furious at being punished so unjustly, he cursed the sage right back.

'Just as I have lost my body, you, too, shall lose yours.'

As Vashishtha stormed out, Gautama addressed Nimi's soul. 'But how will you complete the remaining rituals?'

'I shall do so in this astral form of mine.'

Mantras resumed. The fire crackled again. Oblations were poured and merit was earned. As the yagna came to an end, several gods appeared and offered to merge the king with his lifeless form.

'Vashishtha will soon regain his body and we wish the same for you.'

But Nimi refused.

'I am not besotted with this physical frame like Trishanku. Let me remain free from this prison of flesh and bone. Bless me that henceforth my spirit may reside in the eyelids of all beings. That would be boon enough.'

The devas smiled.

'As you wish. The interval between the closing and opening of eyelids shall now be called Nimesha.'

The assembly cheered, but another calamity was upon them now. Without a body, Nimi could no longer rule. He had no son, and a land without a monarch would be deemed inauspicious. As the gathering debated, the sages recalled the precedent set by the Saptarishi in the case of King Vena. He too had died without an heir, and his successor, Prithu, had been kneaded out of his flesh. The same process was carried out now and it bore fruit once more.

A son emerged from Nimi.

Since the child had been harvested from a man who had lost his body, he was named Vaideha. Since he had been churned from Nimi's flesh, he was also called Mithi. And since he had been sourced from his father, he was also named Janaka. In due course of time, this new king would obtain a daughter in an equally extraordinary manner and she would be called Vaidehi, Maithili and Janaki.

But the universe would remember her as Sita.

70

LOHAJANGHA AND THE SAPTARISHI

Seven ...

He was not counting the shades of the rainbow that was arching before him. Not the group of lotuses in the pond below. Not even the flock of vultures flying above. He was counting the men who were walking towards him. Seven men in lustrous white as if seven stars had fallen from the sky. The number was pleasing him. More the travellers, more the loot. More the blood to adorn his scythe.

They were now half the way to where he was.

He tiptoed ahead, keeping them in sight. Hiding behind another tree, he peered at them. There was something singular about these seven. As if they were the kind of men you would ask for directions if you were lost. As if they were the kind of men you would ask for anything if you were lost.

They had slowed down. They were within his reach.

'Halt!' he screamed as he leapt into their path. 'If you fear for your life, do as I say.'

But his words were ringing hollow. There was no terror in those eyes. Only tranquillity.

'Hand me your valuables or I will kill you all.'

The first one smiled. 'That dry coat of blood on your scythe tells me a different story. Tells me that you will hack us to death even if we give you what we have.'

He bared his teeth. 'I will.'

'You are Lohajangha? The bandit who has been robbing and killing wayfarers on this road since the drought?' the second one asked.

'I am.'

'Why do you prey like a beast?'

'Better to prey than to be preyed upon. Hand me everything precious you are carrying and I might make your death less painful.'

'But pain is good,' countered the third one. 'It leads to repair. Leads to renewal.'

The fourth one nodded. 'As for our valuables, the most prized thing we are carrying is our knowledge. You cannot rob it. You can only absorb it, if you are willing.'

Lohajangha swung the scythe to the base of the man's throat. 'Looks like I will have to chop your heads off since you have nothing for me.'

'We have a question for you,' the fifth one said. 'Answer us and then you may take our lives'

'Ask.'

'We believe that you kill and rob to raise your family,' said the sixth one.

'I do,' he replied. 'And they are grateful for it. They know what I do and readily share what I bring.'

'Will they also readily share the consequences of your sins?'

'Consequences?'

'The hell that awaits you after you die. Will your family burn with you in Naraka? Will they share the price you must pay in your next birth? Share every punishment you will face since your actions are entirely for their sake?'

Lohajangha stood mute. The question was burrowing into his heart. Digging deeper and deeper for an answer but finding none. As he lowered his scythe, the seventh one nodded.

'Why don't you ask your loved ones and tell us? We shall wait here for you.'

The bandit forced a peal of laughter. 'It's a ruse. A wicked ruse. You are trying to baffle me. Trying to send me away so you can escape.'

'We never escape,' the seven of them chorused. 'Look for us and we will be right here.'

Lohajangha turned and walked away. The sages had divested him of all his doubts. Filled him with a strange belief that they would be there for him.

Reaching his house, the bandit posed the question.

'Why should we suffer for your karma?' answered his parents.

'Why should we suffer for your karma?' answered his children.

'Why should I suffer for your karma?' answered his wife. 'Not even your scythe will share your fate since it was your hand that wielded it.'

He walked back in a daze. His fingers were clenching his scythe. Shattering its blade. Standing before the seven of them again, he stretched out his palms.

'I shed so much blood for them but my blood disowns me. Is there hope?'

'There's always hope for it lives in the smallest of things,' they replied. 'In the smallest of acts. In the smallest of words. Like Rama. We give you the divine word Rama. Keep chanting Rama and your soul will be purged.'

Lohajangha tried but failed.

'Mine is the tongue of a sinner,' he lamented. 'It cannot carry the weight of this word.'

'You cannot utter Rama but you can surely pronounce it backwards.'

'Backwards?'

'Mara. The reverse of Rama. Mara denotes death. You can surely say Mara for you have killed so many.'

The bandit spoke and it rolled off his tongue with ease.

'Keep chanting Mara again and again and you shall end up chanting Rama. So hallowed is this word that even uttering it in reverse will absolve you. Your name means one with an iron thigh. Show the universe now that you also possess an iron will.'

Lohajangha folded his hands. 'Who are you?'

'We are the Saptarishi.'

For fourteen years, the bandit chanted incessantly. Seven anthills covered his body, as if the elements were incubating him. When the Saptarishi arrived again and hacked the anthills, he emerged like a newborn from a womb.

'You are no longer Lohajangha,' they blessed him. 'You have unearthed your true self inside anthills or valmika. You shall now be called Valmiki and you shall write down the epic of Lord Rama.'

71

RAVANA SEIZES LANKA

One of the grandsons of Brahma, Sage Vishrava, had two wives. The first one, Ilavida, had given birth to a yaksha named Kubera. The second one, Kaikesi, was a demoness who had begotten four asuras. The younger ones were Vibhishana and Soorpanakha. The elder ones were Ravana and Kumbhakarna.

When Kubera came of age, he invoked the Creator and succeeded in propitiating him.

'What does your heart desire?' Brahma asked.

'Gold. Infinite gold.'

'Why gold?'

'I may have sprung from the seed of a sage, but I wish to be king. Ruler of a city made of gold.'

'The only place like that is Lanka.'

'Lanka?'

'Hewed out of solid gold. Sparkling by the ocean like fire mocking water. The island city crafted by Vishwakarma for the demons Mali and Sumali.'

'Sumali? Father of Mata Kaikesi?'

'Yes. But Sri Hari killed Mali and routed Sumali. Lanka needs a new king and I declare you its ruler.'

Vishrava and Ilavida were soon rejoicing, but Kaikesi's demonic blood was boiling.

'Shame on you!' she snapped at her sons. 'Look what Kubera has wheedled out of Brahma. A yaksha has become Lankeshwar. Lord of the richest city in Brahmanda, which once belonged to my father. You are blots on our asura race.'

'But he's our brother,' Vibhishana countered. 'Should we not celebrate his joy?'

'Not brother. Half-brother. And that means he loves you with only half a heart. And now that he is king, he will take only his parents with him to Lanka and leave us behind. Will you let that happen, Ravana?'

'Never.'

'Then own Lanka like my father once did. Wage a war like asuras. Breathe fire. Rain sulphur. Sharpen your nails and whet your steel.'

Vibhishana trembled. 'How can a mother speak like that? Have you suckled us with your milk or your blood?'

He refused to battle but Ravana and Kumbhakarna stormed the isle. Like the demons who coveted Swarga, these two brothers were craving Lanka. Alas, Kubera was unprepared for such an onslaught. His affection for his siblings was immense and this attack was wounding his heart. As the ocean turned red, he surrendered. Sailing away, he watched the brothers flying in his Pushpak Vimana. Toppling his yaksha flag and hoisting their asura one. Kubera prayed to Brahma again.

'I have lost all that I had earned. Was I not worthy of Lanka?'

'You were. Worthy of that and more. But this victory was predestined as Ravana is Jaya and Kumbhakarna is Vijaya. The sentinels of Vaikuntha who have reincarnated a second time to be killed by Sri Hari. Hence, I also blessed Ravana that he would win against you. All that gold shall soon blind him. He will sin and Lanka will burn.'

'But he is so wise.'

The Creator laughed. 'Because he has ten heads? I have four myself and that's not always emblematic of true wisdom. In Ravana's case, it only denotes that his pride shall be tenfold. He will continue snatching what does not belong to him and finally pay the price. He who has seized your wealth will be slain by someone who shall renounce all wealth.'

The half-brother's eyes were welling up. Brahma touched his forehead.

'Your heart beats even for your foes, Kubera, and that makes you noble. You had wished for infinite gold and I now declare you its deity. The god of wealth. Let Ravana keep Lanka. You shall be lord of all material abundance. Of bounty and prosperity. You shall forever inspire others to lay their hands on riches.'

'And also remind them how swiftly riches can change hands,' Kubera said and bowed.

72

THE GODS TRICK RAVANA

The ice was melting on Kailash. A mammoth pyre was blazing atop it as if Ravana had drilled a tunnel through Brahmanda and hellfire was surging up. The demon king had taken out his Chandrahas. That divine sword, shaped like a crescent moon, which Shiva had awarded him for his rendition of the Tandava Strotam.

Ravana chopped one of his heads now and flung it into the pyre.

The flames crackled louder. Ravana hacked another head. Then another and another and another. Nine of them were fuelling that inferno now. Blood was encrusting the Chandrahas. Kailash was reeking of burnt flesh. As the asura poised the blade above his last head, he heard the voice he had been craving for.

'Enough!'

The Destroyer was standing before him.

'What do you want?'

'You, lord. I want you in my Lanka.'

'From the mountain to the ocean?' Shiva smiled. 'From the snow here to the salt there? You tried that once before too.'

'Yes. I lifted the whole of Kailash to take you with me.'

'Because you were convinced that my abode was another Lanka that you could capture. But what happened?'

'You pressed your toe on the mountain and almost crushed me to death.'

'You failed that day, Ravana, and you shall fail again today.'

'But I am not talking about transporting you,' the asura said with folded hands. 'Just your symbol.'

'What symbol?'

'This lingam here that is on Kailash. Kindly allow me to install it by the sea at Lanka where waves shall forever anoint it.'

Shiva stood quiet as if he was mulling over his words. Then he struck his trident.

'You have my blessing. I give you what you desire and also restore your nine heads.'

Ravana was ecstatic. Gathering that enormous lingam in his arms, he began descending Kailash when the Destroyer spoke again.

'Just one condition.'

The demon king turned.

'You must not put that lingam down on the ground until you reach your isle. Carry it in your arms all the way to Lanka. If it touches the earth before you get home, it shall become rooted to that very spot and you will be unable to lift it again.'

Ravana agreed. Confident of his abilities, he began taking giant strides towards the south. The lingam was bearing down on him but his pace was not slowing. No sooner had he completed half the journey than the gods convened anxiously in heaven.

'Looks like he will make it,' Vayu whined.

'Does everyone realise what will happen if that lingam gets installed in Lanka?' Indra asked. 'That island will become invincible. That seashore will become immune to every force in the cosmos. Perhaps that is Ravana's intention or perhaps this is pure devotion. Either way, he shall become too powerful for an asura.'

Yama banged his fists. 'We have to make him put it down. But how?'

'How about tiring him out?' Chandra proposed. 'There's hardly any sweat on his skin.'

'Water can flow from other parts too,' Agni smirked. 'Varuna should know.'

'Me?'

'Aren't you the lord of water?'

'Sure.'

'And isn't there water in the lower regions of the body? Filthy water that violently demands to be let out.'

'Of course!'

'Clouds gathering within the belly and flesh rumbling until every warm drop is released?'

The gods were cackling. Varuna had grasped Agni's words. 'Brilliant. Let's see how long he can hold it.'

The water god twirled his fingers and right away Ravana felt the uncontrollable urge to urinate. He instantly hastened his steps, hoping that would soothe those pangs but they only flared up. The faster he walked, the faster water surged through his veins. Collected in his loins. The asura redoubled his speed. Then slowed down. Took a pause and resumed with caution. And yet, it was dawning on him now that he was losing this race. That torrent was beginning to push hard. A thought seized him that he could urinate as he walked but he banished it right away. Not only would that pollute his body but also amount to sacrilege as he was carrying a hallowed lingam. Ravana had run out of options. The river swelling inside him was threatening to spill over any moment now.

I have to stop ...

Flood everything in its path.

But the lingam?

He gasped. A lyre. Someone was walking towards him playing a lyre. Singing like a bird.

Narada?

Saffron robes. Matted hair.

It's Narada ...

The demon king bounded towards him.

'Melodious One! Melodious One! Pray, stop.'

'Lankapati?'

'Pray, listen to me. I need your help.'

Bouncing irritably on his feet, Ravana recounted everything as briefly as possible. By the time he finished, a grin was stretching across Narada's face.

'So, what do you want me to do?'

'I am bursting. Please hold this lingam until I am back and make sure it stays above the soil.'

'What makes you think I can carry it?'

'You can, Melodious One!'

'A body of flesh and blood is a weakling, Lankapati. So frail that it cannot uphold the weight of divinity. So flawed that it always crumbles before all that is immaculate.'

'I am sure you are strong enough.'

The demon king transferred his load and bolted behind the trees. As soon as he was out of sight, the Devarshi looked at the heavens and smiled.

The gods smiled back. 'Do it! Do it!'

'No rush,' Varuna assured them. 'I have devised that the asura's stream shall flow for a while.'

Narada touched his head to the lingam and gently placed it on the ground. He could hear the collective sigh from above.

'That was close.'

'Too close. Here comes Ravana!'

73

SITA LAYS FOUR CURSES

The river was watching Vishnu weep.

The Preserver had taken avatar as Rama. Crown prince of Ayodhya. Scion of Suryavansh. Sheshnaga had incarnated as Lakshmana, and Lakshmi as Sita. But like Kubera's stepmother, Kaikesi, Rama's stepmother, Kaikeyi, had also conspired and exiled him for fourteen years. Sita and Lakshmana had joined Rama and the three of them had been living as forest-dwellers for a while now. No hardship had wrung a tear from their eyes but today they had crumbled. News had come from Ayodhya that their father was no more.

King Dasharath was dead.

Both the sons were wailing now on the banks of Phalgu. The river had seen Surya thawing into her every evening as a puddle of red, but today, his descendants were melting. Tears from their eyes were flooding her bed. Threatening to turn her saline. Sita's voice stemmed that flow now.

'You are the eldest, Raghunandan. You must perform the last rites here by the river.'

The brothers picked themselves up and left to get the required materials. Hours went by but they did not return. Sita's eyes were trailing the parabola of the sun. It had begun to ascend higher and higher. Noon was approaching and the rituals had to be completed before Surya peaked. She got up.

I will have to do it myself with whatever we have ...

She bathed in the Phalgu and milked a cow. Plucked ketaki flowers and a banyan leaf. Prepared an oblation and lit a clay lamp. As soon as she made the offering, a cosmic voice reverberated.

'Bless you, Sita. I accept.'

'Father?'

'Yes, Sita. I am Dasharath. You have fulfilled the rites.'

'Have I?'

'You have. I am satisfied.'

'But both your sons are absent. They will never believe that I have completed the ritual.'

'They will. You have five witnesses.'

'Witnesses?'

'River Phalgu, because you did your ablutions in her. Agni, because you lit a lamp. The cow, the banyan and the ketaki flower. They shall all testify.'

Sita's fears soon came true when Rama and Lakshmana returned and rejected her claim outright. Both brothers found it hard to accept that the rites had been accomplished with such frugal means. She summoned her five witnesses now and Rama questioned them one by one.

'Tell me, O Revered Phalgu. Has my wife completed the ritual?'

'No, she hasn't.'

'Tell me, O Holy Cow. Has my wife completed the ritual?'

'No, she hasn't.'

'Tell me, O Sacred Agni. Has my wife completed the ritual?'

'No, she hasn't.'

'Tell me, O Fragrant Ketaki. Has my wife completed the ritual?'

'No, she hasn't.'

Four of them had denied her. Now remained the tree.

'Tell me, O Venerable Banyan. Has my wife completed the ritual?'

'She has.'

'She has?'

'Absolutely. Your father was satisfied.'

Sita was gazing at her husband's face, searching for something.

'Don't you believe me, my lord?'

Rama kept quiet.

'Don't you?'

'I do but others may not.'

Sitting down, he had barely begun the rites himself when Dasharath's voice resounded once more.

'Why are you invoking me again? Sita has already served me.'

'But her witnesses say she hasn't.'

'Whom will you believe, Rama? Others, or your wife?'

The prince grew quiet. He looked into Sita's eyes to find the same question staring at him.

Others, or your wife?

The brothers begged for her forgiveness. She pardoned them but cursed the four witnesses.

'You haven't changed, Ketaki. You are still that liar who lied for Brahmadeva. The truth today could have redeemed you, but you failed again. I curse you that you shall continue to remain unfit for worship as decreed by Mahadeva. I curse you, Phalgu, that you shall no longer flow on Earth but sink into the netherworld, hiding your face in shame. I curse you, Agni, that you must now consume everything poured into you. Not only what is pure but also what is impure. You can no longer make a choice. And since the cow too spoke a lie, I curse that the mouth of every cow shall henceforth be considered impure. Only you were truthful, O Banyan, and I bless you. You shall never shed your leaves but remain perennially green.'

That night, Sita questioned her husband again.

'I live in fear now, Raghunandan. You trusted those witnesses but not me. Tomorrow, if the world denounces me wrongly again, will you forsake your faith in me? Will you not stand by me? Will you not believe me?'

'I will, but others may not,' Rama closed his eyes.

74

MAYA SITA

A pair of eyes at the window were watching from inside the cottage.

Watching her and him standing on either side of that line. A line scrawled on the earth with the tip of an arrow. Cradling an invisible wall of fire that was not letting him enter. She was pleading with him to accept her offering but he was commanding her to step over the line. The pair of eyes were watching. Waiting. Wondering.

Will she? Won't she?

The eyes watched her move. Her feet rose above the line and landed on the other side. She had crossed over. She was standing right next to him now, but he was morphing. That ascetic was turning into an asura. Gripping her and dragging her. She was screaming. Her nails were gouging his face. Her teeth were gnawing at his arm. Her toes were clawing back towards that line. Desperate to take refuge behind it once more but in vain. The line had disowned her.

'Sita.'

The pair of eyes at the window turned towards the deity standing behind her.

'She's gone, Agnideva. Ravana has abducted her.'

'I know, Sita.'

'You say he shall remain blind to our deception?'

'He shall. Already blinded by so many things, Ravana will never realise whom he has carried off to Lanka.'

'Never realise that it is not me? Not Sita but Maya Sita? My replica conjured by you?'

'Yes. He came here as an illusion and has left with an illusion. Brahmanda will forever think that he captured you. Some will shed tears for you. Some will spew venom for you. They will write stories and sing songs about you. But only you shall know the truth. You and the gods.'

Sita gazed at her shadow. 'In another yuga, Sangya had created Chhaya. In this yuga, Sita needs a Maya. Sangya's husband was Surya. My husband is Suryavanshi. Sangya had abandoned her husband and now I, too, must stay away from mine.'

'Yes,' Agni nodded. 'Epochs change but events remain the same.'

'I wonder what I would have done if it had been me standing there.' Sita shifted her gaze outside again. 'Would I have obeyed him or obeyed that line? The universe will forever say now that Sita fell in Ravana's clutches because she violated the code. But did she not uphold another code that dictates that a guest is godlike? Did she not breach one dharma for the sake of another dharma? Did she not defy that line to dignify the hermit standing at her door? Did she not dishonour the line to honour that law? Would it not have been a transgression to not have transgressed that line? Which code of conduct would you place higher? Should she have obeyed Ravana or Lakshmana?'

Agni remained quiet. Sita walked towards the circle of fire that had generated Maya Sita.

'What now?'

'You shall remain hidden in these flames, Sita, until Ravana is vanquished. Once Rama liberates Maya Sita, she will pass through fire.'

'Why?'

'To prove that she's pure.'

She laughed. 'Sati entered fire because everyone called her husband unworthy. But Sita must enter fire to prove to everyone that she's worthy. My grandfather, Nimi, had given up his body. My father, Janaka, had

emerged from one who had renounced his body. But Sita stands defined by her body. She must walk through flames because she was abducted by another man. Because Rama believes her but others may not.'

'Because a trial by fire is the only way we can make the switch again,' Agni explained. 'Maya Sita will walk into these flames and you shall walk out.'

Months later, the exchange happened. Ravana was dead. Kumbhakarna was dead. The second lifetime of Jaya and Vijaya on Bhuloka had ended. Re-entering the fire, Maya Sita looked out to see Rama embracing Sita.

'I hope they never distrust her again. What I just went through was heinous. Nothing can be more degrading than proving your chastity in public as your husband watches helplessly. There can be no bigger shame.'

'There is.' Agni lowered his eyes. 'A shame far worse. A shame like no other.'

'I don't understand.'

'You will when you incarnate once more in Dwapar Yuga. You shall be empress in a Mayasabha. Born again from my flames, you shall be called Yagnaseni, but the world will remember you as Draupadi.'

'But what bigger shame will befall me?' Maya Sita shivered inside the fire.

'You shall see. We all shall see.'

75

RAMA AND THE SHUDRA

'King Rama! King Rama!'

An old Brahmin was tottering towards the throne with his son in his arms.

'You have killed my son, King Rama.'

The court of Ayodhya exploded. A babel of voices was swallowing it up. Rage. Confusion. Horror. Panic. This was not the first time that a Brahmin had accused a Kshatriya. But Rama? Suryavanshi Rama who had served fourteen years in exile for the sake of his father? Who had now exiled Sita for the sake of his people?

A killer?

As Rama bowed before the Brahmin, Sage Vashishtha frowned.

'Can you hear the impiety of your words?'

'Can you hear the enormity of my words? The king of Ayodhya has killed my son. My only son.'

Rama was staring at the old man's face. 'Your eyes! How blank your eyes are, Holy One. Your pain has robbed them of every single emotion. But I have never come across your child before. Are you certain that I have caused his death?'

'Without a doubt. My son was a healthy lad, but this morning he collapsed and died.'

'Collapsed?' Rama echoed. 'Then why do you hold me responsible?'

'Look at me and look at my son. He lies dead in adolescence while I stand alive at this ripe age. Why such an anomaly? Why this reversal of natural law where the young perish and the old live? Anarchy like this befalls only when the king of the land is at fault. Either you have sinned yourself or you have been unable to prevent someone else from sinning. As our monarch, both your action and inaction affect us equally. They touch everything that surrounds us and so I stand here accusing you.'

'He's right,' Vashishtha agreed. 'Such a strange occurrence should be traced back to the ruler. But Rama is beyond reproach. Someone else's actions are the cause here.'

'Find out,' the king commanded his men. 'Find out what took this boy's life.'

Spies were despatched. Inquiries were made. Vassals galloped in every direction and soon one of them returned in an alarmed state.

'It's Shambuka, sire.'

'Shambuka?'

'The Shudra. He's chanting the Vedas.'

Everyone froze. They were failing to process that information because those two words had never been uttered together before. Because those two words forever shunned each other.

Shudra chanting the Vedas ...

A chill had begun flowing through their veins.

Shudra chanting the Vedas ...

The enormity of it was dawning upon them now.

Shudra chanting the Vedas ...

'That's the sin festering in the heart of our land,' a minister hissed. 'That's what has snatched the poor boy's life.'

'Shudras are prohibited from austerities in this Treta Yuga,' Vashishtha concurred. 'Only in Kali Yuga can they carry them out. Shambuka has flouted the law. He must be stopped or many more could perish.'

'Sacrilege!' Others were gnashing their teeth. 'The actions of a Shudra have killed a Brahmin. What darker omens shall plague us now?'

'Death! Death! Death!' The court was reverberating with that word. 'Put that Shudra to death!'

Rama sat listening to the judgement of Ayodhya.

Death ... Death ... Death ...

He rode out. As he approached Shambuka, he could see him hanging upside down from a tree. Chanting the Vedas. Performing austerities. Ayodhya was screaming in his ears again.

Death ... Death ... Death ...

The Shudra had begun another mantra when Rama's voice rang out.

'Halt!

Shambuka blinked as the glare of that crown dazzled him.

'Hail, Scion of the Sun!'

'You are surely aware that Shudras are barred from austerities in this yuga.'

'I am, but I choose to ignore that. I desire to conquer heaven and this is the only way I can attain my goal.'

Rama inched closer. Ayodhya was screaming louder.

Death ... Death ... Death ...

'You made that choice, Shambuka, but someone else paid the price.'

'That Brahmin boy? Your vassal told me. Do you truly believe that I caused his death, sire? Can two fates be so inextricably twined?'

'Your actions are terrifying my people and may bring more harm to my land. As the sovereign, I must enforce the law. The whim of one cannot be above the welfare of many.'

'Is that why you banished your queen?'

'I did what a king had to do,' Rama replied. 'You may question my actions, but I am bound by my throne. By my people. By greater good, which is my only dharma. Which always demands a price. I do not rule. I only serve. I belong more to Ayodhya than to myself. You are disturbing the balance. Inverting the order like how you hang upside down. Challenging hierarchies that have been set in stone.'

'But is stone that enduring? Hadn't you once turned a slab of stone into a woman? You can surely uproot these laws, too.'

'Suryavanshis do not uproot. They uphold. Just as Suryadeva obeys the clouds that cover him. Obeys the moon that replaces him every night. You are violating social codes for selfish ends which I cannot allow.'

'But King Trishanku also belonged to your clan and he had the courage to flout. Like me, he too endeavoured to ascend towards the realm of gods.'

'And so he hangs in limbo. Heed my words, Shambuka, for you are transgressing like him. I command you to renounce this ritual. In return, you shall be provided for.'

'You cannot tempt me, sire. You can only slay me for in your eyes, a Shudra has dared to defy.'

Ayodhya was screeching.

Death ... Death ... Death ...

'You forget, Shambuka, that I had killed Ravana who was half Brahmin,' Rama stated. 'Do you not see the asura you too have become for your aspirations are endangering others? Creating a precedent that could breed more chaos?'

'Why must I care for others when others have never cared for me?'

Ayodhya burning his ears now.

Death ... Death ... Death ...

'So, you refuse?'

'I merely choose.'

Ayodhya possessing him now.

Death ...

The king unsheathed his sword and beheaded the Shudra.

76

AGASTYA TRICKS A MOUNTAIN

Once, while roaming through Earth, Narada passed the valley of Vindhyachal. The mountain greeted him, sprinkling petals of jasmine.

'Divine Devarshi, you honour me by setting foot upon my moss. Like Surya and Chandra, you remain forever on the move for the good of Brahmanda.'

'Yes. Forever drifting. Forever homeless. My destiny offers me no anchor.'

'I envy you for I do not possess that privilege. I stand rooted to a single spot and have seen nothing of the world beyond. None of the wonders that fill this universe. I stare at the same horizon every day and see the same dreams every night.'

'But that sounds so tranquil. Why must you complain?'

'For I have seen nothing else.'

'And I have nothing else to see.'

'Pray, enlighten me,' Vindhyachal pleaded. 'Tell me about your travels. What have you encountered? Where are you coming from?'

'I come from Mount Sumeru. The pillar of Brahmanda.'

'Sumeru. I have heard the name. Is it as majestic as it sounds?'

'Even more,' Narada said, smiling. 'No other mountain has the splendour of Sumeru. Flowers of such colour and smell that even the garden of Indra burns with jealousy. Fruits dripping with such nectar that even the gods have never relished. The sun there is never harsh and the moon splashes it with the whitest milk.'

'And how tall is it? As tall as me?'

'Taller. Much taller. Certainly the tallest among all mountains.'

Narada departed but Vindhyachal could hardly sleep a wink that night. It kept mulling over the Devarshi's words. Questioning them. Loathing them. Rejecting them. Repeating them. Caught in an endless loop of one versus the other. Was Sumeru indeed that unmatched? Were its peaks that immense? Were the three realms serenading Sumeru while it lay abandoned here? Vindhyachal quivered.

This has to change ...

Hours later, as Surya woke up and began encircling the Earth, his chariot came to a sudden halt. Its wheels were no longer moving ahead. The god rubbed his sleepy eyes and stared. His horses were neighing. Kicking at a gigantic wall of stone that seemed to have sprouted overnight. Had Brahma hung a new planet, he wondered? Or created an asteroid belt? Then the truth hit him.

Vindhyachal had made itself soar as high as the sky.

'What have you done?' the sun screamed. 'You are blocking my path.'

'I realise that, but I am helpless,' the mountain tittered. 'Every being in Brahmanda has the right to rise. To better one's condition. I am doing the same.'

'You have every right to aspire but not at the cost of others. Your peaks are hampering natural law. Preventing me from charting my course. Why must Bhuloka suffer for your delusion?'

'Not delusion. Ambition. Someone informed me that Sumeru was superior to me. But not anymore. I am the tallest now. The mountain supreme.'

'Fool. Your body has stretched but your mind has shrunk. You can only be great if you have an equally large heart. Sumeru is not celebrated for its height but its humility. For its soul that breathes even inside that stone. But you are acting like a danava who only tends to himself. This pride that has made you soar had once caused me to plunge. It will not make you paramount but rob whatever merit you have.'

Despite Surya's words of caution, the mountain did not move. With the sun's path now obstructed, chaos ensued. Time stood still, caught between a never-ending day and a never-ending night. One half of Earth was melting, while the other was turning into ice. Excessive light was blinding one half, while pitch darkness was blinding the other. Water was vaporising in half the world and freezing in the other half. As life started to perish, the gods turned to Vishnu.

'Vindhyachal's peaks have swollen with pride,' the Preserver said. 'It does not see that Surya can burn a hole through its body but he's being kind.'

'He's being wise, too, by not doing so,' the devas concurred. 'Vindhyachal shelters not only humans but many forms of animal life. Contains shrines and valuable resources. Destroying it would be wrong. The mountain must lower its height. There's no other solution.'

'What cannot be destroyed can surely be duped,' Vishnu advised. 'Go to Agastya.'

'Agastya?'

'The tiniest of minds can often thwart the biggest of bodies. His wisdom shall clear that path.'

At the behest of the gods, the sage made his way to Vindhyachal at once and addressed it.

'I salute you, O Mount! You rise so high that you seem to hold the very heavens above. Clouds anoint you and stars wreathe a tiara for your head. Truly, you are the loftiest in Brahmanda.'

The mountain beamed. 'You are kind, Sage Agastya. And you honour me by speaking the truth. How can I repay you?'

'I am travelling south. Given my old age, I can barely climb your towering slopes. Could you bring yourself down for me and remain in that lowered state until I am back again? I will return soon, and then you may once more raise yourself up.'

The devas watched as Vindhyachal diminished. Its peaks were coming down, unaware that they were kneeling before the brilliance of Agastya. As the mountain shrank, Surya galloped. The wheels turned once more and light diffused through Bhuloka. Life was reopening its eyes. Time was no longer in a limbo.

'Come back soon,' the mountain told Agastya.

'Indeed. Wait for me in this position. I will be back.'

But the sage never returned. He made the south his home and established his hermitage there.

And Vindhyachal kept waiting.

Narada is still wandering. Sumeru is still humble. Surya is still nurturing.

And Vindhyachal is still waiting for Agastya!

77

DADHICHI OFFERS HIS BONES

Gurur Brahma ... Gurur Vishnu ... Gurur Devo Maheshwara ...

The words were haunting Indra. The mantra that proclaimed that the one who taught was as godly as the gods. That even the teacher was a triumvirate. Creator of knowledge. Preserver of wisdom. Destroyer of ignorance. Worthy of the highest affection and submission. But Indra had offered neither. When the guru of the gods, Brihaspati, had entered his palace, the Devaraja had not even acknowledged him. Frolicking in water with his apsaras, he had ignored the guru's presence. Brihaspati had left and no one had seen him again. Surya had looked during the day and Chandra had searched all night. Indra had scoured the very rim of the universe but to no avail. Their guru had deserted them and the gods were panicking. The Devaraja now stood shamefaced before Brahma.

'Do you ever learn?' the Creator fumed. 'Or are you convinced that, as the ruler of heaven, you can get away with anything?'

'Let's locate Brihaspati first. You can rebuke me later.'

'He is nowhere to be found. We must look at alternatives now.'

'Anyone in particular?'

'Vishrupa.'

'The three-headed son of Sage Twastha?'

'Yes. He's mastered many arts, including the Vaishnavi Vidya. Appoint him as the new guru.'

'Will he be good for us?' Indra asked.

'If you are good to him,' Brahma quipped.

Vishrupa consented and soon proved to be an able guru, securing many victories for the devas. Alas, one small detail had escaped everyone's notice. Vishrupa's father was a sage but his mother was a daitya. With half his blood demonic, half his loyalty was also reserved for that clan. Indra soon discovered that their guru was cutting deals with the foe. Leaking vital information. Even sharing his Vaishnavi Vidya with them. The Devaraja charged. His guilt over Brihaspati and his rage towards Vishrupa now merged to overpower him.

Three strokes of his Vajra and the guru's three heads lay severed. One became a francolin, another one a partridge and the third one a sparrow.

Brahmanda watched as Sage Twastha approached his son's corpse. Struck the ground with his toe and ignited fire. Gathered Vishrupa's heads and began a yagna most terrible. As soon as he offered the three birds, darkness swallowed the sky. The flames were burning brighter. Crackling louder for they were in labour. Their loins were trembling. Pushing out what Twastha had generated. A demon too terrifying to behold. Towering like a burnt hill.

'Vritrasura,' the sage screamed. 'The devas have slaughtered my son. Indra's Vajra beheaded him thrice.'

'And yet your eyes shed no tears?'

'Not a drop. Go forth now. Just as my tears have dried up, go and dry all the water in the universe. Let all of creation wilt and wither.'

The four elements shuddered as Vritrasura pounced upon the fifth one. Sucked the cosmos dry, imprisoning all the water inside him. Captured every drop of rain that belonged to Indra. The Devaraja charged but his Vajra could not even nick the demon's hide. As throats dried up everywhere, the gods assembled.

'Water!' Indra folded his hands before the trinity. 'We must reclaim water or everything shall cease to exist.'

Brahma sighed. 'Seems impossible. You angered a sage long ago and an ocean had to be churned. You have angered another one now and all the oceans have been abducted. Even your mighty Vajra recoiled in fear.'

'Then we need something more potent,' Vishnu glanced at Shiva.

'More potent than my Vajra?' the Devaraja gasped.

Shiva nodded. His tongue uttered a single name.

'Dadhichi.'

The name dropped in their minds like a pebble in a pond. Creating ripples that were reawakening memories long asleep. Dadhichi and Kshuva. That fight. That resurrection. That boon and that curse.

'Of course,' Brahma's four mouths echoed. 'To help him defeat Kshuva, Mahadeva had made Dadhichi's bones mightier than your Vajra.'

Vishnu nodded. 'Asthidaan. We must harvest his bones and Vishwakarma must fashion a weapon from them. The fire of his body alone can bring the waters back.'

The devas immediately descended upon Dadhichi's hermitage. Tears trickled down the sage's face when he heard what they wanted. Tears of absolute bliss.

'It's so simple. So clear.'

'What, Revered One?' they asked.

'I have been wondering why yugas were passing but I was not dying. Now I know. The universe was keeping me alive for this. This death that shall give others life.'

Indra touched his feet. 'Brahmanda shall never forget your sacrifice. The error was mine, but you are paying for it by donating yourself.'

'Who am I to donate anything, Devaraja? I am only giving back what I had been granted. Our cosmos is nothing but a barter of energies. We borrow and then we must ultimately return.'

Dadhichi sat down cross-legged. As soon as he closed his eyes, his flesh caught fire. His psychic energy had sparked that combustion. His soul was devouring his body. Leaving behind only bones. His limbs were melting but his eyes were twinkling. The gods heard his voice for the last time as it wafted joyously through those flames.

'So simple ... so clear ...'

The ashes were glinting as if powered by a strange occult. Indra picked up a piece of his spine.

Adamantine ...

His fingers were confirming Brahma's words.

Mightier than your Vajra ...

The weapon crafted from these bones soon tore through Vritrasura's belly. Plunged deep inside him to release all the waters. As that stream gushed out, so did his life. The demon was dead. Brahmanda was green again. Brishaspati also returned now and celebrations erupted in Swargaloka. But Indra was nowhere to be seen. The devas looked and so did the danavas. His wife, Indrani, searched and so did his Airavata. Even the stars looked everywhere but found not a trace.

Indra had vanished.

78

NAHUSHA BECOMES DEVARAJA

'I have found Indra,' Brahma announced one day.

The gods cheered. They had been searching every peak and pit in Brahmanda for him. Probing the five elements and the ten directions. The Devaraja would always lead the celebrations when a demon would fall. He would drink the most and laugh the loudest. And yet, despite having trounced Vritrasura, he was nowhere to be seen.

'Where is he, Param Pita?' Surya asked.

'Indra has exiled himself. Remorse over what he has done is gnawing at his soul and he is seeking penance.'

'Penance?' Varuna frowned. 'He slew a demon who had become a threat to the universe. Why is he condemning himself?'

'Not for Vritrasura. For the death of Dadhichi.'

'But Dadhichi only fulfilled his destiny,' Agni argued.

'Indra is blaming himself for it. Agonising over how selflessly Dadhichi sacrificed all that he had while he himself always clung to Indraloka. He told me that the smoke from the sage's remains has filled his lungs and he can no longer breathe. This is perhaps the first time that guilt is racking the Devaraja. Beheading Vishrupa has also traumatised him.'

'The guru was betraying us all. Despite his allegiance towards us, he was aiding the demons.'

'He was a Brahmin. The Vedas warn that killing a Brahmin is one of the gravest sins possible and Indra knows that. He remembers how even Mahadeva had to cleanse himself in Kashi because he had severed one of my heads, which amounted to Brahmahatya. Indra showed me his Vajra and wept that it still reeks of Vishrupa's blood. He has fallen in his own eyes.'

'If we talk to him, we can surely persuade ...'

'No,' the Creator asserted. 'Indra has lost his will to rule. Someone will have to take his place.'

He was glancing at them one by one. The devas realised what Brahma was thinking and began excusing themselves.

'I have to cover the whole circumference of Earth every day,' Surya whined. 'I hardly have time for matters of heaven.'

'I stay awake all night and sleep all day,' Chandra reminded them. 'It cannot be me.'

'Keeping a record of each and every death is highly taxing,' Yama said, shaking his head. 'How can I burden myself with anything more?'

'And we are the elements,' Vayu, Agni and Varuna chorused. 'If we occupy ourselves with ruling, who shall sustain Brahmanda?'

The other deities also displayed various degrees of helplessness. Indra's seat was an exalted one and none of them was willing to take charge of it. Brahma turned towards Brihaspati.

'What now?'

'When heaven offers no answer, one must look to Earth.'

'A man? A mortal to lord over immortals?'

'Since the divine find themselves inadequate, we have to choose from humans.'

'It sounds like you have already chosen someone.'

The guru nodded. 'Nahusha.'

No sooner had he spoken than all eyes swung towards Chandra. He was standing transfixed. Elation and confusion were latching on to his face.

'Nahusha? My Nahusha?'

'Yes. The Chandravanshi king. Progeny of Ila and Budh and grandson of Pururava.'

'Is he worthy?'

'He has accomplished a hundred Ashwamedha Yagnas. Wisdom dictates his mind and justice rules his heart. Bhuloka is flourishing under him and so will Indraloka.'

The moonbeams turned a brighter shade of white. That name now had become a euphoric chant among the devas.

Nahusha ... yes ... Nahusha ...

Soon, a delegation headed by Chandra landed in the monarch's court. Nahusha trembled when he heard what the gods were offering him and coiled around his patriarch's feet.

'Every evening I walk up to my roof to perform Chandra Namaskar. To venerate you who is the sovereign of the night sky. Progenitor of my clan. How can I rule over you? Over all of you?'

But the moon held his hand and soothed his fears. Told him it was morality and not mortality that mattered. The trinity crowned him and the universe rejoiced.

'Hail Nahusha! Devaraja Nahusha!'

The king soon proved to be an ideal replacement for Indra. He was safeguarding Swarga and overpowering asuras. The gods were pleased and the sages content. Alas, just as Chandra wanes after waxing, so did Nahusha. His conscience began to fade. His virtues began to ebb. Pride was now flooding his heart and it no longer held reverence for anyone. Neither for the moon god nor for the devas. Not even for Brahma, Vishnu and Shiva. Proclaiming his dynasty as the sole masters of Indraloka, he even declared that his son, Yayati, would be the next Devaraja. Losing more and more of himself, the darkness finally devoured Nahusha when he laid eyes on Indrani in her garden. The wife of Indra.

'You are mine and you shall make love to me,' he hissed.

'My devotion is only towards my Devaraja,' she countered. 'I can love no one else.'

'I am Devaraja now. His throne is mine and so is his bed.'

'One's wife is not an object that changes ownership. You may have replaced Devaraja everywhere but not in my heart. Stay away or your fate shall be like that of Ravana.'

Despite being spurned, Nahusha kept making advances and even tried invading her chamber at night. Finding herself in peril, Indrani now turned to Brihaspati.

'You promised us a flower but you have planted a thorn,' she wailed. 'Will you sit here and watch me bleed?'

'It's this throne, O Queen. Perhaps it blinds whoever occupies it.'

The guru had been observing Nahusha. Observing how he had poisoned everything that he had achieved. How his humanity had buckled under the load of this divine authority. Time had come to get rid of him. He wiped Indrani's eyes and whispered something in her ears.

Her face lit up. 'Will it work?'

Brihaspati smiled. That evening, an envoy reached Nahusha's palace and bowed before him.

'A message from Indrani?' The king exulted. 'What does she say?'

'The queen regrets her behaviour. She seeks your pardon and hopes that you will accept her.'

'Of course!'

'She is at Guru Brihaspati's abode and has requested you to come and fetch her.'

'Right away!' He clutched the man's hand. 'Let's go.'

'Not like this, sire. You will need to make preparations.'

'What preparations?'

'The queen has another small request. She wants you to arrive in the grandest manner possible. A magnificence that befits the Devaraja.'

'I shall come on a bedecked Uchchaishrava.'

'Loftier than that.'

'Airavata then.'

'Even more lavish.'

Nahusha frowned. 'What does she have in mind?'

'The queen wishes to see you arrive in a golden palanquin carried by eight wise sages.'

'And so she will.'

Soon, mounds of gold were procured and a palanquin was fashioned with eight sides. That bright metal outside encased dark silk inside. On the appointed day, Nahusha entered the vehicle and the sages hoisted it up. Eight sages were carrying a side each of that octagon. As the palanquin moved like a gilded star through the sky, its motion began lulling the king to sleep. He was dreaming now. Dreaming that he was making love to Indrani. Licking her lips. Fondling her bosom. Sucking her navel. Their fingers and toes were intertwining as he was thrusting himself into her. Deeper and deeper. Faster and faster. Their nails were digging. Their tongues were fastening into a knot. Deeper and deeper. Faster and faster. Their bodies were melting into a puddle of sweat. Deeper and deeper. Faster and faster. His loins were throbbing now as a river began swelling inside them. Deeper and deeper. Faster and faster. Surging violently to race towards that sweet release. Deeper and deeper. Faster and faster. Just about to pour into her when the palanquin suddenly tilted, jolting him awake.

'Fools!' Nahusha blared. 'Have you forgotten how to walk?'

'It's Agastya,' a sage protested. 'He's short and we keep losing balance. He's also slowing us down.'

That heady rush of blood had inflamed the king. Sticking his leg out, he kicked Agastya.

'Faster! Faster! Or I shall whip you dead!'

The ruse had worked. The king had done the unthinkable. Already reeling under the ignominy of being a human mule, Agastya now turned and pronounced a curse.

'You, Nahusha, are no longer worthy of being Devaraja. No longer worthy of paradise or this human form. I curse you to fall from heaven. Fall like Trishanku but find no refuge midway. Land on earth and turn into a python for all eternity.'

The effect was instant. Nahusha slipped from the palanquin and began plunging towards Bhuloka. As he fell, his limbs shrivelled and his head morphed. His skin turned into scales and his teeth became fangs. No sooner had the reptile landed on earth than music reverberated throughout heaven. Indra had returned. Indrani had found him hiding in a lotus inside the Manasarovar Lake and had convinced him to reclaim his throne. He became Devaraja again and the universe forgot Nahusha. Only Agastya remembered. A few days later, he came across the python shedding tears under a full moon. The sage was touched and he alleviated his curse.

'Years from now, you shall encounter a man who will teach you what being a ruler truly means. That day you shall regain your human form.'

'How will I identify him?' the serpent asked. 'What will be his name?'

'Yudhishthira.'

79

KACHA STEALS A SECRET

The Divine Council in Swargaloka had convened at Brihaspati's behest. It had been a while since their guru had summoned them and his face today was especially grim. The devas were listening now as his long monologue boiled down to a single word.

Mritasanjivani ...

'So, you are proposing that we must steal this secret of reviving the dead from the asuras?' Indra asked.

'Yes.'

'But why? What good has Mritasanjivani done for them? Hiranyaksha. Hiranyakashipu. Taraka. Raktabija. Mahishasura. Vritrasura. All these demons have perished one after the other.'

'Mritasanjivani is not only about bringing asuras back to life,' the guru explained. 'It is also about keeping the fear alive that they possess such a power. Keeping that threat alive in our minds forever. It's a psychological weapon of the highest order and we must neutralise it now. Once the demons realise that we have stolen Mritasanjivani, it will be an assault on their minds, too, and there will be far fewer battles to fight.'

The Devaraja nodded. 'But only Shukracharya knows that secret. How do we steal it from him?'

'I have thought of something. And someone.'

Days later, a young man made his way to Shukracharya's hermitage and requested to be his disciple. The guru tied a thread around his wrist and put a mark on his forehead. Fed him the sacrament of the demons, unaware that he was none other than Brihaspati's son. That he was there to rob his hallowed secret. As the young man stepped out, he found a comely pair of eyes gazing at him.

He smiled. 'I am Kacha. His new disciple.'

Her eyes lowered. 'I am Devayani. His daughter.'

Not long after, she had etched his name on her heart. Every morning, Kacha would sing hymns by Devayani's window to wake her up. Every evening, he would bring her wild flowers from the woods nearby. And every night, Brihaspati would appear stealthily in his room and ask the same question.

'Do you have it, Kacha?'

'Not yet, father. But the guru's daughter is falling deeper and deeper in love with me.'

Soon, Kacha was convinced that Devayani was completely under his spell. Time was ripe to formulate a plan but ideas were evading him. He needed an extreme turn of events, for only that would make Shukracharya yield the secret. Lighting lamps at dusk, he saw the demons preparing wine. As the liquor brewed, they burnt a deer and added all of its ashes to the guru's drink. Watching Shukracharya gulp that wine, a thought now tore through Kacha's brain. A thought so ghastly that he collapsed on the floor. His body was convulsing. His heart was pounding. His senses were questioning if he was desperate enough to take such a risk. Begging him to abandon it right away. But Kacha knew that it was the only ruse possible. The only ruse that would work because the asuras loathed Brihaspati. Because Shukracharya loved his wine. He nodded.

Because Devayani loves me as much as she loves her father ...

Not more ...

Not less ...

As much ...

His mind was racing now. The plan would be activated in three stages. While he would control the first two, the third one would be entirely in Devayani's hands. Kacha was almost tempted to take her into confidence but decided against it. Her ignorance was going to be more valuable than her allegiance. Her love for him would take care of the rest. He stood up. It was time to join the demonic orgy. Time to trade information.

One secret for another ...

Liquor was flowing and flesh was roasting. Some were dancing while others were copulating. Kacha picked up a bowl of wine. Pretending to be intoxicated, he whispered to a daitya.

'Shall I reveal a secret?'

'Tell me.'

'I am the son of the great Brihaspati. Guru of the gods.'

The demon choked on his drink. It was bubbling out of his nose. He was flaring with rage. Turning around, he poured those words into the ears of a second asura. The second one grabbed a third one. Then a fourth one. Fifth one. Sixth one. Kacha was watching as his secret flowed from one demon to another, igniting them all. By the end, an inferno of red eyes and fuming breaths was closing in on him. As they reached for his throat, their guru thundered, 'Halt!'

'He is enemy blood,' they growled. 'We shall tear him from limb to limb.'

'You shall do no such thing.'

'But he has deceived us. Concealed his identity. Who knows what mystery lies inside him? Why do you stop us?'

'Because here in my hermitage, he is under my care. When I agreed to tutor him, I also made an unspoken pact to keep him safe. That thread I have tied on his wrist binds me to protect him. Besides, becoming someone's disciple is also like taking a new birth. Embrace him as one of your own.'

The asuras dispersed but Devayani now confronted Kacha in his room. Pain and fury were oozing from her every pore. Already anticipating this, he began to appease her. To amuse her. Devayani ran out giggling. Her body calmed. Her heart comforted. Lying down, the young man knew that sleep would elude him tonight.

Time for the second stage ...

As soon as dawn broke, Kacha offered to graze Shukracharya's horses. Entering deep into the wilderness, he stopped. Stood still. He was waiting. Looking out for something he hoped was coming after him. Wondering if it would play out just as he had plotted. He had seen their anger and he was now yearning to see them act upon it. The sun had begun to climb the spine of the sky. The herd was falling asleep but his eyes were awake. Watching. Waiting. Then he heard a twig crack.

They are coming ...

Kacha instantly started piling up branches and grass. As he kindled that heap, the footsteps grew louder.

They are close ...

The fire was seething now. Bodies were surrounding him.

They are here ...

Kacha did not look up at their faces. He was only staring at their feet inching closer. Their nails hungering for his flesh. Their blades thirsting for his blood. As that circle tightened around him, it blotted out the sun. He could no longer breathe. His body was quaking but his soul was rhapsodic. All that he had set in motion was falling into place. Every element was playing its part, unaware that he had devised it all. The universe was bending to his will as if he was god. He was going to die and yet not die as if he was god.

Die and yet not die ...

As night descended, it saw Devayani staggering through the forest. Her fingers were clutching a piece of burnt cloth. Clutching it tighter as she stood before her father.

'Kacha's cloth?' Shukracharya gaped. 'What are you saying?'

'Your asuras have killed him. Hacked him and burnt him.'

'How dare they flout my command? I won't spare them. I shall ...'

He paused. Devayani was cackling. Her tears were gushing and yet she was laughing.

'You? You won't spare them, father? You who have gulped down my Kacha?'

The guru froze. Four of his daughter's words had rendered him catatonic.

gulped down ...

my Kacha ...

Advancing close to his face, she scraped a black speck from his lips.

'Yes. I love him. But the demons put his ashes in your wine and you have drunk him up.'

Shukracharya closed his eyes in horror. A moment later, he spoke again.

'I pronounce now that henceforth woe shall befall the Brahmin who consumes wine. It shall be the worst of sins as both virtue and wisdom will desert him in that inebriated state. And when his stupor ends, he shall be holding nothing but regret. What do I do, Devayani? I have failed to keep Kacha safe.'

'You know what you have to do.'

'Mritasanjivani?'

'Right now.'

'If it pleases you,' the guru assented as his voice turned hollow. 'But he is inside me. If I revive him, he must rip through my body.'

'Rip through your body?'

'As a butterfly bursts through a cocoon. Kacha can only emerge by tearing my body asunder. And I am willing.'

She shrank. Blinded by her loss, she had not realised what she was asking for. Kacha's life was demanding another life.

Her father's life ...

'I am willing, Devayani.'

The calm on Shukracharya's face was terrifying her more than Kacha's death. She slumped at his feet.

'Never! Never say that, father. I cannot exist without you. You are my source. I began with you but I must end with Kacha. I want both of you alive for I love you both equally. Not more. Not less.'

'That can no longer be. You must choose.'

'How can I?'

'Him or me?'

Devayani rose. Her eyes were suddenly gleaming. Her voice whispering.

'Not him or you, father. I can have you both.'

'How is that possible?'

'Give me the Mritasanjivani. Once Kacha emerges from your insides, I will resurrect you too with the mantra.'

Shukracharya felt as if icy fingers had clutched his heart. A penance of one thousand years had earned him that secret and he had locked it deep inside himself. But his daughter was asking for it now. And asking a question.

'Don't you trust me, father?'

He had told her to make a choice. Now she was asking him to choose.

To share or not to share ...

The guru nodded. 'I shall write it down. But you must use it yourself. And once you are done, you must destroy it.'

'I will.'

'Destroy it completely.'

'Yes, father.'

'We share many things, Devayani, and we shall now share Mritasanjivani, too. It must not fall in anyone else's hands. Promise me that.'

'I promise.'

Shukracharya closed his eyes again. He was chanting. His right hand was scrawling. Strange words. Mystical phrases. It was as if his arm had become a conduit and the secret within him was flowing furiously through it. Getting deposited line by line for her to read. He stopped. She was gazing at Mritasanjivani.

The pride of asuras ...

The boon of Shiva ...

Shukracharya's belly was trembling now. Faster. Wilder. Now his bosom. His face. Arms and thighs. Everything was pulsating as if a tempest was bulging inside him. Devayani recoiled as a spurt of blood splashed across her cheek. The mantra had reanimated the ash. Kacha's finger was emerging out of the guru's left eye, his nail piercing the eyeball. Now a toe was erupting through his navel. More digits were surfacing here and there. As Shukracharya bled, Kacha's face burst through the guru's skull. His torso was cracking its way through the guru's ribs. His arms were shattering his spine and his legs, his loins. Devayani was watching the old one cave as the young one rose now as if tearing through a womb. Standing naked atop a mass of flesh and bone. Drenched in the guru's slime.

'Kacha!'

She clasped him. She was watching him smile like he had never smiled before. Watching his eyes glint like they had never glinted before. Unaware that she had just completed what he had begun.

'I must bring father back to life now.'

'Let me do it,' he extended his hand.

Devayani backed away, hiding the mantra behind her. 'I must do this myself. Father's secret cannot be shared with anyone.'

'Anyone?' Kacha contorted his face. 'Am I anyone?'

'I have given him my word that only I ...'

He inched closer. 'I am you. You are me.'

His voice was paralysing her.

'The guru has brought me back to life. Let me do the same for him.'

His eyes were peering into hers. Devayani's fingers loosened their grip and the mantra fell. Kacha swooped.

Mritasanjivani ...

Nestling in his hands now. Causing his palms to tingle.

As he read out the mantra over Shukracharya's remains, his mind began to swallow it. Each word. Each line. Every syllable. All of it was getting engraved inside him. By the time Kacha finished, Mritasanjivani had become a part of him.

'Father!'

The guru was standing before them. As he took a step towards Devayani, he stopped. He was staring at Kacha's hand. Staring at the mantra he was holding. Looking up, he caught the twinkle in Kacha's eyes.

He has learnt Mritasanjivani ...

He had come for Mritasanjivani ...

He turned to look at his daughter. There was no fury on his face. Only ache. An enormous ache. Devayani was gazing at him with perplexed eyes. The next moment, Shukracharya collapsed. The young man was walking away.

'Kacha!' She ran after him. 'I have told father about us. Speak to him so we can get married.'

He frowned. 'You still don't understand, do you?'

Now. She saw it now. Saw what she had seen on her father's face. What her father had seen on Kacha's face. The word fell from her mouth.

'Mritasanjivani?'

'I got what my father, Brihaspati, sent me here for.'

Devayani touched Shukracharya's blood streaking her face and gaped at her fingers.

'You made me betray my father so you could fulfil the wish of your father? How could you be so vile?'

'If I was vile, Brahmanda would have curbed me.'

A deluge of tears was flowing from her eyes now as she asked, 'You came for the mantra but didn't you also find me? Didn't you also find love?'

'I only found a friend. A beautiful friend. I never made any other promises, Devayani.'

'But you said you are I and I am you?'

'Yes. Reborn from Guru Shukracharya, I am also his child now, like you are. Don't you see? Having emerged from his body, I have now become his son. And that makes you my sister. How can I tarnish this bond?'

As he took a step, her words gored him from behind.

'I curse you, Kacha. I curse you that you will be unable to use this secret you have stolen from us.'

He paused. Turned and snarled.

'I shall impart it to others then and it will fructify in them. And I curse you back, Devayani. You shall never find the love you seek.'

80

DEVAYANI AND SHARMISHTHA

The demons had now chosen Vrishaparva as their new ruler and Shukracharya crowned him in a glittering ceremony. Soon, the king's daughter, Sharmishtha, and the guru's daughter, Devayani, forged a friendship. So tender was their bond that many would wonder if they had been sisters in another birth. As they shared each other's laughter and tears, the wound of Kacha's betrayal also began to heal inside Devayani. Alas, the powers above resent such peace. Back to his wily ways, Indra now decided to pull a prank when both women went bathing in a pond. Turning himself into a wayward breeze, he exchanged their garments lying on the banks. As a result, they ended up in each other's attire.

'Not bad,' Sharmishtha tittered. 'You could almost pass off for a princess.'

'I would rather remain Shukracharya's daughter,' Devayani seemed to have taken offence. 'Rulers may have power but sages have wisdom.'

'Are you saying my father is inferior to yours? How can you forget that your whole hermitage thrives on his generosity? His untold bounty?'

'The king does no favour. My father is Asuracharya. Guru of your clan. And the gods themselves have decreed that a teacher is above everyone else.'

Voices rose and tempers too. The love for their fathers had suddenly displaced the love they had for each other. Their castes had begun overpowering their hearts as they kept belittling each other. Reaching a boiling point, the pair came to blows now. Their nails were scratching and their teeth were biting. Hair was being pulled and bodies were being pushed. Soon the asura princess gained an upper hand and flung Devayani into a well. As she crashed into that pool of water, Sharmishtha walked away shrieking, 'Die, wretch, die!'

But Devayani's fate was kinder than her friend. Moments later, a young man stopped by the well, thirsting for a sip. As he peered inside, her voice leapt towards him. Her screams were echoing within those cylindrical walls. Soon, she was back on ground and thanking her saviour.

'What's your name, kind sir?'

'King Yayati.'

'Yayati? Son of Nahusha who once ruled over heaven?'

'Yes. Son of Nahusha who now wriggles on Earth.'

They were speaking no more. Only gazing into each other's eyes. Soon, news reached Shukracharya that his daughter and the Chandravanshi ruler were desirous to wed each other. The guru got them married and even soothed away the king's doubts about taking a Brahmin wife. But his rapture gave way to rage when Devayani revealed how she had landed in the well.

'Call Sharmishtha!' he bellowed. 'Call that father of hers.'

Hearing what the princess had done, Vrishaparva fell at Shukracharya's feet. He was quivering with fear. Pleading for mercy. Offering the guru and Devayani all his riches but in vain. The time for words had passed. It was time to punish.

'Go ahead,' the asura king bowed before the Chandravanshi queen. 'My daughter shall abide by whatever you command.'

Devayani glared at her friend. 'It's my turn now to hurl you down but I won't need a well for that. I am royalty now and you shall be a commoner. You shall come with me to my palace and work as my maid.'

Sharmishtha smiled.

'Do you hear me? As my maid.'

But she was still smiling. Smiling when Devayani wrenched off her jewels and handed her rags. Smiling when she arrived at the Chandravanshi kingdom to serve. Smiling when her mistress would abuse her every day. Smiling when the city would fall asleep every night. The queen began to wonder.

Why does Sharmishtha smile?

Soon, Devayani gave birth to two sons. The capital rejoiced as Yayati held up his babies for all to see. Five years passed and it was time now for their Vidyarambha ceremony. The formal initiation into education. Priests were consecrating their foreheads and multitudes were raining flowers. As the queen watched, she saw Sharmishtha approaching. Her pace was fierce. Her face fiercer. Climbing up the royal altar, she bared her bosom.

'Won't you anoint them too?'

Everyone gasped. Devayani sprang.

'Babies?'

'They are mine.'

'Three babies?'

'My sons.'

The queen struck her savagely. 'You whore! How dare you pollute this altar with your filth? How dare you bear children when you are nobody's wife? Was it not enough that you sinned that you now make a public display of it? I shall have you stoned to death. Have this bastard litter trampled under horses and ...'

'A bastard is one who is unaware of his father,' Sharmishtha cut through. 'I know who begot my sons.'

'Show me,' Devayani looked at the crowd.

'Not there,' she said, laughing. 'He stands behind you. Stands silent while the world reviles me.'

The queen turned. The gathering recoiled.

Yayati ...

'The scion of Chandravansha,' Sharmishtha declared. 'He who pulled you out of that well held my hand too. Your husband is my husband too. We share the same seed. When you call my children foul, you abuse your own sons as well. Abuse that same royal blood.'

Devayani had frozen like a pillar of ice. Her tongue scorched Yayati.

'Is she speaking the truth? Have you married her and fathered these sons?'

'I have.'

Sharmishtha advanced and held the king's hand. 'I had told him that since you owned me, he could own me too. He has loved me every day since then. And every night.'

Her lips were curving. Joyously. Blissfully. Contemptuously. The queen saw it now.

She smiles ...

That's why she smiles ...

That's what she had been plotting ...

Devayani spoke no more. Another voice was assailing her ears now. Kacha's voice.

You shall never find the love you seek ...

Something was choking her.

Never find the love you seek ...

Closing in from all sides as she kept staring at her husband.

First Kacha ...

Now you ...

The queen marched back to her father's hermitage. Yayati soon came rushing after her only to face Shukracharya's wrath.

'Did you save my daughter from that well to drown her in grief?'

'Never, Venerable One.'

'That woman left my daughter to die and you are raising a family with her?'

'I love her. I love Sharmishtha as much as I love Devayani.'

'Not love,' the guru roared. 'It is lust. You Chandravanshis have always been carnal. Twenty-seven wives could not satisfy your patriarch, Chandra, and he sinned with Tara. Pururava fell for Urvashi and your father, Nahusha, lusted after Indrani. Your lineage plagues your flesh too. You are all slaves of your body and I shall lay a curse upon it. Curse you like how your father was cursed to lie writhing as a python. Blight you the way Daksha blighted Chandra for tormenting his daughters.'

Shukracharya burnt a blade of grass.

'I curse you, Yayati, that you shall lose your youth that makes you so depraved. May old age set upon your body right away!'

81

YAYATI MAKES A DEMAND

The king was peering into a mirror.

Seeing what everyone had been seeing for the past many years. White hair. Shrivelled face. Pale eyes. All of him that had turned limp. The reflection seemed to transform. Shukracharya was glaring at him from the depths of that glass. Denouncing him once again as he had done long ago.

You are all slaves of your flesh ... I lay a curse upon it ...

Yayati smashed the mirror to pieces. 'What would a yogi know about being a bhogi?'

The glass lay useless like his body had become. No longer vigorous. No longer virile. No longer giving him what he was still craving.

That primal pleasure ...

Devayani walked in. Her beauty was again magnifying his own frailty. Her youth again reminding him of his own decay. Arousing not his itch but his ire.

'Have you come to mock me once more?' he hissed.

'Not today. Today, I bring tidings. Good tidings that perhaps your condition can be reversed.'

Yayati sniggered. 'You pity me now? You are here to heal me? To forgive me? I want none of that for I am what I am. I relish the pleasures of the flesh and I shall do so again if possible. You can love me or leave me.'

Devayani shook her head. 'I shall do neither. Now, I shall only go through this life that I have stepped into with you. Go through this fate that I have been pushed into by Kacha. I have fought long with myself and I shall fight no more. Perhaps if I can live out this birth, I might find love in my next birth. I have spoken to father about you.'

'What can the guru do when he himself cursed me?'

'I told him that his curse was not only sucking the joy out of your life but mine too. My words affected him and he agreed to help you.'

'Nothing can help me,' the king snapped. 'I am but a corpse.'

'You forget that my father can revive the dead,' she was running her fingers over a sculpture.

'What do you mean?'

'He told me that the curse cannot be undone but there is a way out.'

Yayati clutched the woman's waist. His nails dug into her skin.

'Still that animal,' Devayani simpered. 'Hungrier than ever.'

'What did your father say?'

She drew him closer and whispered. The king's body shivered.

'Perfect!'

'But will they do it?'

'Of course! I am Panchananda. Father of five. They shall surely comply.'

Yayati called for his sons right away. Devayani had given birth to Yadu and Turvasu, while Sharmishtha had brought forth Druhya, Anu and Puru. The five young men were standing around his bed now.

'My princes. A father demands many things from his sons. To love him and emulate him. To please him with virtue and valour. To perpetuate his clan and liberate his soul. But today I ask of you what no father has ever asked before.'

'Tell us, father.'

'I will, and I know you shall not refuse.'

'Never.'

'You are all aware of the damnation I live under. My body lies stricken by Shukracharya's words. His curse has kept me away from physical pleasure all these years. Deprived both your mothers too from enjoying the same. But the guru has relented now. He has offered a solution that will work only if one of you agrees.'

'Agrees to what, father?'

The king paused and then spoke again. 'Shukracharya has granted that I can exchange my condition with a young man. Transfer my old age to him and absorb his youth.'

Silence. No one spoke. The five of them glanced at each other as if probing for the right words. Yayati waited. Then he turned to his eldest.

'I am pining, Yadu. Will you do it for me?'

'I cannot, father.'

'Yadu?'

'I have seen how old age racks your flesh. Why would I want to be this decrepit?'

'Because the scriptures say that a son who anticipates his father's wish is gold. A son who acts only after being told is silver. But a son who so flatly refuses is dirt.'

'I would rather be dirt than dust.'

'But as my firstborn ...'

'Precisely. Firstborn. I am to be king. The next Chandravanshi monarch. How can I accept old age? How can I wane so you may wax?'

'Besides, what will you attain by becoming young again?' Druhya berated. 'Haven't you had your fill of women? You should be working towards uplifting your soul but you are still yoked to your body. This carnality of yours shames me.'

'You forget that you three brothers are standing here because of that very carnality,' Yayati fumed. 'Because I embraced your mother despite being married to Devayani.'

'And you are yearning to sin again just as you did when you betrayed my mother,' Yadu countered. 'None of us will barter our youth for that.'

'Not me,' said Turvasu.

'Nor me,' said Druhya.

'Nor me,' said Anu.

'I am willing.'

All eyes darted. The king choked.

'Puru!'

'I will do it.'

'Will you? Will you truly?'

The youngest one clasped his father's trembling hand. 'I will if it pleases you.'

No sooner had he spoken than the curse began to switch bodies. It was now flowing from one to the other like a contagion. And Devayani was watching how this story that began with an exchange of clothes by a pond had arrived at an exchange of conditions. Father and son were still holding hands but the young had turned old now and the old had turned young.

Yayati glared at Yadu.

'You denied your father because of your lust for my throne. I curse you now. I curse you that neither you nor your descendants shall ever rule.'

He cursed Druhya, Turvasu and Anu, too, and declared the youngest as his heir.

'Your deed, Puru, has balanced the misdeeds done by me and my queens. Like Lord Rama, you too have renounced yourself for your father's sake. You shall be king and your progeny shall rule. It shall be a clan that ages will remember.'

After savouring his son's youth for a thousand years, Yayati finally realised that the flames of desire never die but only flare higher. He gave up his crown and returned Puru's youth to him. Yadu would soon bring forth Yadavas, the lineage of Krishna which would never produce any kings. Puru would become progenitor of the Puru clan, which would emerge as the Kuru dynasty. From here would spring the Kauravas and Pandavas whose tribe would rule right through Kali Yuga.

82

SATYATAPA IS TESTED

Far away in the lap of the Himalayas lived a sage who had amassed enormous merit through austerities. So potent was his spiritual self that it empowered his physical self. In the coldest of winters, the aura flowing through his body would keep him warm. He would go without food for days, nourished only by his vital force. And any carnal pang would melt before the glare of his mysticism.

He was called Satyatapa. The one fortified by truth.

One day, the sage was cutting wood for a yagna when he accidentally chopped off a finger. Lo and behold, sacred ash spouted from the wound instead of blood. And when Satyatapa placed the severed finger over the cut, it fused and became whole again. A passing gandharva couple witnessed this miracle and instantly informed Indra. The Devaraja was intrigued and consulted Vishnu.

'He's an enlightened soul,' the Preserver revealed. 'Very few on Earth have insight like him.'

'We should test him then,' Indra proposed. 'Let's find out how wise he truly is.'

Satyatapa had begun hacking another stump when the ground suddenly convulsed. A din of hooves was getting closer. A whimpering sound was turning louder. He looked up to see a boar bounding towards him with an arrow piercing its flesh. The wound was bleeding. Its eyes were brimming. Circling the sage three times, the animal fled towards the hills. Before Satyatapa could react, the hunter arrived out of breath.

'Which way did the boar go?' he queried. 'I shot it but it bolted. I must capture it or else my family will starve.'

Satyatapa lowered his axe. He was staring at the two halves of the wood he had chopped. Equal in shape. Equal in size.

This one or that one?

If he uttered the truth, the boar would die. If he lied, the hunter's family would die.

This one or that one?

The dilemma was cleaving him.

Should I?

Shouldn't I?

The two halves were gazing at him.

Will he?

Won't he?

The sage smiled. 'I remain silent. That's my answer.'

The hunter scowled. 'That's no answer. Like your name, you must speak the truth. There are lives at stake here and you are bound to reply.'

'I am not,' Satyatapa asserted. 'Every organ in the human body has its own function. Its own dharma. They are bound to perform only that and no other.'

'Such as?'

'The mind can only think. The heart can only feel.'

'True.'

'The ear can only hear and the skin can only touch.'

'I agree.'

'Similarly, the eyes can only see. They cannot speak. And the tongue can speak but cannot see.'

'What exactly are you saying?'

'I am saying that my eyes have seen where the boar went but they cannot tell you anything. And my tongue can speak but it has not seen anything. Since my eyes and my tongue have fulfilled their dharma, I am not bound to do anything more. So, I stand silent.'

The sage heard laughter. He turned to see the boar behind him, laughing. He turned back to see the hunter laughing. He glanced behind him again to see the boar transforming into Vishnu. Glanced to the front to find the hunter transforming into Indra. Satyatapa realised what had occurred and fell to his knees.

'Did my answer please you both?'

Indra raised him and embraced him. 'It did, Wise One. But what is the moral?'

'Two morals, Devaraja. One, that we must learn from our faculties to remain content with our own place in Brahmanda and not usurp that of others.'

'And the second?'

'That an ocean of wisdom can be milked even from our limitations.'

83

VISHWAMITRA ACCEPTS MEAT

The yuga was rolling by when a severe drought clung to Earth's breasts, sucking all her milk. Her rivers became rocks and her seas turned into salt. Crops yielded no grain and trees bore no fruit. Men were speaking less for their throats were too parched.

Has Lord Indra deserted us once more?

The question was arising again and again in Vishwamitra's mind. Gazing at the bare bones of Bhuloka, he was wondering what had caused her to turn so barren. Roaming throughout the land, the sage along with his family and retinue, reached the banks of Gautami Ganga. They had been starving for days, and Vishwamitra now asked his disciples to look around for food. The group searched hither and tither but found nothing in that wasteland. Suddenly, something caught their eye.

Could we?

Should we?

The disciples were staring at it and then at each other. The very thought was profane. Unheard of. It would forever condemn them, their fathers and their sons. Saddle them with multiple births to expiate this single sin. Their eyes were shrivelling with fear but their tongues had begun to salivate. Their bellies were growling louder, as if telling them that they could serve their souls only when they served their bodies. The earth was offering them whatever she had. Should they refuse her gesture?

They wrapped it up in a piece of cloth and walked back.

Vishwamitra's family stood up as the disciples arrived and placed the bundle down. The sage's wife uncovered it only to recoil with horror.

A dead dog.

The woman collapsed. She had touched the carcass of an animal that was way down the chain of beings. A filthy creature that roamed streets and graveyards. The sage's wife was screaming at the disciples, saying they had dragged her too into their sin.

'What sin?' Vishwamitra asked.

They turned towards the sage to find him looking calmly at the animal. There was no rage in his eyes. Only resignation.

'Bhuloka has left us with no choice. In these desperate times, we must be like Agni that devours anything. Everything. Prepare the meat. We shall make an offering to the gods and consume it.'

'Offer dog meat to the gods?' His wife covered her ears. 'How can you utter such blasphemy? Have you forgotten your scriptures?'

'Perhaps this drought wants us to beget a new scripture. One that dictates that all creatures in Brahmanda are equal.'

As Vishwamitra proceeded to pick up the dog, Indra panicked. He had been witnessing everything and realised now that the sage had made up his mind. He was not only going to consume the animal but also offer it as oblation. Transforming into a hawk, Indra swooped and carried the carcass away. A furious Vishwamitra raised his right hand to curse the Devaraja when he saw him circling back.

'Do not defile yourself, O Sage. I have transformed this meat into amrita. Offer it to the gods and feed it to your family and followers.'

'Amrita?' the sage sneered. 'You are offering us eternal life when we stand surrounded by death? Give me back the flesh.'

'How can you let your body overpower your soul? Do not transgress like Trishanku. Can anything be higher than dharma?'

'What I am doing is also dharma. It's called Apad Dharma, which can be exercised in such catastrophic times. Since nothing else is available, there is no harm in having the dog flesh. One can only follow dharma if one stays alive. Adharma would be to accept nectar from you when you are denying water to the whole world.'

They saw Indra soaring. He was gathering clouds. Sounding thunder. Beaming lightning. Rain erupted and filled the veins of Bhuloka.

84

THE BIRTH OF KRISHNA

Vasudeva was staring at his hands.

He had just slashed the umbilical cord. The cries of his newborn son were getting louder and louder, and an exhausted Devaki was trying to soothe him. Trying to see his face in the light and shadow of the dungeon. She spoke now and Vasudeva heard a smile in her voice after a long time.

'He has your forehead.'

'My forehead? That's where the gods stamp our fates, Devaki. No wonder our firstborn has barely moments to live.'

'Are you condemning yourself?'

Vasudeva was still looking at his hands. He answered as if he was talking to them.

'You are a princess, Devaki. You married me thinking you would become queen, but you languish now in the prison of Mathura. Our child is delivered not by midwives as you lie on a silken bed but by me as you writhe on a stone floor. The curse on my Yadu clan now singes you, too. Do you know my other name is Anakadundubhi because drums resounded in our palace when I was born? But my firstborn's arrival today meets with silence. Pain. Fear.'

'None of this is because of you.'

'None of this would have happened with you if you had not wedded me.' Vasudeva turned and extended his hands before her face. 'Look, Devaki. Blood. Coated with blood. Listen to what they are saying. They are telling me that my child shall die today because I am his father. I have my son's blood on my hands.'

'It's my brother's doing. A fruit of his actions. Do not look for that darkness within yourself for it lives only inside him. Inside that man who is an animal. If he could imprison our father for his throne, why would he show any mercy to me. His sister. The hour draws near. Guards have left to inform him and he will be here soon. Take our son in your arms. Hold him close, for you will never hold him again.'

Vasudeva stepped back in horror. 'How can I? How can I look into his eyes? How can I forge a bond with him when I can hear the footfalls of his death? Even if I glance at him now, it will bind us together and that thread will rip my flesh when he is wrenched away. Eight times, Devaki. They will be wrenched away eight times from us. How can I look at any of them?'

The infant was wailing again. Devaki hid his face in the folds of her garment but Vasudeva shrieked.

'Uncover him. Let him cry. Let him see what he can. Let his voice be heard. He won't be here long. Let him give a part of himself to us. To this dungeon. Let these walls absorb every sound he makes so that they may echo again someday for someone.'

As he broke down, Devaki's tears began falling, too.

'Pray, give our firstborn a name,' she pleaded. 'There is no priest to consecrate his birth and no butter to place on his tongue, but we must name him. What if we meet him again in another world and he asks us how we could let him die unnamed?'

'The dead don't ask for names, O Sister.'

The voice had hacked through the darkness. The shadow moved forward to stand under the glare of the torches. Colossal frame. Twirling moustache. Burning eyes. Frigid face.

Kansa. Monarch of Mathura.

Vasudeva stood up as that memory began to bleed again. Right after his marriage to Devaki, her loving brother, Kansa, had been escorting them home when celestial words had rained from the sky.

'Beware, Kansa! Your days on Earth are numbered now with the marriage of your sister. She shall become the vessel to carry your doom. Devaki's eighth child will bring about your death.'

Kansa's affection had vanished in a trice. He had furiously pulled out an axe to behead Devaki but Vasudeva had stood in his way. Fallen at his feet and pledged that when their eighth child was born, he would offer it to be killed. He had even agreed to be imprisoned along with Devaki.

Kansa had relented, but then Narada had confounded him. Shown him a rainbow and asked, 'Tell me, O King. Which is the first colour and which is the last? Should one count from above or below? Similarly, how can you be certain which is the eighth child? If you count from the beginning then it's the eighth one, but if you count backwards, it's the first one. Inscrutable are the ways of gods and any child could be the eighth child.'

Ravaged with fear, Kansa had again attacked his sister. Vasudeva had then taken a terrible vow.

'I shall lay all our eight children at your feet. Kill them all but spare my Devaki.'

Kansa was glaring at the firstborn now. The child was slumbering as if the universe had lulled him to sleep. As if the universe wanted him to remain oblivious of this moment when his life would bleed out.

'It's time, Vasudeva,' the king grunted like a boar. 'Bring my nephew here.'

Vasudeva glanced at Devaki. Her body was shuddering but her fingers were firm, clutching their son. As he grasped the child, she held on to him for just a moment longer. Then she let go. The look on her face was terrorising Vasudeva more than what he was about to do. Still not looking at his firstborn, he handed him to Kansa. The king dangled the baby by his feet. Gazed at him curiously.

'How come your parents love you so much? My parents cursed me for being born. My mother cursed me because the gandharva, Dramila, had tricked her into sleeping with him and she was livid. And my father,

Dramila, cursed me because he was afraid of what he had done. Her fury and his fear are all that I got from them. Nothing else.'

A corner of Kansa's eye appeared to have turned moist. Raising the infant high in the air, he smashed his head on a slab. Vasudeva looked away but Devaki watched it all. Something bled inside her as she saw her son bleed. Something died inside her as she saw him die.

It began happening again and again. She was birthing one son after another and her brother was butchering them all. Vasudeva now decided to distance himself from his wife.

'This ache is weighing upon us like a hill,' he pleaded. 'Let's not give Kansa any more sons.'

But Devaki was disrobing. She pulled Vasudeva close.

'It's no longer about us. It's about ridding the world of Kansa. If our eighth one is destined to do that, we shall keep procreating.'

She had collected the umbilical cords of all her dead sons and she would play with them for hours. Count them again and again. Tie and untie them. She had also stopped suckling her newborns. Vasudeva asked her to, but she shook her head.

'There's no bigger debt than a mother's milk. Why burden these doomed souls when I know they can never repay it?'

She had turned quieter. The slab was turning redder. It had drunk the blood of six of her children and she was now pregnant with her seventh one. Her belly had swollen up like a ripened fruit when suddenly it turned empty. Unknown to both the parents, Goddess Yogamaya had transferred the foetus from Devaki to Rohini, the other wife of Vasudeva. Rohini had moved into her brother Nanda's house in Gokul, where she soon gave birth to Balarama. The second incarnation of Sheshnaga after Lakshmana. The mystified guards informed Kansa that the seventh one had perished in the womb and he flung sapphires at them.

'Time now for the eighth one,' he sneered.

Months later, Devaki placed Vasudeva's hand on her stomach.

'It's him.'

'Who?'

'He who will slay Kansa.'

'How do you know?'

She pressed his hand tighter. 'There is a warmth inside that is nourishing me. A flame inside that is guiding me. I am not carrying him. He is carrying me.'

At the midnight hour of the eighth lunar day of Bhadrapada, Devaki brought forth her eighth son. The dark one who had filled her with light. The avatar of Vishnu born with the four symbols of shankha or conch, chakra or disc, gada or mace and padma or lotus.

Krishna.

No sooner had he arrived than the torches blazed brighter. Kansa's guards fell asleep and the dungeon door swung open. A voice from heaven was now reverberating.

'Hail the incarnation of Mahavishnu in Dwapar Yuga. Take him to Gokul across River Yamuna to the house of Nanda and his wife, Yashoda. In a previous birth, they were Drona and Dhara, who were blessed by Sri Hari that he would grow up as their son in this yuga. The time has come for that boon to flower. Yashoda has given birth to a girl at this same hour and there, too, everyone has been made to sleep. Lay your son in their cradle and bring that girl here.'

Devaki touched her child's feet. Placing Krishna in a wicker basket, she handed it to Vasudeva. But his hands were quaking.

'What if the guards awake? What if Kansa sees me? He will sever my head and come looking for you. I have lost everything and I cannot lose you too.'

She walked out of the dungeon towards that slab. The blood of her sons lay congealed on it. Caressing the stone, she stretched out her red palm silently towards him. Vasudeva placed the basket on his head. Something unspoken had possessed him and he was now obeying every word of that divine injunction. Stepping out of the dungeon. Exiting the royal palace. Walking through the empty streets. Standing now before that expanse of water.

Yamuna.

Thunder was searing the sky and rain was lashing the stream. Vasudeva began wading through it. His lower half was struggling for a foothold while his upper half was balancing that precious load on his head. Like his eighth child, the moon, too, was in its eighth phase of the waning crescent tonight. Its final phase before a new cycle would begin, just as Krishna was about to herald a new order. Suddenly, Yamuna surged. Her waters were dwarfing Vasudeva. Rising higher and higher until a liquid wall was enveloping him. As he gasped for air, he heard a voice. The river was whispering.

'Fear not. I only wanted to touch the feet of Sri Hari. I had heard how his foot had sanctified Ganga and I have been pining for the same. Today, I, too, flow blessed.'

The tide receded. The god was traversing Yamuna like how he had once lay floating over primordial waters. Vasudeva had reached the middle of the stream when the downpour intensified. Tottering on, he cried out.

'You bring the rain, Narayana, and you shall bring the shade.'

Something was emerging from Yamuna right behind him. Someone was looming so high that it was blocking the moon. Casting a shadow over father and son. Vasudeva turned and stared in awe. The mighty Vasuki had surfaced from the river. The serpent's ten hoods were spreading over them like a giant parasol. Gods and goddesses appeared now to see this divine spectacle. To see Vasudeva cradling the lord below and Vasuki shielding him from above. To see both man and animal celebrating the Preserver who had taken another avatar for their sake. Vishnu, who helped men to cross over, was being ferried across by a man. Vishnu, who had kept afloat the vessel of Manu, was being kept afloat by a manava. The devas were welling up. The elements were rejoicing. Brahmanda was chanting in a wild ecstasy.

Hare Krishna ... Hare Krishna ... Hare Rama ... Hare Rama ...

Yamuna was narrowing now. Water was making way for land. Stepping onto the bank, Vasudeva looked at Gokul. Tears were pouring from his eyes. Tears because he was again parting from a son. Tears because he had fathered an avatar of Vishnu.

Tears because Krishna would live and Kansa would die.

Not long after, Vasudeva was back inside the dungeon. Standing next to Devaki with the girl child in his arms. The door had locked itself and the guards had woken up. They had rushed out and Kansa had stormed in. He was laughing now as he held the infant above the slab.

'A girl? A girl will grow up to slay Kansa? I am no Mahishasura or Shumbha–Nishumbha whom Durga killed. No Daruk or Raktabija whom Kali killed. I am Kansa.'

But as soon as he raised the child, she flew from his grasp and soared high. A blinding light swallowed the dungeon. In that effulgence, the girl transformed into the eight-armed Yogamaya. Goddess of illusions. The Primordial Supreme.

'Vile Kansa,' she roared. 'Whom are you trying to kill? Me, who is unborn? Me, who is undying? Your nemesis is alive. Alive and well. And each day that he shall breathe, you shall choke. Each day that he shall grow stronger, you shall turn weaker. He is far away, but he will come. And when he does, it shall be the end of you.'

The light went out, leaving Kansa in the dark. His heart was sounding like the battering of a drum. Clutching Devaki, he gnashed his teeth.

'Where is your son?'

She seized his hand.

'Where is he? What is his name?'

Tying an umbilical cord around Kansa's wrist, Devaki smiled. 'The dead don't ask for names, O Brother.'

85

KRISHNA AND YAMALARJUNA

Baby Krishna's eyes were closed. His lips were curving into a smile. His tongue was swirling again and again with rapture as it licked that white mound on his palm. Its taste was filling him with a strange bliss as always. Its smell was exhilarating his senses as always. But that was not the only reason he had broken his mother's pot once more and scooped out the butter. It was also because of how it was dripping down his mouth. Tickling his skin. Staining his clothes. Because of how that lard always frolicked with the lord.

A shadow fell over him now. Krishna looked up to see his mother. The pieces of her pot had tattled about his theft and Yashoda was fuming.

'It's time you learnt a lesson, Kanha,' she said as she hauled him up.

Taking a thick coil of rope, Yashoda tethered her son to a heavy grinding mortar. Because the rope, or dama, had been tied below his belly, or udar, the god now gained a new name, Damodar.

'You can no longer move,' she said, checking the knot. 'Stay here while I finish my chores inside.'

The child squatted in silence. His tongue was licking the remnants of butter sticking to his fingers. Moments later, he was looking at what was towering before him. For everyone else, they were Yamalarjuna or two arjuna trees growing close to each other. But for Krishna, they were two beings who had been pining for his arrival. Two beings who had been hiding a secret for the past hundred years.

Long ago, Kubera's sons, Nalkubar and Manigreev, had been enjoying the company of damsels on the banks of River Mandakini. Soon, they had undressed the women and begun making love to them when Narada had come by, warbling a hymn. Seeing the Devarshi approach, the women had instantly covered their bodies, but not the two brothers. Furious at being interrupted, they had stood up and insolently displayed their naked flesh before Narada. The song had died on the sage's lips. Bristling with rage, he had pronounced a curse turning Nalkubar and Manigreev into arjuna trees. Two entities who would vegetate together for a hundred years until Vishnu released them in his new avatar.

Krishna began crawling towards the trees now. Dragging along with him that mortar he had been yoked to. That massive chunk of stone was obeying the child. Getting pulled by him as if it had no weight of its own. Following him as if it had surrendered to a higher power. The elements were gaping. Envying the mortar for having been chosen by the lord to do his bidding. As Krishna inched closer, the arjunas stirred. The hour had come. Their deliverance had arrived. Their leaves were rustling. Their flowers were blooming. Pale yellow flowers were raining on the child as if the trees were shedding tears. Serenading the avatar.

The child passed between the two trees now, but the mortar got stuck. Wedged between both the trunks, it was no longer moving. Krishna turned. He gazed at the stone. Gazed at the arjunas. The trees were waiting. Brahmanda was watching. The mortar braced itself.

Namo Narayanaya ...

The child tugged and such was the force that the stone lunged forward, yanking both the trees along. They were wobbling now. Their trunks were swaying. Static for so long, Krishna had set the arjunas in motion. Both the trees had been uprooted and they were collapsing together. No longer shackled to earth, they were turning delirious with joy. Crashing headlong as if bowing before the avatar. Liberated from all things past, the arjunas now lay at Krishna's feet.

The child plucked a leaf. As he looked up again, the trees were not there anymore. Only Nalkubar and Manigreev. They were standing with folded hands. Looking at Krishna's body tied to the mortar.

Looking at how the god had got himself chained to set them free.

86

KRISHNA TAMES KALIA

Yamuna was shuddering.

A naga called Kalia was entering her stream along with several of his wives. Yamuna had always embraced every life form that had sought habitat in her but this one—a massive black serpent with multiple hoods—was chilling her. Invading her like an asura. Swirling through her like a pestilence that could turn her into a curse. Yamuna's fears came true in a matter of days. Her waters began frothing with Kalia's venom. Bubbling with lethal vapours from his breath. As she became a poisonous pool, life around her started to perish. Trees shrivelled on her banks and fish choked in her bed. Birds flying above her would drop dead and cows drinking from her would never return. Even at night, the river would gleam with a deadly luminescence. Infesting her to her very core, Kalia had turned Yamuna into a plague that was smiting anyone who came close.

'We may have to relocate,' the dwellers of Vrindavan pleaded before Nanda now. 'Four leagues of the river have filled with poison. Our cattle are dying and soon it shall be us.'

'Perhaps we can speak to Kalia,' Nanda proposed.

'That naga is a vile being. We will end up foaming to death if we go anywhere near him.'

Krishna was standing afar, listening to their plight. Years ago, the terror of Kansa had driven them out of Gokul. The tyrant had identified his nephew and had been making constant attempts on his life. He had sent Putana with poisoned breasts to suckle Krishna, but the infant had sucked the life out of her. Trinavarta had acquired the form of a whirlwind to dash him to the ground, but Krishna had made himself too heavy for the demon. Shakatasura had tried to crush him under the wheels of a cart, but Krishna had kicked it to pieces. The collapse of Yamalarjuna, too, had been perceived as a terrible omen and the whole of Gokul had fled south and created the new settlement of Vrindavan. The assaults on Krishna had not ceased, however. The crane demon, Bagasura, had tried swallowing him up, but Krishna had ripped open his beak. The donkey demon, Dhenukasura, had attacked him, but Krishna had struck him dead. He had also slain Agha, the python, and Keshi, the horse, earning the name Keshava. Now another monster was infecting Yamuna and the elders were shaking their heads.

'Nothing can be done.'

Krishna turned. Tossing a wooden ball in his hand, he smiled.

'Something can be done.'

Gathering all his mates, he led them towards the riverbank. Games ensued and the ball was soon flitting from one lad to another. Round and round. Higher and higher. Charting strange parabolas. Hurtling through curious angles. Krishna was holding the ball again. He gazed at Yamuna. Yamuna gazed at him.

It's time ...

He hurled the ball. As if dodging his mates one by one, it landed in the river and sunk right away. The boys sprinted towards Yamuna only to come to an abrupt halt. Their feet freezing at the very edge of that stream. Their eyes gawking at those hissing waters.

'It's gone!'

'We must fish it out. Someone should dive in.'

'Dive into Yamuna? You are insane.'

'But that's Manasukha's ball.

'And that's Kalia's river.'

'Manasukha will surely raise hell when he finds out.'

Krishna nodded. 'Then there's only one thing to be done.'

Before the others could react, he leapt. As he plunged into the water, he could hear his mates shrieking in alarm. But the deeper he dove, the fainter they became. Fully submerged now, he looked around this reservoir of venom. As the daughter of Surya, Yamuna had always glistened like her father. Always nourished life like him. But now, Kalia had turned her into a toxic tank. Dead creatures were floating around Krishna. Lashings of poison were sullying the stream. As he sank lower, a voice rang out.

'Who goes there?'

A reptilian was slithering towards him. His scales were glinting. Eyes flaring. Fangs dripping. As Krishna watched, his manifold hoods began waving before him now in a terrifying cluster. The gigantic Kalia was looming like an underwater daitya.

'What's your name, boy?'

'That which is yours. I am Krishna and you are Kalia. Both mean the same.'

'Your skin is as dark as mine but why that peacock feather on your head? You stand before me adorned with the plumes of my enemy. Why are you here?'

'To look for my ball. And to tell you that you must leave Yamuna or I shall kill you.'

The snake hissed and a haze of venom diffused in the waters around Krishna.

'You will kill me, boy? And gulp my poison like Mahadeva? You who should have been dead by now swimming in my river?'

'Your poison cannot touch me, Kalia. Take your wives and leave or Yamuna shall bubble with your blood like it does with your venom.'

The serpent lashed out. Unfurling himself, he began looping around Krishna. Imprisoning the boy in his mammoth coils. As he wrapped him from head to toe, Kalia sniggered.

'How will you slay me when I envelop you?'

Krishna began expanding. His limbs were growing. His torso towering.

The feather enlarging. As he grew bigger and bigger, the snake's coils fell shorter and shorter. Kalia was straining. Tightening in an attempt to stem Krishna's surge. Employing every muscle to try and constrict him to death, but only tearing himself. Retching globs of blood. Tangling into a knot. Realising now that the finite was trying to contain the infinite, his coils surrendered. As they collapsed at Krishna's feet, Kalia gaped. Asked in a tone of enormous awe.

'You are no human. Who are you?'

'I am He who reclines on Sheshnaga. He who is revered by Vasuki.'

Meanwhile, the whole of Vrindavan had gathered at Yamuna's bank. The boys had spread the word and Nanda had come rushing with Yashoda. She was beating her breasts. Tearing her hair. Promising her son all the butter in the world if he would come back to her. Cutting loose again and again to leap into the river but being restrained by Rohini. Nanda and others were staring at that stream. Steeling themselves to see the boy's corpse floating up any moment now. They gasped. It was happening. The waters were churning. Something was emerging from Yamuna's womb.

A feather. Krishna's peacock feather, waving in the air.

They were watching.

Krishna's eyes. Twinkling, because he was about to unveil a secret.

They stopped breathing.

Krishna's face. Smiling like a lotus sprouting from that mire.

They were pointing.

Krishna's hands. Raising his flute to his lips.

They inched forward.

Krishna's feet. Planted firmly on Kalia's hoods.

They staggered back.

The boy was standing atop the serpent like the sun crowning a hill. He was playing his flute. Kalia was swaying with enchantment, as if yoked to that melody. The gathering kept looking. Looking at Krishna. Looking at each other. Was it truly happening or were they seeing a mirage? Were the notes of that flute toying with their eyes? Had their pain of losing Krishna conjured this sublime sight? Yashoda heard his voice now.

'Mother,' he flung the ball towards her. 'Kalia helped me find it.'

Yashoda clasped the ball. She was feeling its form. Fondling its warmth. That touch was telling her that this was all real.

'He's alive,' she said as she clutched Nanda. 'Our Kanha is alive.'

Krishna was dancing now. His feet were pounding the hoods of Kalia. Frolicking like a child who had won a game. Rejoicing like the lord who had subdued the naga. Reminded him that nothing was more glorious than the Parabrahman. All of Vrindavan was standing rapt as that divine choreography unfolded. Tears were flowing down their eyes. Rapture was flooding their faces. Pirouetting above Kalia, Krishna had become Natwar. The cosmic dancer who was enthralling Brahmanda with his moves. Whose leela was pervading them all. His tempo was quickening. His feet were battering the serpent. As the god's dance peaked to a crescendo, Kalia's wives surfaced with folded hands.

'The universe resides in you, Nayarana, and our husband is crumbling under its weight as you dance atop him. Pray, release him. Your touch has absolved him and he shall do your bidding.'

Krishna addressed the naga.

'You came here with your wives from Ramanaka Dwipa. Go back to that island and remain there for the rest of your life.'

'I came here out of terror, Narayana,' he wailed. 'Men fear me but I fear Garuda. Your mount is the mortal enemy of every serpent and we had to flee Ramanaka because of him.'

The boy closed his eyes as an image of Gokul flashed. 'I know how that feels, Kalia. But you are destroying the natural balance around Yamuna and dharma says that the lives of a few cannot endanger the lives of many.'

'Am I at fault if we nagas are born violent? Born with venom? How can I relinquish my nature which has been dictated by Brahmanda? We had sought refuge here for our survival because this is the only place that Garuda cannot enter due to a sage's curse. But if you are commanding us, I shall obey.'

Krishna blessed him. 'Return without fear, Kalia. My footprints are now

forever etched on your hood. Garuda will see them and never touch you or your clan.'

The serpent gazed at him with wonder. The lord had not trod on him to take his life. He had done so to take away his death. Kalia was crying. Krishna was laughing for he could hear Yamuna laugh.

87

KRISHNA OUTWITS BRAHMA

Brahma was watching Krishna play.

He was grazing cattle by the Yamuna with his mates. While the cows had found a lush patch of grass, the boys had begun to frolic. They were inventing games and daring each other. Pulling pranks and tumbling with laughter. Climbing trees and plucking raw fruits. Jumping in the river and floating in her waters. Falling asleep now as Krishna's flute hummed.

Brahma was watching that they were no longer watching over their cattle. He grinned.

I also want to play ...

Closing his eyes, he entered the minds of the cows and the calves. Whispered a few words to all of them. The animals were gawking at each other. Sensing this entity that had taken hold of them. Hearing what his voice was instructing them to do. They began to move. One after the other. The whole herd together. None of them was making a sound that would alert the boys. All of them were trudging the same path, for they knew where they were headed. The calves were no longer following their mothers. The mothers were no longer attending to their calves. They were all tethered now only to that voice inside them. Reaching a cave, they faded into its darkness. A faraway cave where they would remain hidden until the god released them. Brahma laughed.

I am just playing, Sri Hari ...

Manasukha woke up with a jolt. Moments later, he was kicking the others awake.

'The cows. The calves. I can't see them.'

A frenzied search began but not an animal was in sight. Neither the tip of a horn nor the edge of a hoof. It was getting dark and they were becoming tense. But the Creator was not done yet.

I want to play some more ...

As they kept looking, Brahma now started invading the minds of Krishna's mates. Possessing their senses just as he had done with the cattle. Surrendering to his enchantment, the boys, too, began to separate from the group. Began walking away one by one as if in a state of trance. Following the murmur of his voice like rivers heeding the call of a sea. Entering the cave, they, too, concealed themselves along with the cows. Moments later, Krishna glanced around. He was all alone. All his mates had vanished. He smiled.

Not all ...

One is still playing with me ...

He was sensing how Brahma had whisked them away. Sensing the glee in the Creator's voice.

Just playing, Sri Hari ...

Krishna nodded.

Then I must play, too ...

He closed his eyes. Rays were shooting from the pores of his body. Sketching outlines of numerous shapes. Filling them with flesh and blood. Adding skin and planting hair. Infusing them with all the colours. When the rays died, Krishna opened his eyes to see them standing before him. All the boys and all the cows. He had crafted exact replicas of each one of them. They were looking at him, unaware that they were optical illusions. Mere extensions of him just as he was an extension of Vishnu. Just as Vishnu was an extension of the Parabrahman. Manasukha called out.

'Come, Kanha. It's time to return.'

An entire year passed but no one in Vrindavan had grasped what had happened. Neither the owners of the cattle. Nor the parents of those children. Not only had they not uncovered the truth but they were also showering them with more love than ever before. Being the handiwork of the lord, the replicas were generating a strange fervour in everyone around them. Brahma realised now that he had lost yet another race to Vishnu. His prank had caused no panic in Vrindavan. His maya had failed before Krishna's maya. He dissolved those replicas and released everyone from the cave. And just like their clones, the boys, too, remained oblivious of this divine mischief. Brahma grinned as he offered Krishna a kadamba flower.

'Creation gets tiring, Sri Hari. Sometimes I wish I, too, could play.'

'And sometimes I wish I could stop playing.'

88

KRISHNA LIFTS GOVARDHAN

A bolt of lightning torched the night sky above Vrindavan. Eclipsed hundreds of clay lamps that were twinkling in the village for Deepavali. Nanda glanced up with frightened eyes.

'Looks like the Devaraja has heard you and he is livid.'

'But I am only speaking the truth,' Krishna replied.

'And I am speaking about tradition. Truth and tradition don't always hold hands, Kanha. We, at Vrindavan, have always worshipped Indra on the day after Deepavali. We are a land of cowherds. Our cows need grasslands and grasslands need rain, which the Devaraja provides. Our ancestors have always sought his grace and we follow the same.'

Krishna picked up a clay lamp. 'What is causing this flame, father? Is it only Agnideva and not this wick that burns itself to give us light? I do not challenge what's celestial, but why ignore what's material?'

'You are asking us to question our beliefs.'

'How else will we find new answers? How else will we evolve if we do not examine things? If we do not reinvent? If we do not keep seeking a higher truth?'

Nanda stood silent.

'The Devaraja may be the lord of rains, father, but it is Mount Govardhan that channels his bounty towards us. It plays a vital role in the gathering of clouds that bring those showers. Not only is it a conduit between Indra and us, but its pastures also provide food for our cattle. The presence of that hill is a blessing for Vrindavan and we must exalt it. Tomorrow, we shall not bow before that distant god but our own Govardhan. Thus, we will perform true dharma.'

Nanda smiled. The lamp in Krishna's hand was showing him a new path and he soon convinced others to walk upon it. The next day dawned to see lavish preparations in motion at the base of the hill. The whole of Vrindavan was assembling to offer their gratitude to Govardhan. Families were arriving with their cattle in tow. Priests were consecrating a triangular altar. Garlands were being strung and hymns were being sung. Strains from Krishna's flute were filling everyone with a strange new piety. Transforming that stone into a sanctum sanctorum.

Soon the yagna fire was blazing high. Women were drawing symbols on Govardhan with rice and vermillion. Shaping miniature hills and decking them with flowers. Milk and butter were being offered along with fruits and grains. The priests stood up holding lamps. The flames were moving in circles. Ascending and descending. Their chants were reverberating. Krishna joined in. Then Nanda. Balarama. Yashoda. Rohini. More and more voices flowed in as the whole of Vrindavan now became a part of this divine chorus.

Govardhan Dharadhar Gokul Trankarak ...

Suddenly, thunder crashed, drowning out their voices. Krishna glanced at the sky. Then, looking at the gathering, he spoke, 'Chant louder!'

Thunder rumbled again.

'Louder!'

Roaring now like an angry lion.

'Louder!'

Threatening now to tear the firmament.

'Louder!'

Deafening now as if their ears would bleed.

'Louder!'

Lightning exploded. Branching furiously above them, it struck Govardhan. The assembly froze. Their voices were now hiding in their throats. Their faces were gaping at the hill, scorched by that flare. Gaping at that crack, smouldering like a wound. The sky was turning dark. Clouds were sprouting everywhere. Amassing like the banners of Indra. The sun, no longer visible, seemed to have fled in terror. The gathering stood up. Their eyes were nailed to the horizon. Their skins were shuddering as drops began to land on them. Bigger drops. Faster drops. Krishna nodded.

First fire, now water ...

Rain pounced upon Vrindavan like a savage army. It was as if Indra had kicked open his gates and unleashed his troops. They were cascading to flood. They were cascading to drown. The downpour was flogging their bodies. Wiping their symbols. Dousing the yagna flames. Washing away the offerings. Everyone was scampering. Looking for a refuge. They were clustering under trees, but the rain was hacking the branches. They were cowering beneath boulders, but the rain was grinding those to dust. Cows were bleating. Trampling their masters. The shrine had turned into a swamp where men and muck were mingling into a mess. The lightning was becoming fiercer. The water was pounding harder. Indra's wrath seemed to be mounting. Commanding the rain to destroy more. Defile more. The elders began to berate Nanda.

'We should have never angered the Devaraja. This is not lightning but Indra glaring at us. This is not thunder but Indra screaming in rage. This is not rain but Indra shedding tears because we have disowned him.'

'Brahmanda often invokes fear,' Krishna said. 'But if one applies the mind, one can engage with it.'

'Engage? Who will save us from this pralaya?'

'Govardhan.'

'This mound of rock that sits with its eyes lowered while we are being swept away?'

'Govardhan means one who nurtures. The hill shall not lower its eyes but raise its head.'

Moments later, no one was blinking. They were standing transfixed. Watching Govardhan soaring high. Forsaking all its ties with earth. Ascending towards the sky as if a giant Yadava warrior was charging towards Indra. As the hill loomed above them, the gathering gasped. Govardhan had not flown up on its own. Krishna had given it wings. Uprooting it, he was holding the hill aloft on the tip of his little finger.

Yashoda gripped Nanda, quaking with disbelief. The others were standing numb as if they were no longer conscious of anything anymore. No longer conscious that rain was battering their flesh. No longer conscious that lightning was striking so close. That the wind was howling or that Vrindavan was drowning. Nothing mattered anymore, for they were all now linked to this miracle that had absorbed their pain. Warmed their bodies. Filled their souls with such wonder that they would no longer wonder at anything else. They had seen Krishna standing above Kalia. They were now seeing him standing below Govardhan. He was beckoning them. They were walking towards him. Their limbs were no longer their own. Krishna was pulling them with invisible strings and they were surrendering. Assembling below the hill. Not long ago, Kurma had lifted Mount Mandara on its back to ensure the churning of Ksheersagar. Today, Krishna had lifted Mount Govardhan on his finger to keep Vrindavan dry. He was smiling. Hearing what Indra was whispering in his ears.

'Forgive me, Sri Hari.'

'Why do you do it, Devaraja?'

'Fear. I exist in a perpetual state of fear that I might stop serving any purpose. That men might stop revering me. That, no longer deemed necessary by Brahmanda, I might be cast aside. Pray, tell me, Sri Hari. How can one defeat fear?'

'You must hold it aloft like how I am holding Govardhan. It will not be easy. Your fear will keep pressing down upon you but you must lift it as high as you can. Hold it as far from yourself as you can. In the beginning, you shall need your entire body to do so. Then just your arms. Then just a single arm. Then just your five fingers. Then only four. Then only three.

Then only two. When you can finally hold up your fear with only the tip of your little finger, you would have conquered it.'

The downpour ceased but Indra's eyes were raining.

'You have filled me with light, Sri Hari. Let me also offer you something. I see this blessed sight of you standing here, surrounded by the cows of Vrindavan. Let me glorify this leela forever. Let me gift you two new names. I call you Giridhar. One who holds the hill. I call you Gopal. One who protects cows.'

89

KRISHNA HEALS KUBJA

'I hear sitars playing, Kanha. I smell flowers. And sweetmeats. Do you see the palace? That majestic archway. Those columns of gold. Turrets of ivory. Do you?'

'No, Dau. All I hear are the wailing sounds of six newborns put to death. All I smell is a slab that reeks of their blood. All I see are prison bars whose shadows are now engraved on the bodies of our parents. You are talking about Kansa, the monarch. I am looking for Kansa, the murderer.'

Krishna's countless feats had been finding their way to Mathura and trickling into the ears of Kansa. Everyone was marvelling at this cowherd who had raised Govardhan with his finger and lowered Kalia with his toe. Everyone but Kansa. Not only had he failed to eliminate his nemesis but Krishna was now being hailed as a superhero. A possible Yuga Purusha. Furious and fearful, Kansa had despatched one of his chiefs, Akrura, to invite Krishna and Balarama for a wrestling match. On their way to Mathura, Akrura had taken a dip in the Yamuna and seen a beatific vision. Seen Vishnu underwater, reclining on Sheshnaga. Seen that the faces of the Preserver and his serpent were also the faces of the two brothers seated in his chariot. Coming out of the river, he had fallen at their feet. Euphoric that he was escorting Narayana himself. Aghast that Kansa was so brazenly challenging the prophecy.

When he comes, it shall be the end of you …

Krishna and Balarama were now standing before Kansa's palace as the whole of Mathura gathered. They were staring at his peacock feather. His blue limbs. His lotus eyes. His golden flute. Their minds were questioning if this rustic lad had performed all those miracles. Their hearts were answering that only this rustic lad could have performed all those miracles.

'Such compassion!' the elders said, gazing. 'He must be the greatest of sons.'

'Such strength!' the men said, admiring. 'He must be the greatest of saviours.'

'Such beauty!' the women said, sighing. 'He must be the greatest of lovers.'

All eyes were on Krishna, but his eyes were on a hunchback. A woman whom Mathura reviled as Kubja. Reviled as Trivakra as her body was deformed in three places. Kubja was a palace maid whose task it was to prepare fresh sandalwood paste for Kansa every day. Today, however, she had brought it for Krishna. The sight of him was filling her with delight and yet she was troubled. A vision she had seen in her sleep last night was still haunting her. She could still hear those sounds of mourning. Still see those three hazy figures. A woman and two men. They were clad like hermits. Standing by a river. Their eyes were laden with sorrow, but they were smiling at her. Trying to tell her something.

'Beautiful One!'

Kubja's reverie broke. Krishna was addressing her.

'O Beautiful One!'

Coming close to her, he inhaled the sandalwood in her hands.

'Many are standing here with fragrant offerings for me. I see blossoms of rose, marigold and jasmine. I smell perfumes of champa, padma and kewda. Each one wants to please me, but it's your scent that draws me, Beautiful One.'

Kubja's voice quivered.

'You too mock me, Krishna? You, who stand in Tribhanga, are mocking this Trivakra? Calling me, whom the world shuns, beautiful? Whose crooked body evokes either horror or disgust in others? Many have pelted stones at me but even those have never wounded me as much as your words today. I had heard that you are kind, but it's a lie. When the universe taunts me, why would you be any different?'

'I utter the truth, Beautiful One, for I see what others do not. I see your soul that holds no malice towards those who scorn you. Your soul that blesses even those who scar you. Thus have you been following dharma and asking for nothing in return. You are like this sandalwood, Beautiful One, for your allure lies deep within.'

Krishna lifted his foot now. Kubja began to step back in fear, when she heard him speak again.

'Have you become so used to hatred that you no longer recognise love?'

She paused. Krishna put his foot gently on her toes. Placing his fingers below her chin, he raised her up. A tremor was rushing through Kubja. Her spine was jolting awake. Stretching in an upward motion. Her body was uncoiling itself. Her torso was turning erect. As the spasm dissolved, she saw everyone gaping at her. As Rama, the Preserver had turned a rock into Ahilya. As Krishna now, he had turned a hunchback into a beauty. Kubja looked down at herself.

'What have you done?'

'I have only made you as glorious outside as you are inside. Your body now reflects your soul.'

Tears were streaming down her face. Krishna took the platter of paste from her.

'The gopikas in Vrindavan love to apply sandalwood on me. Won't you do the same?'

Kubja was serving Krishna just as Shabri had served Rama. As she dotted his forehead, a strange consciousness filled her core.

'I have seen you before, lord.'

'You have?'

'I have seen this face. You were just as radiant then. I was just as hunchbacked then. We have met before. When was it, lord? Another yuga? Another place?'

'Another birth, Kubja.'

She was standing before that vision again. Gazing at those three figures again. Realisation was flooding her like a shaft of light. Making it all so clear. So vibrant. She knew now whom she had encountered in her dream. Why they were clad like hermits. Why there was such mourning. Why the three were smiling.

I remember ...

The river was Sarayu. The place was Ayodhya. The three figures were Rama, Lakshmana and Sita. They were leaving the palace to begin their exile. She heard now what they were telling her.

'We bless you, Manthara.'

Kubja collapsed at Krishna's feet. Smearing them with sandalwood, she kissed them again and again.

'My Rama. My Krishna. I see now that my back was hunched with the burden of my sins, but you have purged me.'

'It's time I purged this city, too.'

Not long after, both brothers had mangled every wrestler in the royal arena. Mathura watched as Krishna dragged Kansa by his hair and smashed him to death.

90

PRADYUMNA AND THE MAID

I have not fathered you ...

Krishna was cradling Pradyumna, his firstborn. A montage of past events had begun playing in his mind. The slaying of Kansa had infuriated his father-in-law, Jarasandh, and he had raided Mathura seventeen times. Aware that the city had now become perilous for his Yadava clan, Krishna had arranged for a mass exodus. He had acquired twelve yojanas from the sea on the western coast and commanded Vishwakarma to create a citadel. Flanked by waves, the magnificent Dwaravati had now become the domain of the Yadavas. Krishna had later eloped with Rukmani and married her despite opposition from her brother, Rukmi. He was holding his newborn now and whispering in his ears.

I have not accomplished any of that ... It's the Parabrahman ... I am but an expression of it ...

Rukmani entered. The sight of her husband and her son filled her with bliss. Hearing Krishna's thoughts, she tittered aloud.

'What are you teaching him? You are Mahavishnu. The one who preserves.'

'I am indeed. But those who wield power must often remind themselves that theirs is not an absolute state. That power has merely been granted to them and will be taken back when the time comes. I am only a form of that which is formless and I am here to carry out its bidding.'

As she gathered Pradyumna to suckle him, Krishna gazed wistfully.

'Feed him well for it shall be long before you feed him again.'

Rukmani looked up. He saw no fear. No pain. No rage. Only a query.

'What is about to happen? Tell me what you know for you are the omniscient one.'

'Yes. The omniscient one. Do you know the curse of being omniscient, Rukmani? I do not possess the comfort of hope like humans do. Hope that eases their burden. That helps them live out each day. I cannot hope because I already know.'

'But he is our son. Our firstborn.'

'And he shall adhere to dharma by submitting to the will of the Parabrahman. Mahadeva had done so when he had lost Sati. And I when I had defiled Vrinda. When, as Rama, I had banished Sita. Now, as Krishna, I must detach again. Engage with maya but not surrender to it. Do not grieve, my beloved. Hold on to the thought that nothing in Brahmanda happens without intent. That everything is by design. That it must happen to us so it can happen for others.'

Six days later, Rukmani was standing beside an empty cradle. The demon Shambarasura had discovered that Pradyumna was ordained to kill him and had abducted the infant. The whole of Dwaravati had plunged into sorrow. Yadava men were scouring the land while Yadava women were consoling Rukmani. She was looking at Krishna. Hearing his words again and again.

It must happen to us so it can happen for others ...

Shambarasura had flung Pradyumna into the sea, but a large fish had gobbled him up. Such was the decree of destiny that the fish got caught in a net and landed in that very asura's kitchen. Hardly had his wife carved its belly when she recoiled. The child lay encased inside, wailing in hunger. Hearing the commotion, her maid, Mayawati, came running and froze at the threshold. She was gaping at Pradyumna.

Those eyes ...
That forehead ...
Those lips ...
That face ...

Her mistress was still raving and ranting. Mayawati lifted the infant and pressed him to her bosom.

'I will raise him as my own.'

And thus it came to pass that, unaware of his divine parentage, the boy embraced Mayawati as his mother. Having turned ten now, he would still insist on her bathing him and feeding him. And sleeping next to her every night, he would clamour to hear about the feats of Krishna.

'Tell me again how he tricked King Kalyavana.'

'The king had attacked Mathura, but Krishna devised a crafty plan. Making sure that Kalyavana was watching, he pretended to flee from the battleground. The king began pursuing him and even called him Ranchhod, which means deserter. Krishna now entered a cave, followed by Kalyavana. As the king wandered inside, he spotted Krishna sitting still. Covered in his yellow robes. As soon as Kalyavana kicked him, the robes fell away, revealing someone else. It was not Krishna but Muchukunda of the Suryavanshi clan. The gods had blessed him that he would sleep undisturbed in this cave and anyone who woke him would burn to death. Kalyavana realised that Krishna had duped him, but it was too late. Muchukunda opened his eyes and reduced the king to ashes.'

Years passed and Pradyumna had turned into a charming adolescent. As Mayawati was bathing him one day, an eerie confusion gripped the lad. There was something different about the woman today. She was gazing at him in a way she had never before. Touching him in a way she had never before. Caressing the nape of his neck. The curve of his back. The tip of his nipples. The hollow of his navel. He was squirming. His heart was racing. An odd electricity was slicing his flesh. Igniting his blood. He glanced at Mayawati to see her eyes half-closed. Her face tremulous. Her mouth moaning. She appeared to be deriving a secret pleasure from his body. Her fingers were now sliding below his navel. Feeling his loins. Inching softly towards the innermost depths of his thighs. Pradyumna lunged. As he wrapped a piece of cloth around himself, Mayawati simpered.

'Won't you bathe?'

'I am done. Let's eat.'

She sat down to shape a morsel of rice for him but he held her hand.

'Leave it. I should start eating on my own.'

He asked for no stories that night. He was squeezing his eyes shut to drive himself to sleep when his body froze. Mayawati was fondling him again. Kindling that nameless fire inside him again. Turning him over, she pressed her lips over his. As she sucked them hungrily, his eyes snapped open. Leaping to his feet, he flung a handful of ash on her face.

'Mother!'

He was simmering. But she was laughing.

'I am not your mother.'

'Not my mother?'

'I found you in the belly of a fish.'

Pradyumna stood motionless. Unable to process anything, as if a fog was swirling inside him. Shrouding all of him. But before his disbelief could react, his rage resurfaced.

'Is that why you are tainting our bond? You may not have birthed me, but you have raised me as your son. That makes you my mother. How can you do what you are doing?'

'I can because I have been waiting for ages and I cannot wait anymore. I can because of who I am. Because of who you are.'

'Who am I?'

Mayawati placed a platter of flowers before him.

'This is who you are.'

The lad was staring.

'Remember these?'

Four flowers.

'Remember?'

Lotus. Ashoka. Mango. Mallika.

'The flowers you love the most.'

Their colours were penetrating his eyes.

Lotus ...

Their aroma was attaching themselves to his soul.

Ashoka ...

They were tearing apart the present.

Mango ...

Resurrecting the past.

Mallika ...

He seized the flowers and inhaled deep.

The blossoms that adorn my bow ...

He was staring at the ash coating his palms. Staring at her face that he had blackened.

'Ash had separated us,' she spoke. 'It brings us together now.'

Every layer that had been covering the truth had melted away. Moving towards her, he called out her name.

'Rati.'

She closed her eyes. 'Say it again.'

'Rati.'

'Again.'

'Rati.'

'Again.'

He clasped her tight. 'You are my Rati.'

'And you are my Kamadeva.'

Their bodies were dissolving into each other. Their tears were making love.

'I recall, Rati. Mahadeva had opened his third eye and charred me to death.'

'But he had given me his word that you would be reborn in Dwapar Yuga and we would be one again.'

She was wrapping herself around him. He was thrusting himself into her. Stoking flames that were burning them alive. Moments later, they lay panting in each other's arms. Drenched in sweat. Smeared with ash. She spoke again.

'One prophecy has come true. The other one must, too.'

'Which one?'

'Shambarasura. You have to kill him.'

Mayawati now imparted the wondrous Mahamaya Vidya to Pradyumna. The art of beguiling anyone in Brahmanda. The lad challenged the demon and slew him with ease.

'We must return to your parents now,' Mayawati exulted. 'Your mother has been pining for years. And your father, too.'

'Who is my father?'

'The one whose exploits have regaled you every night.'

Not long after, Pradyumna was touching Krishna's feet. Relishing sweets from Rukmani's hands. The city burst into celebrations as their prince married Mayawati. Rukmani was embracing the newlyweds. Recalling Krishna's words again and again.

It must happen to us so it can happen for others ...

91

THE THEFT OF SHYAMANTAKA

Satrajit was awaiting the sun.

A Yadava nobleman of Dwaravati, he was an ardent devotee of Surya. Every day, before the crack of dawn, he would walk to the sea to venerate the god. He was standing again on the shore today, watching the sky. Waves were crashing against his body as if asking him to revere water. Sand was embracing his footprints as if asking him to revere earth. The breeze was fondling his skin as if asking him to revere air. But Satrajit was gazing at the fire that was now kindling the horizon. That flush of red as if the sky was littering rose petals in the path of the sun. The rim of Surya was rearing. More and more of him was becoming visible as that cosmic flame glowed brighter. More and more of the darkness was fading as his rays burnt away the night. The moon was bowing out. The stars were falling asleep. The sun had reclaimed the sky. Just as that dazzling orb hovered over the sea, Satrajit folded his hands. This was the moment he craved.

When fire floated on water. When water caught fire.

The sun had lit up Dwaravati. Satrajit began chanting. Invoking that primordial deity.

Tat savitur vrinimahe vayam devasya bhojanam ...

He paused. Surya was morphing. Elongating into a torso. Sprouting limbs and a face. The sun god was manifesting before him and calling out his name.

'Satrajit.'

His eyes clamped shut. His ears were rejoicing at the sound of that voice. His heart was hammering knowing that Surya had descended. His soul was craving to seek his grace but his eyes were refusing to gaze upon the god. Satrajit was trying again and again. Forcing his lids to open but they were shutting in alarm lest the glare blinded them.

He fell at the sun's feet. 'Forgive me, lord. You have deemed me worthy enough to appear in person but my eyes cannot bear your splendour. They dread that the very fire that nourishes life could be the death of them.'

Surya laughed. 'That is what Sangya used to tell me long back. You can look at me now. Look without fear.'

Satrajit could sense a sudden waning of that blaze. He opened his eyes to see the deva smiling at him. His light now muted. His heat now mild.

'How did you do this, lord?' he asked in wonder.

Surya opened his palm. 'I took off the object from around my neck that magnifies my lustre.'

He was staring at what the god was showing him. A luminous red jewel, as if Brahmanda had bled to birth it. As if the sun was holding a tiny sun.

'Shyamantaka.'

It was ravishing Satrajit's body. Paralysing his soul.

'Your devotion has pleased me,' Surya was saying. 'Ask me what you want and it shall be yours.'

But Satrajit was no longer looking at the deva. Only at the jewel that had imprisoned him inside its magnificence.

'What do you wish for, O Yadava?'

'Shyamantaka, O Lord.'

Satrajit shrank. He had heard himself. Heard the word that had fallen from his mouth. His flesh turned into ice.

Did I just blaspheme?

Surya was advancing towards him. Satrajit took a step back.

Will he burn me alive?

The god handed him the jewel. 'Shyamantaka is a miraculous stone and will reward you with eight measures of gold every day. No human has ever possessed it and I hope it brings you good fortune.'

Soon, Satrajit was flaunting his prize before the Yadava council. Some were gazing at it in awe. Some with mirth. But most with envy. As he finished narrating the sun's visitation, Krishna spoke.

'You have made a truly divine acquisition. My advice is that you deposit the Shyamantaka in our Yadava treasury.'

Satrajit frowned. 'But Suryadeva has gifted me the jewel, saying I shall prosper with it.'

'You shall. But if it goes into our treasury, our whole clan shall prosper. Just as the sun shares his light with the entire world, it would be dharma if his Shyamantaka, too, is shared for greater good.'

The council nodded but Satrajit shook his head.

'This is the blessing of Suryadeva. A covenant most holy. I cannot disregard it by giving it away.'

The matter seemed to end there, but days later terrible news rocked Dwaravati.

'My brother, Prasanjit, had gone hunting wearing the Shyamantaka,' Satrajit ranted before the assembled Yadavas. 'It has been days and he has still not returned. I am certain that he has been killed and the jewel has been stolen from him.'

'Do you suspect anyone?' the council asked.

Seething, Satrajit pointed. 'Krishna.'

The Yadavas gasped. Krishna remained silent, but Balarama's anger exploded.

'Careful, Satrajit!' he roared. 'How dare you accuse my brother?'

'Didn't your brother steal butter as a child? Didn't he steal Rukmani from her father's house? Didn't he kill Kansa, his own uncle? Your brother is a thief and a murderer. I had seen how that cowherd was ogling my jewel that day. He didn't want me to have it and now he has ensured it.'

Krishna stood up. He was looking at the council. Hearing the silence that was encircling him.

'I can see that Satrajit's words have tunnelled into your hearts. You all have the same doubts about me now, and even if I pass through fire, you will not believe my truth. There's only one recourse. I shall find the Shyamantaka and prove my innocence.'

Convinced that Prasanjit's absence held the key to this mystery, Krishna immediately left for the forest. The day passed but he found nothing. Just as the sun was sliding down the horizon, the stench of rotting flesh invaded his senses. Moving in that direction, Krishna halted his horse. The ghastly remains of Prasanjit lay scattered before him. His limbs dismembered. His body half-eaten. The pawprints of a lion were revealing that he had been slain by the beast. Galloping further, Krishna spotted the carcass of a lion. Its belly had been ripped open and the marks of bear claws were all over the ground. Krishna nodded.

'While devouring Prasanjit, the lion must have swallowed the jewel. Then a bear killed the lion and found the Shyamantaka.'

Gazing at the blood everywhere, he sighed.

'Neither man nor animal has benefitted from this jewel. Not everyone can carry the load of a hallowed object. The Shyamantaka should never have left Surya. In the wrong hands, even divinity can become a curse.'

Following the bear tracks, Krishna was soon standing before the animal's lair. A red glow emanating from inside was affirming that he had found the jewel. As he entered the cave, he saw a comely bear princess frolicking with the Shyamantaka. Her eyes seemed bewitched by how it was sparkling even in that darkness. Krishna took another step forward and a voice echoed.

'Halt!'

A massive bear lunged towards him.

'Men like you keep invading my cave to steal my daughter. Is there no end to your lust?'

'I have come for this jewel that you plucked from the lion's belly,' Krishna replied. 'It belongs to Surya and must be returned to him.'

The bear came closer. 'If you want it, then fight for it.'

The cave began rumbling. The ground pulsing. Rocks crumbling. Dust flying. The god and the beast were battling over the Shyamantaka. Soon, the bear slumped half-dead.

'You are no mere mortal. Who are you?'

'Have you forgotten me, Jambavan?' Krishna smiled.

'You know my name?'

'I do. Don't you know mine?'

Jambavan stared.

'Is it because I wear these yellow robes now instead of saffron?'

The bear gasped.

'Is it because I have a peacock feather now in place of matted hair?'

Jambavan inched nearer.

'Or is it because I hold this flute now instead of a bow?'

The bear collapsed, his face glowing with the epiphany.

'Lord Rama! Lord Rama!'

'I was Rama then but I am Krishna now. You are one of the very few who have encountered both the avatars, Jambavan. Yugas have changed, but one thing has remained constant. You aided me then when I was searching for Sita. You aided me now when I was searching for Shyamantaka. One that did not burn. One that forever burns.'

The bear placed the stone at Krishna's feet.

'Pray, accept my jewel too, lord. My daughter, Jambavati.'

Soon after, Satrajit was also standing with folded hands before Krishna. And he, too, was solemnising his daughter Satyabhama's marriage with him. Days later, Surya materialised before Krishna.

'Perhaps none of this would have happened if I had not given away the Shyamantaka.'

'I agree. Sometimes one must curb one's charity.'

'I may do that, but not my son,' the sun god exulted. 'My Karna. His generosity has eclipsed even that of Bali. That demon king from whom you had taken everything as Vamana. I often fear for Karna, but I know that he stands invincible as long as he is clad in that gilded armour and earrings.'

Krishna nodded. He was gazing far away.

And I shall ensure that they are taken from him ...

92

KRISHNA AND SUDAMA

The grains of puffed rice were giggling.

That night ...

That rain ...

That tree ...

That branch ...

Recounting those moments. Reminding him of that gesture. That one act of love that had bonded them forever. Sudama grinned.

'Again?' his wife frowned as she scooped the grains into his platter. 'What is it about puffed rice that always makes you smile?'

'A memory. It keeps tickling me.'

'Laugh all you want. I can only weep for we have nothing to eat but these grains.'

Sudama held her hand fondly. 'We should be grateful that we have rice for our bellies. There are so many out there with not even this much.'

'And we shall be joining them soon,' she said, pointing at their vessel. 'That is all the puffed rice we have left. You won't be smiling for much longer.'

'Despair not, beloved. The universe that feeds everyone will feed us, too.'

'I would rather put my faith in your friend. You know Krishna has become quite powerful in Dwaravati. I have asked you several times to reach out to him but you don't listen.'

'You are asking me to milk my bond with him. How can I do that?'

She shoved their son's half-empty platter towards him. 'If we were just by ourselves, I would never have asked you. I would have knotted a wet cloth around my belly every day to stifle my hunger. But how can I see my child starve? Can your dharma bear the weight of a dead son?'

'I cannot beg anyone for anything. Not even a friend.'

A voice chimed at their doorstep. A beggar was eyeing their rice. Pleading for a handful. She glanced at her husband again.

'Won't it be better to beg once from a friend than to beg forever from others?'

Sudama was trudging through Dwaravati now. His wife's question had silenced him and he had finally journeyed towards the sea. He was gawking at the magnificence of his friend's citadel. At crystal palaces studded with sapphires. At silver walls glistening with emeralds. At pillars of coral and canopies of pearl. At delectable smells wafting from windows. He was soon standing before Krishna's palace. Its gilded gates were turning his rags even uglier to behold. He was pleading with the guards now to let him in. Telling them that he was Krishna's friend. Narrating their days together as students at Sage Sandipani's hermitage. But they were sniggering. Shooing him away with spears. Threatening to lock him up. Sudama took out a handful of puffed rice from his bundle that his wife had packed as a gift.

'Take this to your master. He will know who I am.'

Krishna had sat down for his meal when a guard entered holding the rice. He got up at once. Before the guard could utter a word, he was sprinting towards the gates. His robes were in disarray. His feet were bare. Reaching the entrance, he pulled Sudama to his heart.

'Sakha!'

His arms were nestling him. His eyes were shining as if they had found something precious.

'It has been long. So long.'

Before Sudama knew it, Krishna was placing him on his seat and washing his feet with scented water. Fanning him with peacock feathers and plying him with a feast. Fifty-six dishes were spread out before him on an enormous platter. Concoctions of rice and milk. Fruits and vegetables. Sweets and savouries.

'Eat, Sakha,' Krishna said, beaming.

Sudama sat numb.

'Eat.'

But Sudama had frozen as if unable to process this abundance. He had never seen such delicacies. Never inhaled such aromas. His eyes were darting here and there as if trying to find a way through this culinary maze.

'What is the matter?'

Sudama looked at him. 'Where do I start?'

'Wherever you please.'

'And your meal?'

Krishna grinned. He was clutching Sudama's bundle. Opening it, he began munching fistfuls of puffed rice. The grains were breathing life into that memory again. When, as students at Sandipani's hermitage, they had lost their way in the forest one night. When a sudden downpour had forced them both to scramble up a tree. When, resting on a branch, they had felt hunger gnawing at them. When Sudama had taken out puffed rice and Krishna had stretched out his hand.

'But you are the son of the chieftain of Vrindavan,' Sudama had exclaimed. 'Will you eat this lowly fare?'

Krishna had polished it off and laughed. 'I owe you these grains, Sakha. And as dharma is my witness, I shall return them tenfold.'

For the next few days in Dwaravati, Sudama felt as if he had wandered into a fantasy. He was sleeping on the softest of beds and relishing the choicest of dishes. Wearing silken robes and sporting golden chains. Watching yagnas at sunrise and enjoying carousals at sunset. But the more he was revelling, the more he was aching. The sound of his son's empty platter was ringing louder in his ears. The promises he had made to his wife were weighing heavier on his heart. Unable to hold himself any longer, he walked up to Krishna to share his miseries. But not a word stemmed from his mouth. Something was seizing his tongue. Gagging him fast. Was it that smile on the face of his friend? Or that look in the eyes of his queens? Or perhaps it was his own voice inside his head. The voice that was engulfing him as he saw beggars lining up before Krishna for alms. That night, Sudama stood gazing at a mirror in his chamber. He removed the jewels from his body. Cast off the robes and melted into a puddle of tears.

'Forgive me, beloved. I can't beg him for anything. I can't. I shall leave Dwaravati now.'

The next morning, he was back in his rags as Krishna walked with him towards the gate. As Sudama stepped outside, he suddenly turned.

'What is it, Sakha?' Krishna asked.

Sudama's eyes were clutching his friend. Those words inside him were surging again. Standing now at the edge of his mouth.

'I ...'

'Yes?'

'I want ...'

'Tell me.'

'I want ...'

'What?'

He let go. 'Nothing.'

'Nothing?'

'No. Nothing.'

Soon after, Sudama was nearing his home. He had been composing his defence throughout the journey back. Arranging and rearranging the lines that he would tell his wife. Editing them over and over again. He paused.

My house?

He was staring here and there. Front and back. Up and down.

What maya is this?

He realised what was happening. The splendour of Dwaravati was still coating his eyes. Swindling his senses. Why else was he seeing a palace instead of his hovel? Why was he seeing his wife decked in muslin and gems? Why was his son rushing towards him licking a sweetmeat? The boy clasped his hand.

'Eat, father!'

Sudama gasped. This was no mirage. Neither that edifice nor those riches. Neither his son's laughter nor his wife's tears.

'I woke up today morning to find all this,' she sounded dazed. 'Coins. Robes. Food. Cows. Your friend has showered us with everything and more.'

The bundle fell from Sudama's hand. He was gazing at the puffed rice that had spilled out. Hearing once again what Krishna had told him that night.

As dharma is my witness, I shall return them tenfold ...

Days later, Draupadi was celebrating Sankranti with Krishna. Their kites were flying high when a string gashed his finger. Tearing a piece of her cloth, Draupadi instantly dressed the wound. Krishna touched her forehead.

'I owe you these threads, Sakhi. And as dharma is my witness, I shall return them tenfold.'

93

KRISHNA AND
NARAKASURA

'The earth has invoked me,' said Brahma.

'The earth has invoked me,' said Vishnu.

'The earth has invoked me,' said Shiva.

The trinity fell silent. They could see Bhuloka approaching them as a cow. Her eyes were welling with tears. Her udders were swelling with milk.

'I am blessed that all three of you have heeded my call,' she bowed. 'Blessed indeed to gaze upon you together for it is a singular sight. It fills me with joy and yet I am racked with sorrow.'

'What sorrow?' Brahma asked. 'What are you seeking?'

'A son. Grant me a son. Just one.'

'But we have granted you so many,' Vishnu reminded her. 'Not only sons but daughters, too. Men and women. Animals and birds. Trees and plants. All the forms of life that you cradle in your lap are your children.'

'They are indeed and they call me their mother. I house them on my land and suckle them with my rivers. I nourish them with my fruits and adorn them with my flowers. But I crave a son. A son born of me. A son I can call my own.'

Water was spilling from her eyes now. Shiva stroked her with affection.

'Who can refuse a mother anything?'

The triumvirate raised their palms.

'May your desire be fulfilled. And just as you will give him life, it's you alone who can give him death.'

Often in the past, Brahmanda had witnessed darkness springing from the loins of light. Brahma had created Daksha who had forced his own daughter to burn herself. Shiva had given rise to Andhaka who had lusted after his own mother. It happened again now when the earth spawned an asura. The combined grace of Brahma, Vishnu and Shiva brought forth Narakasura. A demon so filled with greed that on becoming the ruler of Pragjyotishpura, he annexed many other kingdoms. So filled with lust that he caged thousands of women for his debauchery. Bhuloka was quaking now at this plague that she had unleashed. Tired of terrorising humans, Narakasura soon stormed Indraloka. The gods fought back but were thoroughly trounced. Perched now on the celestial throne, the asura beheld the devas kneeling before him. Their bodies in chains. Their pride in tatters. Standing up, Narakasura kicked the throne away.

'You can keep this gilded chair, Indra,' he snickered. 'But you are no longer king. Just as my maids look after my palace, you will look after my Indraloka. You and your deities. I shall march back to Pragjyotishpura seated on Airavata.'

Grasping one of that elephant's tusks, he began twisting it viciously. As the animal cried out in pain, a clanking of chains erupted behind him. The asura turned to see the Devaraja glaring at him.

'I see fire in your eyes and I don't like it,' he snarled at Indra. 'A slave's gaze must never rise above his master's feet. Lower your eyes.'

The Devaraja continued to look at him.

'Lower them.'

Kept staring as if his eyes would burn holes in Narakasura's body. The demon hissed.

'I don't just dominate, Indra. I decimate. See how I bring down your gaze.'

He began walking towards someone. The Devaraja was watching. The devas were watching. Narakasura stood before Aditi. Mother of Indra.

'Your son refuses to obey. You and I must teach him a lesson. I will have to take something else now besides Airavata.'

He inched closer. His breath was colliding with her face. Scalding her skin. Stretching both his hands, he wrenched off the Devamata's earrings. As she bled, the gods winced. Narakasura was running his fingers over her body now.

'You must have been ravishing in your youth. A pity that you have aged or you would have dazzled in my harem.'

Aditi was shrinking. Her flesh was cringing as the asura continued to fondle her. She glanced at Indra. She was seeing it now. All those tears that he was not shedding. Hearing it now. All those words that he was not speaking. The demon taunted him again.

'A spineless king. A spineless son. Will you still look me in the eye?'

The Devaraja had turned inert. Unblinking. Unuttering. Unbreathing. Then he slowly lowered his gaze. Before Narakasura could gloat, Vayu thundered.

'Woe upon you! Was it not enough that you routed us all that you now degrade a woman?'

The demon lunged towards him and snatched his parasol.

'Don't you slaves ever learn? The more insolent you are, the more possessions you shall lose. Your parasol will now accompany me to my kingdom along with Aditi's earrings and Indra's elephant. Who else dares to scorn me?'

The gods stood quiet but Vayu spoke once more.

'You are the son of Bhuloka. Mother Earth. What will she say when she learns how you treated another mother?'

Narakasura's voice sounded strange. 'She will say nothing for she disowned me long back.'

No sooner had the demon departed than Indra sought out Brahma.

'My mother bleeds and so do I. How do we slay Narakasura?'

'Go to Dwaravati,' he counselled.

Hearing the Devaraja's plight, Krishna instantly began manifesting his arms. His Sharanga and his Sudarshana. His Kaumodaki and his

Panchajanya. Indra bowed as he gazed upon this divine warrior form.

'You will battle him?'

'I will, for he has disgraced two mothers,' Krishna answered. 'His own mother, Prithvi. Your mother, Aditi, who also birthed me as Vamana. I, who have two mothers in this yuga, cannot pardon this.'

'But how could divinity bring forth an asura?'

'Just as some asuras are more divine than devas.'

Satyabhama expressed her desire now to accompany her husband.

'I have heard such tales of your valour, my lord. May I come along to watch how you vanquish this demon?'

'You must,' Krishna held out his hand. 'Or I won't be able to vanquish him at all.'

As they prepared to leave, they heard Indra speak again.

'I often feel that we should have shared amrita with the asuras. Perhaps that nectar from the Ocean of Milk could have brokered some peace. Will this conflict with them never end?'

Krishna smiled. 'Peace can also lead to stasis, Devaraja. A state of inertia that does nobody any good. Sometimes conflict is also dharma. A bit of strife can goad the universe into action. Provoke a change so that we keep evolving.'

Soon, the couple was descending upon Pragjyotishpura. Narakasura's five-headed general, Mura, had installed stakes throughout the city to prevent anyone from infiltrating it, but Krishna's chakra sliced them all. It also beheaded Mura and his sons as they tried to launch an attack. Krishna and Satyabhama were now standing before Narakasura. The battle raged with no end in sight. The demon was proving as mighty as the deva and repelling all of his weapons. The blessings of Brahma, Vishnu and Shiva appeared to have coated him with a layer of impregnability. Narakasura hurled a trident now and it seemed to render Krishna unconscious. Seeing this, Satyabhama's blood boiled. Grabbing the Sharanga bow, she launched an arrow and, lo and behold, it cleaved the asura into two. As she stood aghast, a cosmic voice pierced the sky.

'The prophecy comes true. Narakasura was destined to die by his mother's hand. Born as an incarnation of Bhuloka, Satyabhama has fulfilled that condition.'

She looked down at her son. The demon cackled as he breathed his last. 'We bond in death, mother, if not in life.'

Krishna opened his eyes and nodded at Satyabhama.

'I told you he cannot be conquered without you.'

Entering Narakasura's harem, the couple now came across a group of women. As they stood up with fear, more women joined them. Then more. Some more. Still more. Lots more. Satyabhama finished counting.

Sixteen thousand one hundred ...

The demon's concubines. Queens and princesses. Maidens and maidservants. Apsaras and gopikas. Yakshinis and ganikas. So many trembling bodies but the same dead faces. The same dead eyes. Satyabhama was peering into them.

Thousands of women defiled by a single man ...

Krishna addressed them now.

'Narakasura has been killed. You are free to return.'

'Return where?' one of them asked.

'To your homes. To your fathers and brothers. To your husbands and sons.'

'They will never take us back,' another one said. 'We were concubines of an asura. He violated us for years. Our families would have already performed our last rites.'

'The demon may have soiled your bodies,' said Krishna, 'but has he soiled your souls?'

'Souls?' she laughed. 'Which man goes beyond a woman's body to peek into her soul? Even Rama had to banish Sita despite knowing that she was pure. Why will our men embrace us knowing that we are impure?'

Krishna stood silent. He was hearing what these women were asking. Hearing what the primordial woman, Shatarupa, had asked at the very beginning of creation.

Who shall heal them if everyone wounds them?

He replied, 'Rama could not accept Sita but Krishna will accept you all.'

They were listening. Satyabhama was listening.

'You shall henceforth be my wives and live with me in Dwaravati.'

The women shuddered as if blocks of stone were coming to life. Their eyes were suddenly flickering. Their hearts were suddenly pounding. Wondering if it was possible for fates to so utterly reverse. If it was possible for concubines to become consorts. Then another question crept into their minds.

'But we are thousands here,' one of them pointed out. 'How can you alone ...'

She froze. She was watching. They were all watching.

He is splitting ...

Krishna was splitting into many Krishnas. Like a cell multiplying itself, his body was dividing into manifold bodies. Surrounding itself with its own replicas. It was as if the universe had become a giant kaleidoscope that was reflecting infinite Krishnas. Brahmanda was gazing spellbound. Gazing at how Vishnu was breeding his own selves. Birthing more and more of himself the way he generated avatars. One Krishna was standing next to each concubine now. Pledging her all of his heart. Promising her all of his love. The cosmos was welling up. Bowing before this multiform. Witnessing again why he was truly the omnipresent one. Satyabhama finished counting once more.

Sixteen thousand one hundred Krishnas ...

She was smiling.

Thousands of women deified by a single man ...

94

THE BATTLE FOR PARIJAT

The ornament was twinkling in Aditi's left ear.

'And this one for the right ear,' Krishna said, handing it to her. 'It's only when both are adorned that one attains harmony.'

As soon as she wore them, her lobes stopped bleeding. The devas cheered. Drums echoed. Trumpets blared. Indra was kissing Krishna's feet. The Yadava had not only brought back his mother's earrings but also Airavata and Vayu's parasol. Brahmanda had been liberated from yet another demon and the Devaraja was back on his throne. Aditi touched Satyabhama's forehead.

'You have saved our Indraloka. Prevented it from wilting in the hands of an asura. I bless you that you, too, shall never wither with age.'

Gandharvas were bursting into melodies. Apsaras were dancing. Smearing each other with golden dust. Indrani appeared now before Krishna and Satyabhama carrying strings of flowers. She wreathed roses around their heads and marigolds around their feet. Honeysuckles around their necks and jasmine around their wrists.

'I have never seen blossoms this alluring,' Satyabhama exclaimed. 'I must take a walk through your garden.'

Moments later, she was strolling with Krishna through the famed Nandana Vana. Gazing at brooks gurgling with water. Flowers glittering like multi-coloured gems. Birds singing in dulcet tones and foliage sprouting every shade of green. Suddenly, Satyabhama froze. A scent was coiling around her as if it had been waiting for her. A scent like no scent she had ever known. Clutching her like a lover. Infusing her every cell. Awakening a strange desire. Asking her to seek where it was hiding.

'Satyabhama,' Krishna called out.

But she was no longer listening. She was only lusting after that fragrance. Drawn to wherever it was taking her. Aching to find out the root of that sorcery. She saw it now. A tree was towering in the heart of the garden. Its bark was of gold and leaves were of copper but she was gazing at its flowers. White flowers with six pointed petals as if a cluster of stars had made it their home. A speck of orange in the centre of the flowers as if every star was clasping a sun.

'What tree is this?' she asked.

'Parijat,' Krishna replied. 'One of the ratnas that had surfaced from the Ocean of Milk during the churning.'

'From Ksheersagar?'

'Yes.'

Enchanted, she walked up to it. Wondering if those blooms had drunk all the milk of that ocean to be so white. Or perhaps they had absorbed drops of amrita to be so ambrosial. A heap of flowers was lying around the tree. As Satyabhama picked them up and inhaled, tears rolled down from her eyes. The scent was piercing her heart. Pleasuring her core. Merging with her soul to spark such an alchemy that she felt as if she had died and taken birth again. Everything around her had become insignificant. The garden. Indra. The devas. Even Krishna. Her whole universe had contracted into a handful of parijat blossoms.

'They are ethereal,' she moaned.

'They are.' Krishna nodded. 'Found only here, in Indra's Nandana Vana.'

The spell broke.

Indra ...

She glanced at her husband as if that name had suddenly gored her flesh. Her rapture was giving way to rage.

'You battled Narakasura for the sake of Indra. I killed the demon and made him Devaraja again. And yet, his wife welcomed us with ordinary flowers and not the parijat?'

Krishna kept quiet but Satyabhama's eyes were screaming. She tore the roses from their heads and the honeysuckles from their necks. The jasmine from their wrists and the marigolds from their feet.

'Take the parijat,' she hissed. 'We shall plant it in Dwaravati. Indrani has slighted us and we cannot let this pass.'

'Is that the only reason?' Krishna asked. 'Or is it because you are smitten by it?'

'This is no place for this ratna.'

'Your father had once accused me of stealing a jewel. Now you want me to steal a tree?'

'Not a single deva here rebuked Indrani for how she treated us. They hardly deserve something this wondrous.'

'If you say so.'

Seizing the trunk, Krishna uprooted the entire tree. As he placed it on his shoulder, Indrani's maids came running in fear.

'Pray, do not take the parijat. The queen is especially fond of it.'

'The tree emerged from Ksheersagar,' Satyabhama retorted. 'That makes it a universal entity. Indrani has no right to hoard it in her garden.'

The maids rushed to alert their queen who informed her husband at once. Soon, Indra was standing in Krishna's way, brandishing his Vajra.

'Ungrateful wretch!' Satyabhama fumed. 'The ocean shared the parijat and the parijat shares its fragrance but you refuse to share anything. This is why the demons keep attacking you. Will you battle us now who made you Devaraja again?'

'Because I am Devaraja again, I must battle. Confront you for carrying away one of the ratnas that sanctifies my loka. The mortal world below is unworthy to possess the parijat. Narakasura had robbed us and now you are doing the same. Your slaying of that demon does not entitle you to my riches.'

As Indra hurled the Vajra, Krishna released his Sudarshana. The weapons were blistering the air. Flaming towards each other. Portending a collision that would be nothing short of cataclysmic. Brahmanda cowered as they inched closer.

Closer.

Closer.

Closer.

Right at the critical point, they passed each other and continued ahead. While Krishna grasped the Vajra, Indra squealed in terror. The chakra was hounding him. He was scampering for refuge. Hiding here and there. Glancing now and then to find the disc hovering above him like a bird of prey. Satyabhama laughed.

'Observe, Devaraja. The realm you were trying to defend does not defend you.'

Indrani collapsed before the chakra with folded hands.

'Forgive us! We were unwise to resist Mahavishnu. Unwise to refuse him anything when the whole of Brahmanda resides within him. Ratnas like the parijat have elevated us but they have also tied us down. We live in constant fear that they might be snatched away from us. It is this maya perhaps that has sullied our souls. Take the parijat with you. Let it flower by that very sea it had emerged from. We shall have one less ratna to worry about.'

Not long after, Krishna and Satyabhama were back in Dwaravati with the parijat. All the Yadavas had assembled to marvel at the flowers. Noticing the awe in Rukmani's eyes, Krishna duly instructed Satyabhama.

'Plant the tree in a spot where you both can enjoy it.'

Alas, the splendour of the parijat had blinded Satyabhama too. Like Indra, she also could not find it in her heart to share the tree. Looking at the wall that stood between her and Rukmani's quarters, she devised a wicked plan. She got the parijat planted on Rukmani's side but ensured that its branches hung across the wall on her own side. As a result, while Rukmani found herself tasked with watering the tree, Satyabhama got to relish the flowers. Rukmani was soon protesting before Krishna. As she whined, he gazed at the parijat.

Humanity buckles under divinity again ...
First that jewel ...
Now this tree ...

'We are both your wives and you must be fair,' Rukmani was saying. 'Let me remind you of what you had told Devamata Aditi. Only when both are adorned does one attain harmony. What does your dharma say?'

Krishna turned.

'My dharma always says that one must restore balance,' he said and embraced her. 'I give you my word that the parijat will now blossom only when we are together. Let Satyabhama enjoy the flowers, but whenever she sees the tree bloom, she will know that I am making love to you.'

95

THE FALSE VISHNU

On the eastern edges of the land was a region named Pundra, which was ruled by Paundraka. His affection for Jarasandh could only be equalled by his aversion towards Krishna. The feats accomplished by that Yadava and the rising fortunes of Dwaravati had been stoking the lava inside him for years. It erupted now when Krishna brought about Jarasandh's death. Paundraka had not only lost a friend but also a powerful ally. As he raged and raved, the sycophants around him began to fan those flames.

'That Krishna is nothing but a common thief. He stole the Shyamantaka. Stole the parijat. And he now steals your glory.'

'What do you mean?'

'He has beguiled everyone into believing that he is Vishnu incarnate when clearly you are the avatar. The human form of the Preserver born to rule over Earth.'

'Am I?' the king gazed at his reflection in a mirror.

'Absolutely. Your very bearing is godly. It is time everyone knew that he is an imposter and you are the one who should be venerated.'

Alas, a lie uttered innumerable times acquires the garb of truth. Hearing those words again and again, Paundraka gave in to the delusion that he was truly divine. The chorus around him was drowning out everything else inside his head. All he could hear were a thousand voices whispering in awe.

You are Vishnu ...

You are Vishnu ...

You are Vishnu ...

Soon, he was hearing only a single voice. His own voice.

I am Vishnu ...

I am Vishnu ...

I am Vishnu ...

Paundraka now renamed himself Vasudeva and despatched a decree for Krishna.

'I, monarch of Pundra, hereby declare that I am the Preserver Supreme,' his emissary read out from a copper scroll. 'The descended deity who blesses Bhuloka with my birth here. You, cowherd of Vrindavan, have falsely declared yourself as Vasudeva and you continue to propagate that lie. I command you to relinquish the title and hand over my sacred symbols that you have usurped. The Sudarshana chakra. The Kaumodaki mace. The Sharanga bow and the Panchajanya conch. Surrender before me and I might pardon your life. Continue with this charade and you will find yourself in battle. Choose wisely.'

Krishna smiled. Then he laughed. And finally nodded.

'Tell your king that I shall battle.'

'But you are inviting your death,' the emissary claimed.

'If he is truly Vishnu, then such a death shall be dearer than life.'

A week later, Paundraka was marching towards Dwaravati. His men were watching in silence at how their king had tailored himself to acquire a facade of Vishnu. None of them were pointing out at how ludicrous he was appearing. He had painted his whole body blue and clothed himself in yellow. Two wooden arms were protruding awkwardly from behind him to fabricate a four-armed deity. His chest bore a fake Srivatsa and around his neck hung a fake Kaustubha. He had garlanded himself with lotuses and hoisted a Garuda banner atop his chariot. Brahmanda gaped in amusement. A false god was about to denounce a true one.

Paundraka smirked now as he stood before Krishna's troops.

They shall flee this shore seeing my glory ...

But they were laughing. Each one of them. Some were pointing and cackling. Some were wiping merry tears. Some were rolling on the ground while others were making faces. He glanced at Krishna to find him trembling with mirth.

'Your adornments won't make you almighty, Paundraka. Gods create humans but humans have constructed your godliness. Assembled you like a toy. Just as a toy can never be human, a human can never be god. You are nothing but a man behind a mask. Not even a man but a monkey who imitates. A fake deva with a fake dharma. You have duped yourself with this farce and now you wish to dupe others.'

'Enough,' Paundraka snapped. 'I have heard how your words trick the mind. How they conjure doubts that bewilder your enemies. Not today. You are calling me false when you yourself are a liar. Far removed from the true ideal that I am. The sun rises in my kingdom in the east because I am Mahavishnu. And it sets here on your western coast because you are a fraud. A cowherd who yearns to be king. Hand me my weapons or your blood shall stain this sea.'

Krishna stepped forward. 'You want my weapons. Take them. Take them all.'

He hurled the Panchajanya and the Sharanga. The Kaumodaki and the Sudarshana. As they tore through the air, clouds crackled. The sky turned indigo with flashes of gold as if it too was mimicking the body of Krishna. The conch burst into a death wail while arrows from the bow razed Paundraka's army. The mace smashed his chariot and the disc severed his head. As it rolled off his torso, those wooden arms also detached. Pieces of Paundraka were lying all around now. The rain was washing off the blue paint from his skin. Krishna's voice echoed.

'Beware everyone! Beware of the Paundrakas of the Earth. Beware of them for one false god shall plague you more than a hundred demons.'

96

ARJUNA IS HUMBLED

One ... two ... three ... four ... five ... six ... seven ...

Krishna was counting. Balarama was counting. Pradyumna was counting. All the Yadavas were counting. Seven sacred threads were lying before them.

'Seven sons,' the Brahmin's voice cracked as if someone had crushed it underfoot. 'All my seven sons have vanished.'

'Vanished?' the council echoed.

'Every time my wife gives birth, the newborn disappears. As if stolen by the sky. As if hidden by the earth. I look everywhere but I fail to find even a trace. It has happened seven times now and I am left holding these threads. These sacred threads that I had prepared for each son.'

His eyes veered towards Krishna.

'What sins have I or my wife committed that our house remains childless? Or are we somehow suffering for Kansa's sins? That tyrant who slaughtered your siblings as soon as they were born?'

Krishna did not reply. The Brahmin showed him another thread now.

'My wife is pregnant again with our eighth one. You, too, were the eighth son. The gods saved you. Will no one save my child?'

The council remained quiet but a voice thundered.

'I will, Holy One.'

Prince of Indraprastha. Son of Kunti. The archer supreme. He, whose marriage with Balarama's sister, Subhadra, had united the Yadu and Puru lineages for a second time.

Arjuna.

'You are our guest at Dwaravati,' Balarama reminded him. 'You should not get entangled in these matters.'

'I am a warrior wherever I am. And the dharma of a warrior is to defend the meek. I am willing to step back if someone here assures this father that he will not lose another newborn. Will someone among you promise him that?'

Nobody did. The prince laughed. Brandishing his Gandeeva bow before the council, Arjuna addressed the Brahmin again.

'These Yadavas may not safeguard their own but you have my word. An archer's word. No danger shall touch your infant.'

'Why should I trust you when even Krishna and Balarama seem helpless?' he asked.

'Because only I can do this.'

Arjuna aimed and released an arrow. The council watched as it pierced the seven threads lying before them. Pierced them one by one and deposited them in the Brahmin's palms. He was trembling with awe. The prince broke the arrow in two.

'Call me the day your wife goes into labour. In my presence, no harm shall befall your eighth one.'

'And if it does?' the Brahmin asked.

Arjuna clasped the man's hand. 'Then I shall offer myself to Agni.'

The Yadavas gasped. Balarama shot a glance at Krishna but he only smiled. Subhadra rushed into Krishna's chamber that night but he only smiled. Draupadi despatched an anxious letter to Krishna but he only smiled.

On the appointed day, Arjuna arrived at the Brahmin's house. Taking the Gandeeva in his hands, he began shooting one arrow after another. The shafts were unceasing as if all the arrows in Brahmanda resided in his quiver. Unrelenting as if they would gore even Brahma, Vishnu and Shiva if they barred their way. The arrows were aligning themselves in impeccable rows. One next to the other. One atop the other. Like a succession of bricks, they were spanning horizontally and vertically. Each one winging towards its assigned place as if following an invisible blueprint. As Arjuna released the final shaft, the Brahmin gazed at the formation in wonder. Ninety tiers of arrows were soaring up high. Surrounding his house like a metal fortress.

'Proceed with the delivery,' the prince gloated. 'As long as this structure stands, nothing shall endanger the baby.'

Soon, the woman's cries were renting the air. Echoing deep within that sealed space. As Arjuna sat listening, the wails of a newborn began to ring out. The eighth one had arrived. The prince leapt to his feet. The infant's racket was sounding like a victory chant to him. As if apsaras were ululating. As if gandharvas were singing. As if Brahmanda was serenading him for this lofty deed. Arjuna raised his Gandeeva.

I have done what even Krishna could not ...

At once, the wailing ceased. Not a sound was emerging from the house now. Not even a whimper, as if the baby had never been born. Then a scream erupted. The woman's scream. Rising from the belly of that silence. Drowning Arjuna in that well of arrows. He was standing still. His legs were refusing to move. The Gandeeva was slipping from his hands. As the woman's cry demolished his shafts, he pushed himself towards the hut. His heart was cowering. His blood was curdling. Stumbling inside, he saw now what he had already seen.

An empty cradle.

Moments later, his arrows had kindled a pyre. Folding his hands, Arjuna beseeched the flames.

'Venerable Agni! Pray, accept this worthless soul who failed to keep his word.'

Hardly had he taken a step when Krishna grasped him.

'You don't need to do this.'

'I must. I have already sinned by failing to keep the Brahmin's newborn safe. If I do not fulfil this vow, I shall be sinning again.'

'But if you find his children, you can absolve yourself.'

Arjuna spun. 'Find them?'

'Absolutely. The eight of them have vanished from Bhuloka so they must be somewhere else. Just as I had located the missing Shyamantaka, you can find the infants.'

'Yamadeva!' the prince exclaimed. 'Surely Yamadeva has taken them.'

He boarded Krishna's chariot and soon the two were hastening towards Yamaloka. Alas, the god of death swore that he had never laid hands on the Brahmin's brood. Arjuna now pleaded with Krishna to take him to every realm in the universe. He wandered through Indraloka and Brahmaloka. Climbed the eight mountains and covered the seven islands. Scoured Atala, Vitala and Patala. Even questioned devas and danavas but found no answer. Crestfallen, he loaded his Gandeeva once more.

'Let me ignite the pyre. I must offer myself.'

'Are you conceding that despite every attempt you have failed?'

'I am.'

Krishna steered his chariot again. 'Let me show you something then.'

Galloping through Brahmanda, they came to a cavern. The deeper they were entering, the murkier it was becoming. Soon, every particle of light had died and the darkness seemed to be ingesting them. Appearing infinite as if they were moving inside the spine of the cosmos. The horses panicked. Wrenching themselves free, they sprinted back towards the entrance. As their hooves faded, the prince got down from the chariot.

'Now what, Keshava?'

'When it gets dark along the way, see how the higher powers shine a ray.'

Krishna raised his hand. Sparks sprung and became the Sudarshana. The disc was hovering above them, casting a circular beam on their path.

'Let's follow the chakra.'

Arjuna began walking behind it. He had heard how, in Satya Yuga, eight sages had followed this disc and discovered Naimisharanya. Today, he, too, was following the chakra and asking himself a question.

Will it lead me to the eight infants?

They paused. The cave had come to an end, opening up to an immeasurable expanse of water. Sunlight streaming from above was splitting into a legion of colours. The air was pregnant with the scent of the sea. The taste of salt was clinging to their tongues.

'Where are we? This looks like the very nadir of Brahmanda. Its lowest point.'

'It is, Arjuna. The bottom of Ksheersagar. Look.'

The prince froze. Vishnu was reclining on the coils of Sheshnaga. The Brahmin's children were asleep next to him.

'Sri Hari!' He folded his hands. 'You had those infants?'

'Yes, Arjuna. I had instructed Yogamaya to bring them to me one by one. I brought them here so you would come looking for them and I could remind you of who you are.'

'Who am I?'

'You are Nara and Krishna is Narayana. My twin aspects who have incarnated on Bhuloka to rid her of chaos. But you, Arjuna, have become occupied with dazzling the world with your arrows. You pierced the eyes of the bird and the fish, but it's you who have turned blind. You have forgotten that you do nothing. That whenever you utter "I will", you carry out my will. The will of the Parabrahman. You have not taken birth to prove yourself mightier. Your purpose is so much higher. So much nobler.'

The prince fell to his knees. The Gandeeva was bowing before the chakra.

'The Earth I inhabit now has tainted me, Sri Hari, but you have held my hand. Pray, hold me again when I need you the most.'

Vishnu nodded. Krishna smiled.

97

VEDA AND BHILA

Veda was reeling with horror.

Sacrilege!

An ardent Shaivite, the setting sun would find the sage in an abandoned shrine in the woods every day. He would sprinkle the sanctum with water. Anoint the Shiva idol with dhatura flowers and honey. Chant a new strota and offer a portion of the alms that he had collected that day. This routine had become Veda's life for many years now. He would go begging at dawn and place some of what he received before Shiva at dusk. He had arrived today, carrying fresh bilva leaves for the lord, when something had caught his eye. Walking closer to look, he had cringed so violently that his fingers had ripped the leaves.

Flesh ... Deer flesh ...

Veda closed his eyes as if that would somehow make it vanish. But when he looked again, it was still sitting there. Someone had moved his alms aside and placed the meat right before the idol. The sight was sickening him. The stench was churning his insides. Flinging it far away, the sage scrubbed every inch of the shrine. Then, rushing home, he performed a ritual bath to purify himself. But the next evening, the flesh of another animal had been offered again. It became an everyday occurrence now. Veda would dispose of the meat and cleanse the sanctum only to find fresh kill placed before the god the next day. Sometimes a skinned rabbit. Sometimes the joint of a boar. Sometimes a pair of doves. The flesh varied but its intent seemed the same. Usurping his place before Shiva. Someone was not only destroying his rapture of visiting the shrine but also leaving behind a daily chore.

A furious Veda now resolved to confront the person. As the sun began its descent the next day, it saw the sage crouching behind a pillar. Eyes alert. Limbs braced. Body taut. Waiting. Wondering. He suddenly inhaled deep. The breeze was now carrying the scent of raw meat. Footsteps approaching the shrine were quickening their pace. Standing up with the softest of motions, Veda peered from behind the pillar. A young man was kneeling before the idol. A bow slung over his shoulder and animal hide covered his loins. The sage fumed.

A hunter!

Fumed more.

A low-caste wretch!

The hunter moved Veda's offering and placed a heart before Shiva. A blood-stained animal heart that he had carved out with his own hands. The sage's anger boiled over. Hardly had he taken a step to accost this man when he froze. The shrine had lit up. Luminous rays were radiating from the idol. Turning the walls white as if they were standing inside an ice cave at Kailash. The hum of Om was everywhere. The statue had come to life. Shiva was smiling at the hunter. Addressing him with love.

'You are late today, Bhila. I have been waiting.'

Veda stood catatonic. He was watching Shiva bless the hunter. Watching Bhila depart, promising the lord that he would arrive early the next day. He quaked now as the Destroyer's voice called out his name.

'I have three eyes, Veda. Where can you hide from me?'

The sage began walking towards the sanctum. His senses were neither registering delight nor devotion. Neither fear nor disbelief. Only awe. A wave of awe seemed to be carrying him out of his body. Taking him to a higher plane from where he was looking down at himself standing before Shiva. Looking at so much that Shiva was trying to show. But the sage frowned again. He was glaring again at the heart that Bhila had placed. The heart that had displaced his own offering. As his anger swallowed his awe, he came crashing down. The Destroyer was shaking his head.

'Perhaps you wish to question me, Veda.'

'I do, Mahadeva,' the sage said, bristling. 'I have known no other life apart from you. For years I have been coming here to revere you and to offer what I can. I have made this altar my sole pilgrimage but not once have you appeared before me. Instead, you choose to appear before that hunter. That lowly creature who kills. Who defiles this place by dumping flesh. You wait for him but not me. You bless him but not me. How can I keep my faith when you do not reward my love? Where have I gone wrong, Mahadeva? What have I done that you forsake me?'

'You utter the word "I" too much.'

The sage stood numb. Shiva spoke again.

'Come back tomorrow. You shall get your answer.'

The next evening, as Veda entered the sanctum, he found drops of blood on the idol. As soon as he wiped them away, he spotted Bhila arriving. The sage ducked behind the pillar again. Craning his neck to peek, he gasped. The drops of blood had appeared once more. Bhila was standing before the idol, staring at them. The next moment, he collapsed in agony.

'Forgive me, Mahadeva. I have soiled your statue. I have always placed my offerings with care, but it appears that I erred yesterday. There's only one way to atone for this. I must bleed myself for smearing you with blood.'

Taking out an arrow, Bhila began to gore his arm. The shaft was slashing his skin. Shredding his flesh. He flinched as a shadow touched him. Veda had bent over, tearing a piece of his cloth.

'Who are you?' the hunter asked as the sage tended to his wound. 'Why are you weeping?'

'I weep because I now see that purity and pollution lie inside us and not outside. That Mahadeva sees karma and not varna. And that he offers himself only to those who offer all of themselves to him.'

98

KRISHNA BATTLES SHIVA

Her eyes were opening just like her name.

For Usha meant dawn and her gaze was coming alive like the morning sky. Looking at the divine pair that was standing before her. Soaking in their halo that was enveloping her. Bowing before his rudraksha and her palash. They had heard her prayer. They were calling out her name.

'Usha.'

'Mahadeva! Mata Parvati.'

'Your austerities have pleased us, O Daughter of Banasura. What do you seek?'

Her face flushed red. 'A husband, lord. I wish to marry the most handsome man in Bhuloka.'

Parvati smiled as she glanced at Shiva. 'I, too, had once prayed because I wanted the greatest among the gods to be my husband. My desire came true.'

'That's why I have invoked you, Mother,' Usha folded her hands. 'Who else but you knows this ache of the heart.'

'I had granted Parvati her wish,' Shiva said. 'She will grant you yours.'

'It won't be long now, Usha,' the goddess assured her. 'In the coming month of Baisakh, you will see the face of a man in your dreams. A face like no face you have ever seen. He shall be the husband you desire.'

Baisakh had come and almost gone now. Every night of the month, Usha had lain asleep, pining for that face. And every morning she had awoken with her heart in pieces. Was that vision eluding her, she began to wonder. Was that man toying with her like how men did? Or had her own dreams turned against her, showing her so much else but not what she had been promised. As the nights passed, Usha's chaos peaked. She was no longer speaking. No longer eating. No longer smiling. Only counting.

Twenty-seven ... Twenty-eight ... Twenty-nine ...

As she climbed into her bed on the last night of Baisakh, her lips were praying. Her fingers were grasping a vial of poison. The night lamp watched as sleep gradually embraced Usha. The dark was turning brighter. The stars were giggling louder. A gong pealed outside as the sentinel's voice announced, 'One hour to dawn!'

Usha stirred. Her eyelids were twitching. Her body was sweating. Her breath was quickening. Her heart was hammering. Suddenly, her muscles spasmed. Her fingers clenched. Her toes curled. The lamp recoiled as she sat up with a jolt. She was crying. She was laughing.

I saw him ...

Tossing the vial away, she hastened towards the chamber of Chitralekha. Her childhood friend, she was the only one with whom Usha had shared Parvati's prophecy. She was also a mistress of the dark arts and had trained herself in sorcery. She sat rapt now as Usha recounted her dream.

'What does he look like? As handsome as you desired?'

'More than that! The goddess was right. I have not come across a more captivating face in my life. Now that I have seen him, I want him even more. But how do I find out his name? Where do I look for him?'

Chitralekha leapt from her bed. 'We need a bit of magic for that.'

She was holding up a silver chain with a large, hollow pendant. Her eyes gleamed and a circle of light began revolving inside the metal.

'The face of every prince in Bhuloka will appear in this pendant,' Chitralekha revealed. 'Tell me if you see the man you are destined to marry.'

Usha gazed as faces began to fade in and fade out. She was seeing all kinds of men. Dark. Fair. Bulky. Slender. Striking. Revolting. Virile. Senile.

Coming and going in rapid succession. The pendant seemed to be jesting with her like her dreams. Parading every face but not the one she was longing for. She was turning restless. Itching to smash that pendant. Douse that wheel of light. Suddenly, she sprang.

'That's him.'

She clutched Chitralekha's hand as if that face would vanish if she let go.

'Who is he?' she asked.

'Prince Aniruddha of Dwaravati. Son of Pradyumna. Grandson of Sri Krishna.'

'Sri Krishna?'

'Yes. King Banasura will be so proud of you.'

Usha's eyes were devouring the image. Absorbing every bit of it. She gasped as a ray of the rising sun now struck the pendant. It was carving the face of the prince on that metal. Carving every ravishing feature that she had fallen in love with. Her friend was chanting. The ray was etching. That circle of light was waning. As the glow died, Aniruddha's face seemed to have come alive on that pendant. Chitralekha hung the chain around Usha's neck.

'There. He rests now forever by your heart.'

'I, too, want to rest my head on his heart,' Usha sighed.

'I know. I shall transport myself to Dwaravati right away. Once I tell him about the prophecy, he will surely come here.'

'What if he refuses to believe you?'

Chitralekha smiled. 'If my words fail, your beauty shall entice him.'

She was displaying another chain now. This pendant had Usha's face on it. The next moment she vanished. Usha walked back to her chambers and slumped on the bed. Her eyes closed. Her fingers clasped. She was hearing voices. Mahadeva's voice.

'Usha.'

Parvati's voice.

'Usha.'

Chitralekha's voice.

'Usha.'

A man's voice.

'Usha!'

She opened her eyes to see Aniruddha standing before her. The pendant bearing her face was hanging around his neck. His eyes were whispering that he, too, wanted to be with her forever. That he, too, was hungering for her touch. Craving to make love. Usha could feel a wave flooding her body. A flame scorching her loins. As she rushed and wrapped her arms around him, she knew that their heartbeats had blended. That their souls were holding hands.

Crash!

The palace trembled. Banasura woke up.

Has it come to pass?

As he darted joyously out of his chamber, a distant scene began to flash in his mind. He, too, had propitiated Shiva years ago and asked for a boon.

'I have been born with ten thousand arms, Mahadeva. Pray, grant me that I find an adversary worthy enough to battle.'

'You will,' the Destroyer had blessed him. 'A day shall come when you will find your royal banner lying broken on the ground. That shall be the omen for the battle you wish.'

The demon was now staring at his flagpole lying cracked. His banner at his feet. He ordered his guards to probe and soon one of them was scuttling back in alarm.

'It's the princess!'

'Usha?'

'She is with a man. A stranger.'

Banasura bellowed and his soldiers instantly stormed Usha's boudoir. But before they could lay a finger on Aniruddha, he butchered them with his club. The demon descended now. Aniruddha wielded his club again but was routed and chained.

'Identify yourself,' Banasura hissed.

'Prince Aniruddha of Dwaravati. Grandson of Sri Krishna,' Usha spoke up.

The demon spun.

Krishna ...

His blood was suddenly aflame.

Krishna ...

His ten thousand arms were shuddering with ecstasy.

Krishna ...

Shiva's boon was about to bring the greatest possible adversary to his doorstep.

A battle against Krishna ...

News soon reached Dwaravati and the Yadavas came galloping to liberate their prince. While Balarama and Pradyumna engaged with the commanders, Krishna now stood before Banasura.

'This is the moment I had been thirsting for,' the demon exulted. 'The moment for which I was endowed with multiple arms. Mahadeva has kept his word. They say you trampled upon Kalia's many hoods. Can you win against my ten thousand arms?'

Krishna laughed. 'I can. You have yourself ensured that. You and your daughter both prayed to Shiva. But while she asked for love, you sought hatred. And dharma says that hatred can never win.'

As Banasura charged, Krishna let loose his Sudarshana. The disc swooped and began to slice off his arms one by one. Banasura kept trying every trick of combat but in vain. The chakra was powering through as if felling trees in a forest. His arms were piling high. His blood was creating a pool. Only four arms remained now when suddenly the disc fled towards Krishna in panic. A being had materialised before Banasura like a colossal shield. His serpent was dripping venom. His damru was striking terror. His trishul was lacerating the air. His moon was eclipsing the sun. Everyone gasped.

'Mahadeva!'

Krishna smiled. 'Will you battle me now?'

'I must,' Shiva replied. 'Banasura has invoked me. I can disregard you but not my devotee.'

'Must I use the Sudarshana against you? You are the one who armed me with it.'

'And you are the one who saved me from asuras.'

'You are the one who calmed me as Sharabh.'

'And you are the one who unburdened me from Sati.'

'You are the one who soothed my pain for defiling Vrinda.'

'And you are the one who had filled me with pleasure as Mohini.'

They were gazing at each other. The Destroyer spoke again. 'But we must do what must be done.'

Krishna nodded, 'What must be done.'

One raised his mace. The other aimed his trident. One was astride Garuda. The other was bedecked with a naga. The battlefield froze. The devas froze. The daityas froze. Brahmanda froze. Vishnu and Shiva were about to clash. Hari and Hara were challenging each other. Preparing to hurl their weapons at each other. The impact would ignite a supernova so immense that it would engulf the universe whole. Reduce every loka to a pyre. Every life form to ash. Cries began resounding now from every realm.

Trahimaam ... Trahimaam ... Trahimaam ...

At once, Brahma appeared. Folding his hands, the Creator beseeched both the gods to retreat. He also chastised Banasura, who now realised his folly. A truce was called and the marriage of Aniruddha and Usha was duly performed. Days later, as the new bride stood on the shore of Dwaravati at dawn, she heard Krishna's voice.

'What are you doing, Usha?'

'Praying to the rising sun that our clan stays blessed.'

Krishna looked at the horizon. A tear fell from his eye.

But the sun is about to set ...

99

END OF THE YADU CLAN

Under the banyan tree, Krishna sat awaiting death. He had placed his left leg on his right knee and stretched out his sole. He smiled.

That will do ...

Thirty-six years had elapsed today since the Mahabharata War had ended. Since that eighteen-day-long carnage. Kurukshetra had heard the symphony of the Gita. Seen a family slaughtering each other. Tasted the blood of thousands of men. Smelled burning flesh on countless pyres. The Pandavas had won. The Kauravas had lost. And a livid Gandhari had cursed Krishna.

'If you are wondering why I am doing this, ask Devaki when you return to Dwaravati. She who had lost her sons in that prison in Mathura will know my pain. I curse you, O Yadava, that just as my clan has been annihilated, so will yours be. Just as Kurukshetra is bathed in blood, so will the waves on your shore turn red. Just as I stood powerless while my sons were being butchered, so will you. Just as my kingdom lies drowned in tears, so will your Dwaravati drown in the sea. And you shall die in a forest, hunted like a beast.'

Under the banyan tree, Krishna stirred. He could hear faint footsteps. He smiled.

He has arrived ...

A few months ago, Krishna's son, Samba, and his mates had visited the pilgrimage of Pindarika where they had seen Durvasa in the company of sages. Itching to tickle his vile temper, the lads had decided to play a prank. They had obtained female robes and draped it around Samba. Stuffed his belly to resemble a pregnant woman and presented him before the sage.

'Tell us, Enlightened One. Will she give birth to a boy or a girl?'

Durvasa had divined the truth right away. Quaking with rage, he had uttered ominous words.

'He will birth an iron club which shall be the death of your Yadu clan!'

In a matter of hours, a club had indeed emerged from Samba's body. The Yadavas had gazed at it with horror just as Kansa had gazed at Devaki's newborns. Their council had instantly commanded it to be pounded to dust and thrown into the sea. But alas, the sea had refused to swallow this metal of doom. Its waves had spat the dust back on the shore where it had germinated into reeds. Thick iron reeds as if the elements were nurturing Durvasa's curse. Only a tiny chunk of the club that could not be pulverised had been gulped by a fish.

Under the banyan tree, Krishna caressed his flute one last time. He was hearing all the notes that he had ever played on it. Hearing those footsteps become louder and louder. He smiled.

He is closing in ...

The Yadavas had soon passed new laws to ensure their survival. Men had been forbidden from gambling and carrying arms while assembling in large crowds. Alcohol and other intoxicants had also been barred from public gatherings. The threat was too real and every Yadava had strived to safeguard the clan. Only Krishna had known how futile it all was. How inescapable were the words of Durvasa. The curse of Gandhari. This plan of the Parabrahman to decimate his people who had begun to stray from dharma. Only Krishna had known that Samba was but a form of Shiva who had taken birth to bring about that destruction.

It had finally come to pass today when the Yadavas had assembled at the Prabhasa coast on the anniversary of the Mahabharata War. Despite the rules of conduct in place, many of them had consumed wine. An argument had erupted between Satyaki, who had favoured the Pandavas, and Kritavarma, who had sided with the Kauravas. With liquor enflaming their blood, the debate had soon turned into a scuffle. Watching them come to blows, their supporters had also pounced upon each other like wild animals. They had gored with their teeth. Scratched with their nails. Trampled under their feet. Like a spark igniting a forest, their ire had spread from one to another and finally engulfed them all. Krishna had stood helpless while Balarama tried to cheer him up.

'They are carrying no weapons as decreed. This won't last long.'

But Krishna had pointed. One of the Yadavas had plucked something from the shore. Balarama had recoiled.

'Reeds! From that iron bolt!'

Krishna had nodded. 'The metal has been waiting for us on this coast.'

Both brothers had stood paralysed as that Yadava had bashed the skull of Pradyumna with the reed. More wrath had started exploding. More bonds had begun dissolving. More and more of them had begun uprooting those reeds. They had battered limbs. Fractured spines. Crushed ribs. Mangled flesh. The curse seemed to have possessed each one of them like a vengeful spirit. Samba had perished and so had Aniruddha, as the Yadavas had reduced each other to pulp on that shore. Soon the chaos had ended. The men lay in a heap. The clan had wiped itself out.

Under the banyan tree, Krishna glanced up. A shadow was flitting now through the foliage in the distance. He smiled.

He has spotted it ...

The sea had turned red. As a wave of blood had drenched Krishna, he had watched Balarama entering those waters. His eyes had closed. His mouth had opened and a thousand-headed serpent had emerged from within. Its white body had slithered out of him as if it was shedding its skin. The reptile had entered the waters and vanished. Sheshnaga had given up its mortal form as Balarama and returned to the womb of the ocean.

Under the banyan tree, Krishna could hear a bowstring tighten. He smiled.

He is taking aim ...

The arrow touched his feet, piercing his sole. Vishnu winced. Brahma winced. Shiva winced. The universe closed its eyes as tears trickled down its face. When it looked again, it saw Jara advancing eagerly. A tribal hunter, he had mistaken Krishna's rosy sole for a deer's ear. The smell of blood was drawing him closer now. Proclaiming aloud that he had hit the mark. He was seeing his arrow protruding from that flesh. His steps were quickening. His heart was pulsing. As he sprang towards the tree, he slumped in terror.

Vasudeva ...

Jara was staring at his prey.

Vasudeva ...

'Do not fear,' Krishna said. But all of Jara was crumbling. All of his insides were thawing.

I have hit Vasudeva ...

He was gaping at his shaft.

I will burn in Naraka ...

His body was shrieking. His soul was shrivelling.

I am forever damned ...

Krishna smiled. 'No. You are not.'

And all the horror vanished from Jara's heart. The god was bleeding away but he had healed Jara.

'Didn't you fashion this arrow from a piece of iron?' Krishna asked.

The hunter sat down beside him. 'I did, lord.'

'Where did you find that piece?'

'In the belly of a fish.'

Krishna nodded. 'It was all ordained. That metal had been created to destroy the Yadu clan. You have done nothing to kill me just as I could do nothing to save them. You did not come across me, Jara. I was waiting here for you.'

'But why me, lord?' the hunter sobbed. 'Why by my hands?'

'Because it's you I had given my word to, Vali.'

Jara frowned.

Vali?

He was hearing that name for the first time. But it seemed as if he had heard that name many times.

'You were Vali in Treta Yuga,' Krishna reminded him. 'And I was Rama. I had killed you with my arrow from behind a tree when you were locked in a fight with your brother, Sugriva. And I had willed that you would get your vengeance by killing me in the same manner. You have aided the cosmos today in completing that cycle. In fulfilling the dharma that no one can flee their karma. Not even I. You have not sinned, Jara. It's I who have been absolved.'

'From Treta Yuga to Dwapar Yuga,' Jara said as he recalled everything now. 'So much has changed, lord.'

'Yes. As Rama then, the battle was against others. But as Krishna now, I saw men battling their own. And yet, so much remains the same. Sita was dishonoured then. Draupadi was dishonoured now. Men have forgotten Rama. Men will forget Krishna. And then will arrive Kalki to herald the dissolution of Brahmanda.'

'Will I see you again, lord?'

'Beyond life and death is a stretch of epiphany. We shall meet there.'

They could hear the sea roaring. Krishna closed his eyes.

'It began with the flute, Jara. And it ended with iron reeds. It began with Yamuna. And it ends now with the sea.'

Not long after, waves were surging towards Dwaravati. Ravaging its walls. Tearing down its palaces. Consuming the city whole. Leaving nothing but saltwater everywhere, as if Bhuloka was shedding tears. As if she was mourning because she knew that god would no longer walk the Earth. Because dharma would henceforth stand only on one leg. Because with Krishna renouncing the mortal world, Dwapar Yuga had ended and Kali Yuga had begun.

100

JANMEJAYA'S SNAKE SACRIFICE

Now you saw Takshak. Now you did not.

He was coursing down the highest tier of the palace. The sun, setting now, was watching. The stars, rising now, were trembling. He was passing under torches burning atop pillars and that light and shadow had turned him into a spectre. He was appearing. He was disappearing. His eyes were glinting. His tongue was flicking. His body was cavorting with the colours on the floor. Only a while ago, he had arrived coiled inside a fruit, and as Parikshit had taken a bite, the serpent had dug his fangs into him.

'I have kept my word,' Takshak had whispered in the ears of the dying king.

When Krishna had forsaken his mortal form, the Pandavas, too, had renounced Hastinapur. Coronating Parikshit, the son of Abhimanyu, they had embraced death on the Himalayas. So wisely had this Kuru scion ruled that he had acquired the title of Vishwajanina. The Universal Monarch. Parikshit was aware that he was the first ruler of Kali Yuga and had strived to strengthen that single leg on which dharma now stood. Gods had been blessing him. His people had been hailing him. But Takshak had been waiting to bite him. It came to pass now in the sixtieth year of Parikshit's life when the serpent had penetrated his palace and struck him dead.

'I am avenged,' Takshak hissed as alarm broke out.

Guards were now scrambling to locate the snake. Physicians were labouring to revive the king. When both efforts failed, Parikishit's son, Janmejaya, thundered at his men, 'What is the meaning of this?'

He was pointing at the colours on the floor. At the name that the assassin had spelt with them.

TAKSHAK

The minister shuddered. 'He had taken an oath. It has come true now.'

'What oath? Who is Takshak?'

'A serpent king who once ruled over the nagas of Khandava. Your grandfather, Arjuna, had set that forest on fire to clear the area for Indraprastha. The entire clan of snakes had been charred alive, but Takshak had escaped. He had sworn revenge by either killing Arjuna or one of his descendants. That vow stands fulfilled.'

Janmejaya clutched his father's hand as if he could wring the venom out of his veins.

'Call the Brahmins. Prepare for a yagna.'

'What yagna, sire?'

'Sarpa Satra.'

The minister gasped. 'Sarpa Satra?'

'Yes. All the snakes in Brahmanda shall now suffer for what Takshak has done. I, too, will feed them to Agni, like my grandfather. They shall pay with their lives for taking my father's life.'

'But his cremation? Your coronation?'

Janmejaya snarled. 'Not until I have burned every serpent will I burn my father.'

Hours later, a galaxy of sages had descended upon the palace. They were seated in a circle around a massive altar. Symbols in white, red, black, pink and yellow had been etched all around, the five colours denoting the five primordial nagas. Janmejaya was seated next to his father's corpse like coal smouldering next to ice. The sacrificial fire was leaping high. Its jaws were opening wide.

'Now,' he roared.

The sages began chanting. Their voices were swelling like a tidal wave.

Higher.

Higher.

Higher.

Higher.

Mounting to the highest possible crest, it crashed over them with hallowed fury. It was sweeping through that circle now. Through that livid prince. That lifeless king. That palace in mourning. Spilling into the lanes of Hastinapur that had been deserted today by its inhabitants. Mantras arising from this Kuru altar had always filled them with bliss. But today they were generating fear, for today they were invoking the dark. Today they were summoning death. The populace had locked themselves in. They were covering their ears. Blocking out those sounds. Only Janmejaya was inhaling every bit of it. His pulse was racing. His gaze was turning towards the sky now as a shadow lashed his face.

'It begins.'

A snake was plunging through the clouds. Falling into the altar, it began to burn alive. Before the prince could exult, more and more serpents began pouring from everywhere. Cobras. Vipers. Kraits. Pythons. A mass of entangled bodies tumbling to their death. The mantras were now reverberating across Brahmanda like the ominous strains of a snake-charmer. Sucking those reptiles from every realm into this fiery pit. They were wriggling. They were writhing. The more snakes were landing, the more fuel they were providing for the flames to char. Fat from their bodies was flowing like a river. Fumes from their flesh were choking Hastinapur. Never had the universe seen such massacre of a species. The entire naga race seemed to be hurtling towards extinction today, but Janmejaya was still hungry. Hungry for the one who had still not appeared.

'Where is Takshak?'

He despatched his men, who soon returned with startling news. The serpent had coiled himself around Indra's throne to stay safe. Janmejaya signalled the sages.

'Chant louder.'

The voices surged. As the tempo of their words increased, snakes from the farthest corners of Brahmanda now began falling into that fire. The circle of sages seemed to have become a hell-hole that was devouring them all. The Brahmins were reciting. The city was quaking. As the chorus peaked, it finally began to drag Takshak towards Bhuloka. The serpent curled some more around the Devaraja's throne but the mantras had begun to overpower him now. He was holding tight but they were pulling strong. He was holding tighter but they were pulling stronger. Tighter. Stronger. Tighter. Stronger. Tighter. Stronger. The universe was staring at this harrowing tug of war when it gasped. With Takshak clinging on so fiercely, the throne was also getting dragged now towards the altar, along with Indra. As the Devaraja froze, his attendants tried to pull him back, but the throne was fast descending into that fiery grave. The mantras had reached a crescendo. Takshak was hanging above the flames. Indra was right behind. Janmejaya leapt up. The gods shrank back.

Was this holy holocaust about to claim the Devaraja?

Suddenly, a voice as clear as a temple-bell began to sing praises of the prince and the yagna. So endearing was this ode that Janmejaya instantly longed to see the person. Guards rushed out and in walked a Brahmin boy, his face as sublime as his voice. As he continued to eulogise, the gathering marvelled at the wisdom and piety flowing from someone so young. Janmejaya even appeared to have forgotten about Takshak as he asked the boy now to seek any boon he desired. The Brahmin folded his hands.

'Pray, abort this ritual of vengeance. Let the Sarpa Satra end right here.'

Janmejaya glared. His face was seething but his eyes were veering towards a wall. Towards a mural of the demon king, Bali, bowing before Vamana. He glanced at the sky to see that Indra had fled and Takshak had paused mid-air.

'Who is shielding that serpent?' he screamed.

'This Brahmin,' the sages replied. 'His words have nullified our mantras.'

'Who are you, boy?'

'Astika. The nephew of Vasuki.'

A lotus bloomed now near the altar, with Brahma seated atop.

'Heed his words, Janmejaya. It was Parikshit's fate to die of snakebite. When he was destined to live, Krishna had revived him in his mother's womb despite being dismembered by Ashwathama. And when he was destined to die, Takshak poisoned his blood. We are all tied to our fates and none of us can undo that knot.'

'If what you say is true then what about these snakes who lost their lives today? Why did they have to burn to death?'

'Because, like your father, they, too, were fulfilling their destiny.'

'What destiny?'

'Have you heard of Kadru?'

'Mother of the naga race.'

'And Vinata?'

'Her sister. Mother of Garuda.'

'Kadru and Vinata had once placed a bet.'

The prince nodded. 'About the colour of Uchchaishrava's tail.'

'Kadru had wagered that it was black.'

The prince stood up. 'And Vinata was certain it was white.'

'When Kadru was informed that she was about to lose, she had decided to deceive Vinata.'

The prince took a step forward. 'And she had asked her sons to conspire with her.'

'Most nagas had agreed but many had refused and Kadru had put a curse on them. What was the curse, Janmejaya?'

The prince halted.

'What was the curse?'

The prince turned towards the altar. 'That their progeny shall burn in a yagna in Kali Yuga.'

He was seeing it now. How everything in Brahmanda was entangled with each other. Reciprocal in nature. A continuum, like a serpent swallowing its own tail. A Mahagatha of kindred stories. Hearing now what the Creator was telling him.

'Those who had to die have died. I speak for those who have to live.'

He was gazing at his father. Gazing at the snakes.

'Takshak ensured that Parikshit achieves his fate, Janmejaya. You ensured that the nagas achieve theirs. It is now time for you to achieve yours.'

The prince knelt before Brahma.

'I was floating in an ocean of darkness, Param Pita, but you have shone an orb of light. I call off the Sarpa Satra. Enlighten me some more. Enlighten my people. Is there anything in this Kali Yuga that can give us hope?'

'There is. In the previous yugas, even after engaging a lot with the Self, one could earn only a little merit. The reverse is true now. In Kali Yuga, engage just a little with the Self, and you shall earn enormous merit.'

'And how do we do that?'

'Examine the Self. Cleanse the Self. Realise the Self. Are you willing?'

Janmejaya bowed. The serpent coiled into a disc as the lotus folded.

ACKNOWLEDGEMENTS

The journey of *Mahagatha* began five years back and it's so fulfilling to see my labour of love find a home at HarperCollins India. Thank you to the entire publishing team for embracing this book. For making it your own.

Thank you, Ridhima, for everything. For your faith. For your vision. For your patience. For your passion. For the loads of affection, you have showered on the book. For this wonderful collaboration, which I hope shall see many more odysseys together.

Thank you, Diya, for being my sun. For blazing through the dark when the night seemed endless.

Thank you, Saurabh, for the stunning cover design. For the delightful aesthetics throughout these pages that have raised the book many notches high.

Thank you, Onkar, for the gorgeous illustrations. For capturing the perfume of these tales in your art.

A very special thank you to Devdutt Pattanaik for being a friend in need. For being a phone-call away. For those words of wisdom when I wanted them the most.

Thank you, Dipankar, for being my lighthouse. For showing me the way.

Thank you, Vanaja Aunty, for being my fairy godmother. For being that spot of magic when I was looking for one.

Thank you to my mother and my sister for being my wings. For those hundred little things that have made this book of hundred tales possible.

And thank you to you. My reader. Writing a book is only half the circle. It's when you read the words that the circle completes itself.

ABOUT THE AUTHOR

Satyarth Nayak is an author and screenwriter based in Mumbai. A former SAARC Award-winning correspondent with CNN-IBN, Delhi, he holds a Master's in English Literature from St. Stephen's.

Satyarth's bestselling biography, *Sridevi—The Eternal Screen Goddess*, published by Penguin in 2019 and charting the journey of the screen legend from child star to becoming India's first female superstar, met with high acclaim. His debut novel, *The Emperor's Riddles*, that released in 2014, became a bestselling thriller, earning comparisons with Dan Brown for being a 'history meets mystery'. Satyarth followed it up with his second thriller, *Venom*, in 2020. He has also scripted Sony's epic historical show, *Porus*, touted as India's most expensive television series that aired from 2017 to 2019. His short stories have won the British Council award and appeared in Sudha Murty's Penguin anthology, *Something Happened On The Way To Heaven*.

Named one of the Top 50 authors to follow on social media and a regular speaker at national and international literature festivals, Satyarth is currently scripting a high-profile web series, working on his first film script and writing his next book on mythology based on the Mahabharata.

HARPER
VANTAGE